Exaholics
Breaking
Your Addiction
to an **Ex** Love

Exaholics
Breaking Your Addiction to an **Ex** Love

Dr. Lisa Marie Bobby
LMFT, BCC

STERLING
New York

I WROTE THIS BOOK FOR YOU.

— *L.M.B.*

STERLING
New York

An Imprint of Sterling Publishing
1166 Avenue of the Americas
New York, NY 10036

ISBN 978-1-4549-1825-7

Distributed in Canada by Sterling Publishing
c/o Canadian Manda Group, 664 Annette Street
Toronto, Ontario, Canada M6S 2C8
Distributed in the United Kingdom by GMC Distribution Services
Castle Place, 166 High Street, Lewes, East Sussex, England BN7 1XU
Distributed in Australia by Capricorn Link (Australia) Pty. Ltd.
P.O. Box 704, Windsor, NSW 2756, Australia

For information about custom editions, special sales, and premium and corporate purchases,
please contact Sterling Special Sales at 800-805-5489 or specialsales@sterlingpublishing.com.

Manufactured in Canada

2 4 6 8 10 9 7 5 3 1

www.sterlingpublishing.com

Contents

PART 1
THE EXAHOLIC EXPERIENCE

ARE YOU AN EXAHOLIC?

"I thought I was the only one who felt this way."

—JANE D., EXAHOLIC

"YOU HAVE TO MOVE ON."

"They weren't good enough for you."

"Just let it go."

Your friends say these things to you with such sincerity.

You look into their kind eyes and wish you could believe them. In fact, you would trade everything if only you could take a bottle scrubber to your brain and scour out the obsessions that are consuming you. If there was a magical sword that would slice through the attachment you have to your Ex, you would swing it with all your might, severing the connection completely and finally setting yourself free.

But you can't. You feel helplessly trapped in grief, pain, and longing. That is what they don't understand.

You try to explain. You use the most dramatic, searing words you can think of to describe the unbearable agony you cannot escape from.

"Destroyed."

"Ripped apart."

"Shattered."

You try to tell them how the pain throbs constantly—an aching pit in your stomach that is with you throughout the whole day, from the moment you open your eyes in the morning, if you sleep at all. That your self-esteem has been ground up like raw hamburger. That you want to stop them, but you can't. That every time you think of your Ex (which is constantly), and the injustices you endured, and the ruin of your life together, it feels like being stabbed over and over again. You try to make them understand how you feel trapped in the hell of your inner experience: The worse the pain gets, the more insistent your mind is in torturing you with new obsessions. That you can't get away from the waking nightmare your life has become. That you can't make it stop.

That you're an Exaholic.

There is finally a word that describes your experience. One that captures not just the pain of a breakup, but that encapsulates the addictive nature of relationships. It's a word that conjures the emotional, psychological, and social destruction of a relationship that ends traumatically, and which finally acknowledges the support and guidance brokenhearted people need to put themselves back together again.

People struggling to heal from other problems have support. Alcoholics have recovery groups. Drug addicts have rehab. But until now, people stuck in unhealthy attachments to other people have only had invalidating platitudes: "Get over it."

What's an Exaholic?

An Exaholic is anyone who is addicted to a toxic, hurtful relationship that they can't let go of or who is struggling with intense emotional pain in the aftermath of a breakup. An Exaholic is someone tormented by thoughts of a lost lover, and may be nursing hopes of reunion. Exaholics know they should let it go, but they can't. They want to move on but don't know how. Their craving for connection and communication with their Ex makes them do things they know they shouldn't.

We all have the capacity to be Exaholics, because we are all built to fall in love and bond deeply with another person, as you will discover in later chapters. Most of us have fit this description at one point or another, because love is the human experience. Being an

Exaholic means that you've stepped into the temporary identity we can all inhabit when we're suffering deeply in the pain and obsession of a lost love. When you heal, you will step out again. But during the time you inhabit this terrible place, it defines you.

How Do You Know If You're an Exaholic?

- Are you longing to get back together with someone who has rejected you?
- Are you struggling to finally let go of an unhealthy relationship?
- Are you obsessed by thoughts of your Ex?
- Do you feel compulsions to search for information about your Ex?
- Are you afraid that you will never find another relationship that is as meaningful and special as the one you lost?
- Do you feel that your self-worth has been badly damaged in the aftermath of your relationship?
- Are you feeling isolated and alone, and that your friends and family don't understand what you're going through?
- Is your emotional pain so great that you are having difficulty in functioning?

If the answer is yes to some or all of these questions, you are likely an Exaholic.

But being an Exaholic is not about "criteria," because unlike alcoholism or substance abuse, this is not a formal mental health diagnosis. Being an Exaholic is simply a shorthand way of saying that you can currently relate to a nearly universal experience: feeling absolutely gutted in the aftermath of a lost relationship.

I'm frequently asked, "How is someone who is an Exaholic different from someone who's going through a 'regular' breakup?" Embedded in this question is the assumption that there is such thing as a "normal" breakup—some imaginary civilized parting that ends with a handshake before turning and walking in opposite directions.

There is no such thing as a "Normal Breakup."

All breakups are unique, and exist on a spectrum between mutual agreement and the frantic, enraged clinging of one person to another. There is a range of pain and madness in our breakups because there is a continuum of love and attachment in our relationships.

The degree to which we are traumatized in the aftermath of a split is directly in proportion to the degree to which we were in love with, and emotionally connected to, our lover at the time of the breakup. Love and pain create a balanced equation in the emotional algebra of the human experience.

There are, in fact, relationships that can end without intense pain.

As is so often the situation, our fond feelings can fade, eroded by the pecks of small disappointments. Over time, you stop believing that the other person can be who you want or need. Finally, the spell is broken and it feels like the house lights coming up at the end of the show. There is nothing left to see. Its just time to find your keys and go home.

Then there are relationships that can last a long time and end for ages too, like soft taffy pulling apart until the gossamer thread breaks. It feels over for a long time before the fact is formalized. Someone eventually says the obvious truth out loud, and then it is so.

It's also possible to like someone very much, and have sincere feelings of care and love for them that never catch fire and roar into the passion of romantic love. In those cases, ending a relationship is a process akin to relocating for a new job after discovering the old one just wasn't a good fit. You pack boxes, you forward your mail, you say goodbye to the neighbors, and drive off feeling a little sad, a little guilty, but hopeful about your new future. It's bittersweet, but necessary.

In these cases you're not an Exaholic. You just didn't care that much, at the end.

In contrast, the one-sided severing of a deep attachment feels exquisitely traumatic. Being abandoned while you're in the flaming fire of love feels like death itself. To be rejected by someone that you love desperately feels as terrifying as being trapped in an airless room, but with the additional horror of knowing that you were locked in by the person you trusted and who should love you more than anyone.

Exaholics Breaking Your Addiction to an Ex Love

Worse, you're left alone to scream in your confused panic, agony, and rage as they walk away.

The torture of an Exaholic is so fundamentally traumatizing because it is being inflicted on you by the person who should have loved you the most. The cruelty is in the fact that it feels voluntary. You haven't just lost your beloved. It's not like they died. That would be terrible enough. The real torture is that they *could* come back. They could stop this if they wanted. They could change. They could love you again. But they can't . . . or they won't.

All you wanted was for them to love you as much as you love them. You once had their magical, precious love. You entered an enchanted world together, where your love had thrilled both of you and everything had seemed perfect. You felt so special, so cherished. You let yourself believe in love—and believe in this person.

But then something changed. It was like you woke up one day and your true love turned into a cold stranger. It felt like your beloved was replaced by their dark, evil twin. You don't know this new person, or even like them. You keep coming back to them, hoping to reconnect with the person you loved—and who loved you back. But the cold or hostile stranger your beloved has become just disappoints and hurts you.

Now, all you want is for them to turn back into your beloved, so that you can have a life together again. You try everything you know to make them come back to you, but they seem lost forever. Now you are alone, and in pain—and the evil twin that looks just like your beloved is going about their business, blind to your pain.

The truth is that the rejection—and the confusion—can be even worse than the trauma of being apart from your beloved. As your insides are wracked with grief over the loss and you mourn the life you had together, "Why? Why? Why?" blares in your mind as you try to make sense of what happened.

"Where did they go? What did I do wrong? Why did they stop loving me?" are the questions that occupy your every waking moment. "How could this possibly have happened? Why did they change? Are they coming back?" are the obsessions endlessly digging at the bloody scab of the unanswerable question: "Why?"

You search for information. You need to know where they are, and what they are doing. You are driven to know how they feel. Are they upset too? Do they still care about you at all? You search for clues even though you know you shouldn't. The anxiety and obsessions make you feel like you're going crazy.

The most terrible question you wrestle with night and day, stabs at you over and over: "What does this mean about me?" In your most painful, most vulnerable moments, the scariest voice whispers your ugliest fear to you:

"This happened because you weren't good enough."

In this way, the relationship didn't just end. It smashed your self-worth to bits on the way out.

Worse yet is that in the midst of this firestorm of horrible emotions, you may feel very alone. You try to explain the torture you're going through to others, hoping for comfort or guidance, but are met with platitudes instead:

"It was for the best."

"Time will heal."

"You'll find someone else."

Their lack of understanding makes you want to scream. The only way you could make your friends understand is to have the person *they* love and trust the most set their guts on fire . . . then stand next to a bucket of water and watch while they burn. Could they "get over that" while it's happening? Their "advice" feels entirely invalidating.

Even more terrible, when you try harder to make people understand how serious this is and how helpless you feel, they start to seem annoyed and impatient with you for being such a mess. Then, because your self-esteem has already been battered and bruised by rejection, you start to feel like there may be something seriously wrong with you because, after all, why else can't you get over it? Everyone thinks you should.

The combination of rejection, invalidation, and helplessness is a recipe for shame. Not only have you been rejected and abandoned by the person who knew you best, and who you love more than anyone, now people are making you feel, even if not explicitly, like there is something wrong with you for being as hurt as you are. As much as you want to, you can't change how you feel. The ground-up hamburger that is your self-esteem is smushed into the dirt every time you're made to feel foolish for feeling the way you do. It seems to confirm your worst fears about yourself: *Something is indeed wrong with me.*

You feel alone in your pain. You have been betrayed by your beloved. You fear that you are broken and not good enough. You are tormented by obsessions. The pain is emotional, but it is physical too: it's hard to breathe, eat, and sleep. Is it any wonder that you can't focus on your work? That tasks of life go undone? That you prefer not to spend time with people you need to hide your feelings from, so they won't judge you for your pain?

It starts to feel like your entire life is getting shredded, and that it's your fault because you can't deal with the situation. When this happens, self-doubt finds fertile ground to grow roots and bloom into mushrooms of self-loathing. Shame then piles up, on top of rejection, abandonment, loss, and fear as you feel like your life is falling apart. Worse, it feels like *you* are falling apart, which is possibly the most terrifying part of this whole experience.

But something inside of you is still hoping that you can recover. Your hope led you to search for help. And you found this book.

I am here to tell you that there is a name for what you're feeling, and what you are going through. You are an Exaholic. There is nothing wrong with you. Everything that you are thinking, feeling, and going through right now is normal. What is happening to you is what normal people go through when a relationship ends traumatically.

And here is the unimaginable good news: It will get better.

You Are Not Alone

The first thing you need to know is that you are not alone. Many Exaholics who connect with others say, "I thought I was the only one." They find great comfort in knowing that there are other people going through the same thing. This is because one of the key experiences of a bad breakup is isolation.

Even though you probably feel enormously alone right now— rejected by the person who was supposed to love you the most, misunderstood by friends and family, and in a newly awkward social landscape—you need to know that many, many other people are feeling the same way you do. Because the experience of obsessive craving and grief-unleashed heartbreak is so common, there are thousands and thousands of people all over the world who are feeling the same way you do right now.

In fact, nearly everyone has gone through what you're going through. And most people who haven't, just haven't *yet*. What you are experiencing is a universal phenomenon.

Everyone who has ever felt a deep connection to another person who wouldn't or couldn't love them in return has felt the despair that only lost love can elicit. Your friends, strangers on the street, rock stars, world leaders, and captains of industry have all curled up on their beds like a shrimp being seared alive by loss and rejection, wishing for their beloved to return.

Our losses are so traumatic to us because of our capacity to love—and our legitimate need for love—is ingrained so deeply. The pain we experience when a relationship ends is in direct proportion to how much we want it to continue. It's simply the nature of love.

Everyone who has been in love with someone who shattered their trust has walked through days with an aching gut, and the face of their once-perfect lover hanging in their mind. Everyone who has been discarded has lain awake at night seething at the injustice of their betrayal and abandonment. In the aftermath of rejection, we have all gathered up the weight of our many flaws and descended into the depths of shame and self-doubt. Every person has replayed scenes from the drama of their failed relationship over and over again in an effort to detect the small moments when things shifted, rippling out into the earthquake that created rubble of their once-happy lives.

Now it is your turn to descend into this madness and experience the agony that only the loss of a profound love can inflame. This is your moment to be an Exaholic.

As a marriage counselor and therapist, I hear many stories of love and loss. I help people repair their relationships, when I can, and I sit with people in the aftermath of their losses when I can't. I have never heard the same story twice. I know that we are all unique, perfect snowflakes falling through our one-of-a-kind lives. I know that there are many flavors of horror that you can endure in a terrible breakup, and that they are all traumatizing in their own way.

If you are young and fragile, your frail resources can be entirely overwhelmed. You don't know how to cope, so you fall apart. The trauma of your loss can impact the trajectory of your life, for better or for worse.

If you are older, you might feel like everything you've ever known has collapsed around you, leaving you with nothing. In the midst of your pain and suffering, you need to function well enough to take apart a carefully constructed life. You may despair at how you'll possibly rebuild.

If you're a parent, you get to wrestle with the unique indignity of possibly helping your child or children maintain a healthy relationship with the person who crushed you. Worse, even though you can protect yourself from your Ex, you may be helpless from keeping your child or children from having their heart broken by your Ex, too.

Having a relationship end amid the betrayal of infidelity is a special kind of sadistic trauma that cuts deeply into soft places that are hard to repair. The knowledge that your beloved chose someone else over you chops your sense of self-worth to bits with cruel knives of shame and self-doubt, and the scars linger long after the relationship has ended.

Some relationships end in a roar of silence, with the beloved winking out of existence—a ghost who simply stepped out without a word of explanation. You're left with a shocking hole in your heart, and a head full of unanswered questions.

Other relationships end when your better judgment rejects your beloved for extremely good reason, but goes to war with your heart in the process. You know that this person is not good for you, you know you need to leave, but your attachment and obsession are over-powering. You try to get away but you can't. It feels as if your beloved has a supernatural control over you, severely limiting your will.

I don't know what your story is. But I do know that this is your time to walk through the seemingly endless night of grief, pain, and longing. Whatever has happened to you, I know that you are feeling confused, crushed, isolated, humiliated, obsessed, and powerless to help yourself end the madness.

I know this because in the aftermath of abandonment, shattered trust, and rejection, we all share the same agony, because we are humans. Love is the common language across every culture, through every time. We are hard-wired to fall addictively in love, to need each other, and to bond together. And when those bonds are broken, we despair. We throb. We obsess. We crave. We feel alone. When the flipside of love—pain—shatters our lives, we sit among the shards attempting to make meaning of what happened.

The purpose of this book is to help you understand what is happening to you, why you feel the way you do, and to guide you towards recovery. We'll talk about different aspects of breakups, including the biological and neurological basis for your feelings, the addictive nature of relationships, cravings, obsessions, compulsions, the toll on self-esteem, different kinds of breakups and their unique challenges, and ways to cope with all of it.

My hope is that this book will be your shield aganst shame. Above all else I want you to understand why your current experience of heartbreak is normal and expected.

Finally, we'll talk about the healing process, and how you can begin to design the invisible staircase that you will eventually walk up, step by step, and into the light of a new day.

2

IT'S NOT JUST YOU

"Love . . . What is it else? A madness most discreet,
A choking gall and a preserving sweet."

—WILLIAM SHAKESPEARE, *ROMEO AND JULIET*

SOMETHING STRANGE HAPPENS TO US
WHEN WE FALL IN LOVE.

The phrase "falling in love" in itself is evocative—conjuring up images of an out-of-control, unintentional descent into a pool of something warm and gooey. "Possessed by love," "love struck," and "love drunk" are terms that people have used to convey the madness that overtakes us when we become enchanted by another person. William Shakespeare wrote of love as the enduring and profound spell that binds lovers to each other, using words such as "madness," "blindness," "vexation," and "folly" in his various works. But my favorite of his astute observations on the nature of love is this:

> "And therefore is Love said to be a child,
> Because in choice he is so oft beguiled."
> —*A Midsummer Night's Dream*

When people fall in love, it's like their rational minds fly out the window, and they begin living in a reality-distortion vortex of two that can mystify their friends and families. They seem intoxicated by their lover and become deeply and irrationally bonded to them. Once that beguiling and bonding process happens, relationships become very, very sticky. Even when bad things start to happen, people who have fallen in love and bonded continue to hang on. They may be angry, frustrated, hurt, and despondent—but they cannot let go of their lover. They cannot stop thinking about them, craving them, caring about them . . . and hoping that the relationship can still work.

Even when their lover does shockingly terrible things to them, and new evidence emerges that the person they are in love with is not trustworthy, emotionally safe, or even compatible, it doesn't matter. It's like they are under the influence of a drug that has hijacked their better judgment and wrapped them in a fog of delusional fascination with an unworthy or unavailable person. Over time, they may come to realize with certainty that their attachment to their Ex is toxic, but they still feel powerless to stop themselves from thinking about their Ex, checking up on them, contacting them, and wishing that they could just come to their senses, be decent, and love them back.

Jen's story is a good example of this:

When Jen met Matt, he seemed nearly perfect. She knew he had some kind of girlfriend when they first started talking, but he was gracious, funny, charming—and focused on her like a laser beam whenever they ran into each other. He always knew exactly what to say and do to make her feel like a million bucks. After a while, his girlfriend dissolved into the past and they were free to be together. They lived in Boston and seemed to love all the same things: music, parties, and people. It seemed like they never stopped laughing. Jen had never met anyone like Matt before, and the fact that he was so into her seemed like a dream.

His love for her seemed absolute—so strong that it made him endlessly accommodating. She'd had a longtime dream of leaving the East Coast for San Francisco. After she found a job there, he followed. She wasn't sure if she wanted children, and that was fine with him. The religion of her childhood—Judaism—became increasingly important to her as she got older. He converted, seeming to relish the rules and rituals of the ancient religion. They went to temple together, and eventually married there. Life went on, and they both climbed the rungs of their professions, living a full life of hard work punctuated by romantic getaways in Big Sur, international vacations, and lots of parties. They went to concerts, shows, and had many accomplished and interesting friends. Jen was happier than she'd ever been and lucky to have such a wonderful husband.

Then the hand of fate once again spun the wheel of fortune, this time turning up a spade. Jen's mom got sick, complaining of migraines and mystifying, hallucinatory symptoms. She was finally diagnosed with a well-established brain tumor, and her prognosis was dicey. Jen took a leave of absence from her job to be with her mom back in Boston as much as she could. There was the obligatory radiation and chemo and a Hail Mary brain surgery, and Jen's mother suffered terribly through the treatment. Jen took care of her, spending her days in a haze of disbelieving dread about what was apparently happening to her formerly powerful and larger-than-life mother. There was a much anticipated test result that would show whether the months of agony in treatment had been successful. Jen sat by the phone, anxiously awaiting the call.

But when the phone rang, it was not the doctor. It was the boyfriend of a woman that Matt worked with. Jen had never met him before, but as soon as he introduced himself a sickening feeling started in her throat and spread throughout her body. The voice on the phone told her that he'd just found out Matt and his girlfriend had been flirting and carrying on for months, and had spent the previous weekend together in Big Sur . . . while Jen's mother was having the painful tests that would reveal whether she would live or die. Jen felt like throwing up when she realized that while she was texting and talking to him throughout the previous weekend, leaning on him for support through the nightmare she was living with her mom in Boston, there had actually been another woman (perhaps even naked!) in the room with him the entire time.

Then the doctor called. The treatments had been in vain. Jen's mom was going to die, and probably soon.

The one-two punch of the trauma was more than anyone could bear. Jen called Matt and screamed at him, and then collapsed into a barely functional fog of anxiety, obsession, grief, and pain. Matt quickly admitted fault, announced that he was a sex addict, and entered treatment. As the months leading up to her mother's death unfolded too quickly, Matt revealed himself in ever more shocking layers that blew apart Jen's entire concept of their marriage.

Matt told her he'd never been faithful to anyone. He had been cheating on Jen with random people during the entire time of their courtship, and only with great effort during the first few years of their marriage had he been able to be faithful to her. Then his old, flirtatious, attention-seeking ways had gotten the better of him—leading him to seek out sex with anonymous strangers, his co-workers, and more than a few of their mutual friends. Jen was devastated beyond words. Matt cried, apologized for being so terrible to her—blaming it on his illness—and begged for another chance. Then her mother died. Over the objections of her friends, Jen stayed. She was still in love with the Matt she'd known, and the thought of losing both him and her mother was simply more than she could bear.

The months that followed were occupied largely by Jen's enormous grief and their attempts at sex addiction recovery, consisting of marathon marriage counseling sessions, support groups for both of them, workshops, relationship-repair retreats, plus individual therapy for both. At one time, Jen estimated that between the two of them they were attending eight sessions a week.

As Matt's immediate fear of rejection was soothed by her commitment to working on the marriage and the emotional safety of their therapy sessions, he shared his true perceptions: that what had happened was really her fault. He felt that she was "sexually anorexic" to begin with, and that her protracted time away from home during her mother's illness had left him no choice but to gratify his sexual needs with someone who was more available. He criticized everything from her appearance to her personality to the fact that she was sad and withdrawn now, unlike her usual gregarious and happy self, in the months after her trauma. He would often disintegrate into name-calling rages that left Jen feeling like she'd just been beaten within inches of her life by his words. At times Jen felt like her loving husband had been replaced by a sadistic stranger, but the flock of counselors they were attended by supported his right to "expression" and validated his perspective, encouraging Jen to have more empathy for him as he was healing from his disease.

Jen, in the shock and trauma of her grief, fury about the mistreatment she'd experienced, and her unwillingness to lose her husband, descended into blaming herself: This had happened because she wasn't good enough. She wasn't sexy enough, or interested in sex enough, or able to be the kind of woman a charismatic and intense guy like Matt needed. If there was any fault in his actions at all, it was only because he was a sex addict. And he was in treatment now, so she needed to be more mature and forgive him for a disease over which he had no control.

So she did what any conscientious person would do (who was completely confused by what was happening in a marriage she was committed to saving). She tried harder. She had moments and glimpses of the person that she'd fallen in love with. The charming, funny Matt would show back up and say all the right things—making her feel hopeful that the "real" Matt could be salvaged. She worked hard in therapy on her "trust issues" and "anger issues" and "father issues" in hopes that she could once again be the person that had been so special and important to Matt. She debated leaving sometimes but felt like she couldn't since he was so consistently attending therapy. She felt like if she left, the failure of the marriage would be her fault. As the months of treatment stretched over a year, Jen was left struggling in the purgatory of this quasi relationship. It was not emotionally safe for her or satisfying for her, and it crushed her self-esteem—but it was there, unlike her mother.

New evidence emerged that gradually tipped the scales in favor of divorcing: A chain of recent flirtatious emails with one of his coworkers was discovered, and Jen was able to see that the charming, interested, delightful person that Matt appeared to be when they first met was simply the "Casanova Mask" that he wore with all potentially available women. Matt disclosed in a therapy session his view that many women were so desperate for love that they were basically "prostitutes that he didn't have to pay." Some of Jen's old friends revealed to her that Matt had been sexually suggestive or inappropriate with them, causing them great discomfort. All signs were pointing to the fact that Matt was a serial sexual predator.

Jen left. But even after leaving, she was still in love with the person she thought he had been. She missed *that* Matt terribly. She knew all the horrible things that he had done to her. She knew that she was suffering, stuck in rage and pain, and retraumatizing herself every time she thought of what had happened. But she couldn't lose hope that the Matt she'd fallen in love with could return. She would start to feel better when there was distance between them, but then would talk to him and fall back under his spell—enchanted by hope. Each time she thought she was done for good, they would reconnect and he would say exactly what she wanted to hear, making her wonder if reunion was possible.

It was only after nearly two years of continued disappointments, traumas, and emotional abuse—plus the efforts of a dedicated therapist who challenged Jen to see the reality of the person she'd fallen in love with—that she was finally able to let go. With continually applied pressure, over many months, this therapist was finally able to pry Jen's unhealthy attachment to Matt loose, like a hopeful starfish away from a radioactive rock. At the end, Jen finally understood that the situation was not going to change, and that her continued attachment to Matt was going to bankrupt her emotionally. She had to accept the truth, let go, and give up. And in doing so, she was set free.

You may be tempted to think that only flawed or emotionally damaged people would cling so tightly to an unhealthy relationship. You might believe that the only people who would have so much trouble letting go of a toxic attachment (or who would fall in love with such a troubled person in the first place) must have low self-esteem, traumatic childhoods, or abandonment issues. Those core beliefs about "What kind of pathetic person this happens to," may be fueling

Exaholics Breaking Your Addiction to an Ex Love

your feelings of shame around your own recent experiences, if you too are stuck in an unhealthy attachment.

But I want you to know that this is simply not true. Jen, like all the other people I describe throughout this book, is someone who I came to know very well. Obviously I've concealed things and changed certain details in order to protect everyone's identity, but I can tell you truthfully that she is—in all other aspects of her life—an incredibly resilient, emotionally healthy, attractive, and all-around lovely person. She had two devoted parents, a privileged life, swarms of friends, a sparkling personality, and an enviable career. You would love her if you met her. She is not a "damaged" person because this happened to her, and neither are you.

Consider the emotional, psychological, and personality qualities that supported Jen's difficulty in letting go: love, tenacity, optimism, commitment, personal responsibility, and hope—all undeniably positive character traits that created happiness and success in all other areas of her life. She employed them all in efforts to salvage a marriage. Is that bad? It's easy to look back in hindsight and see that she hung on too long, but how do you know—when you're living the ups and downs of the experience—that its gone past the point of no return?

The truth is, the feelings of love you have for someone, or the anxiety and despair you experience at the thought of being without them, can be confusing in themselves—making you hopeful, determined, committed, and loving. You think and feel differently when you are in love, and there is a biological basis for that. Being in love is akin to being in an altered state of consciousness that can lead you to do things you never would have thought possible in your normal, "rational" state. And assuming that feelings of love are the most important part of a relationship can cause a huge amount of confusion and pain for many people.

Take Anna's experience:

> Anna never married. A beautiful woman, she'd had many lovers. She
> was intelligent, competent, and successful in her career as a nurse.

However, she found herself attracted to men who could not love her back. There was the hard-drinking and wild guitar player that she lived with for a good chunk of the 1970s. She finally left him when he failed to come home again, for the last time. There was the artist she became involved with in the early '80s, whose brilliance was balanced in equal measure by his depression. He lived in darkness punctuated (infrequently) by visions of light that he was able to frantically capture before they faded away, leaving him alone again in the swamp of his inner landscape. His self-absorption was so absolute that Anna wasn't sure if, when she finally left, he'd noticed at all. Then there was the small-town real-estate tycoon with the lake house, fast boat, and ski condo. She was thrilled to be his perma-tanned, leggy blonde trophy for several seasons of après-ski happy hours. An excellent cook, she was frequently at the lake house in the summertime whipping up gourmet marinades for BBQ parties on the wraparound deck. She was happy. But that relationship failed around the time of the savings-and-loan scandal, and she was alone once again. She was crushed each time—she'd loved all three of them madly.

Interspersed between her three exciting, passionate, and ultimately disappointing long-term relationships had been briefer dalliances with kind, quiet, "normal" men who she quickly became bored with after a few months. "They were wonderful men," she told me, "I'm friends with nearly all of them to this day." The longest of these relationships was with the school teacher, Greg, who'd made home-cooked meals for her, took her camping, presented her to his parents, and eventually proposed. "I couldn't do it," she said. "I just didn't have the passionate feelings for him that I'd had for the others. It felt like I was making out with my brother." So she broke up with him feeling, at the time, that it was the honorable thing to do. She still sees Greg and his wife socially, decades later, and counts them among her closest friends. But after Scott the real-estate developer traded her in for a newer model with the same matter-of-factness with which he leased a new car every two years, Anna decided to take a break from trying to find love. Pushing forty now, she'd had enough.

So she got busy doing other things. She moved to Palm Springs. She became involved in a transcendental meditation group. She rose to the apex of her career as a supervising nurse practitioner. She was passionate about fitness and spent time every single day exercising or doing something active. Years slid by; as her peers finished raising their children and sent them off triumphantly to college, Anna took extravagant, fitness-related vacations alone.

Then one day at the gym, Dave appeared. He was witty and attentive. Anna felt a flutter that she hadn't felt in a long time. She thought about him that night as she went about her usual evening routine. "Where did he live? What does he do? Is he married?" His smiling face floated in her mind. Her heart surged the next time she saw him at the gym. They ran together and had kale smoothies after. She laughed the whole time, breathlessly. She asked him about his life: He was in construction, divorced, lived a few miles away—and apparently loved to exercise as much as she did. They made plans for a hiking excursion to Joshua Tree for the next weekend and had a magnificent time. Saturday morning hikes followed by leisurely lunches became a weekend staple, and Anna felt more alive than she had in many years. She felt excited again.

However, there were aspects of her relationship with Dave that were frustrating and confusing. He was very rigid with his schedule. For months, the only time she ever—ever—saw him was Saturday mornings and Tuesday and Thursday afternoons at the gym. Their time together on Saturdays never went past two p.m. He left promptly from the gym at six p.m. She invited him to dinners, movies, paid-for vacations—anything she could think of to entice him to spending more time with her. Nope: Tuesdays and Thursdays at the gym from four to six, and Saturday mornings until two. Chiseled in stone. He was also secretive about his phone. On the infrequent occasions he answered it in Anna's presence, he hurried away from her to speak, and never left it sitting out.

Anna's friends were suspicious. Through a blend of spy-craft and interrogation techniques that would have impressed a Guantanamo psychologist, Anna finally arrived at the truth: Dave was married. Like, extremely married. Thirty-plus-years-and-not-going-anywhere married, with four kids to boot. She was devastated. She cried, and raged, and sent him away . . . and then suffered so badly with pain, anxiety, and cravings that when she saw him the following week at the gym she melted into his arms, relieved. She'd missed him terribly. He was all she could think about. Their time together—limited as it was—had become the most important thing in her life. By the time she found out who and what he really was, it was too late. She had bonded.

She'd felt satisfied and entirely happy without him, previously. But now that she pounded with passion for Dave, his absence made the rest of her life feel like a pit of longing to be with him again. So she waited on him. She accommodated his schedule and bent her life around it. On the infrequent occasions he was able to give her more time, she was elated. The time they were not together she spent stewing, imagining his conversations in the kitchen with his wife, their evenings of TV and errands, and their retiring under the same blanket at night. She knew that he was doing all the things that she wanted to do with him, but with someone else. Her churning anxiety was enormous, and relieved only by the few hours she could have with him each week. Years went by, with Anna dangling on the end of Dave's string. She tried to break up with him a couple of times, knowing full well that this relationship was a toxic dead end for her but felt such a panic of loss and pain that she was relieved every time he called to make Saturday plans—like nothing at all had happened.

Holidays were the hardest. The days when he was with his family, when everyone in the world was with their family, Anna was alone with her cat, obsessing about Dave. The final straw came on Christmas Day, when he was able to break away to see her, briefly, on his way to the grocery store to pick up some suddenly necessary item for his family's holiday meal. He stood in the doorway, not even taking off his coat, and with empty hands. The fact that he had not even cared enough to bring her a present snapped something inside of her. She was finally done. She sent him away and stopped taking his calls. She stopped going to the gym. She joined a hiking group that met every Saturday.

But still, she pined for him. Even though she knew that she was done, and that she needed to be done, she thought about him every day. She cried rivers of tears. She felt ashamed of herself for being "the other woman," something that went against every one of her most important values. But worst of all was the fact that she still craved him and wanted to be with him, even after knowing full well that he was absolutely unavailable and ultimately uncaring of her.

It was also a familiar experience for her. It was a revelation to Anna to realize that she had been confusing feelings of anxiety and excitement for "love" her whole life. She'd thought that love was about feeling butterflies, and angst and obsession and passion. Her core beliefs about love had led to her consciously discarding the men who could have been solid, reliable, and satisfying partners, instead choosing to follow the piper of passion down the exciting path toward pain over and over again. Now in her sixties, she is struggling to be free of Dave's spell and make peace with the reality that the feelings of anxiety and torment she associates with being "in love" are not necessarily healthy emotions to take guidance from.

But it's not just feelings of love or passion that can keep people trapped in an unhealthy attachment. People often linger in hopeless situations as a way of protecting themselves from the pain of the grief they will feel when they let go for good. Denial and bargaining are way stations most people go through as they traverse the long road of grief. When you stop hoping that things can be better and when you decide for yourself that the relationship is over, once and for all and forever, you lose any hope of going home to the life you loved. You also lose your dreams for the future you imagined together. Facing these realities can be so painful, they feel paralyzing.

That's why Martin couldn't let go.

Martin was sad. He'd been married for nearly thirty years to Gina. When he first came to see me, they'd been separated for two years. He was living in a small apartment a few miles down the road from their spacious family home. I asked about his marriage and he shared that even from the time they first started dating in the '80s, Gina had been a bitch in boots. She was hard, judgmental, critical, and entirely absorbed by her own priorities. I pressed him as to why he'd chosen her in the first place. He said that she was pretty, she was fun when she was not being mean, he'd liked her perfume, and they'd had a really magnificent time together at one particularly memorable Police concert. Martin's difficulty in articulating a coherent basis for his marriage proposal reflect the truth of what happens to us when we fall in love: it defies logic, intellect, or rational thinking. It just happens. Martin fell in love with Gina. So they got married.

Life rolled on. They had three girls and went about the business of being a suburban family. They took trips during summer vacations. They gardened. But as the plants in their yard grew ever more lush and well established, Martin withered in the relationship. He was never good enough for Gina. She criticized and berated him for everything from his clothes to his job to his hobbies. He felt bullied in his own home. At one point, in the early '90s, he had a very brief emotional affair with a woman he worked with. When I asked him why, his answer was as simple as it was heartbreaking: "She was nice to me."

Of course Gina found out and felt entitled to punish Martin for his transgressions for the next twenty years as their marriage continued to hobble along. He attempted marriage counseling, retreats, and did everything he could to show his remorse and earn back her trust. He hadn't ever been good enough before and certainly had no hope of proving his worth to her now. As the years slid past, her negativity and belligerence piled on top of his own regrets and self-recriminations, sinking him. At some point, there was a fight so severe that it rallied his basic sense of self-preservation and he moved out of their home and holed up in an apartment down the street—emerging only to go to work (to pay for half of the household bills), and to go back to their family home for yard work and visits with their adult daughters.

When I brought up the subject of divorcing and moving on from the no man's land of his current existence, Martin resisted. He insisted that there was still hope to salvage the relationship. "What relationship?" I asked. The truth was that even though the actual marriage had been extremely difficult, Martin was, at his core, a loyal and committed family man. No one in his family had ever been divorced, and he had deeply held beliefs about what it would mean for him to "leave his family." despite the fact that all his adult children encouraged and supported his moving on.

He also would have to grieve the loss of his family as he'd known it—it felt like the precious memories of the three little blond heads asleep in their beds, the Christmas mornings, the afternoons of peaceful mowing and raking, and the infrequent moments of quiet companionship that he did have with his Ex would all be gone forever. He'd also be losing the visions he'd held in his mind's eye for his entire adult life about what his later years would look like, and the retirement he anticipated spending with Gina, watching their grandchildren enjoy the well-tended green estate he'd worked his whole life to create.

He could intellectually walk right up to the precipice, and talk about all the reasons he should let go, but the intense pain of grief he experienced when he imagined actually doing so, kept him trapped. Martin needed a few things in place before he could move on, including the ability to tolerate his own emotions, as well as a life. He spent time preparing for the end. He made new friends, doubled down on therapy, joined a sports league, and started volunteering at the local animal shelter. Finally, he had enough support in place that he was able to grieve the loss of his old life . . . and step into his new one.

There is an interesting paradox when it comes to how people typically respond to these stories. Nearly everyone has had their heart broken at least once and remained emotionally attached to a person who could not return their love for longer than they rationally should have. And yet many people feel frustrated when they see other people going through the same thing—it's so *obvious* that the people involved need to move on. You may have thought to yourself when you were reading Jen's, Anna's, and Martin's stories, "If *that* happened to *me*, I would totally be done." You may be currently experiencing a similar judgment from friends and family, as they peer into your life from the safety of their emotional distance. It's easy for them to say, "What are you doing? Get over it! They aren't good enough for you." But they aren't having your experience. They don't know how you feel. They aren't currently "under the influence" of love, and you are. The fact that you can't turn off your feelings and do what they want you to do (and which perhaps you know you should), makes you feel ashamed, like there is something wrong with you.

There is nothing wrong with you. The truth is, if you've never had your heart broken and spent too long pining away for an unrequited love, only one of three things is true:

- You've never been deeply in love with or profoundly attached, to someone in the context of an unsustainable partnership.
- You separated psychologically and emotionally from your partner before your relationship ended.
- You fell in love with a person who loved you back, and currently have an ongoing relationship with them.

If you are reading this book in hopes of helping someone in your life who is stuck, I'd like to remind you of how easy it is to forget the universality of this experience when you're observing someone else's process in the aftermath of their breakup. Being in love creates a biologically based madness that only makes sense when you are either in it or using your emotional mind to understand it. You must have empathy for the emotional truth of someone living through their long period of irrational hope and their grinding, obsessive fixation, as they work through their stages of healing.

Otherwise, being in a relationship with them while they recover can be as frustrating as soberly babysitting a drunk friend who keeps saying dumb things (loudly) and/or falling over at inappropriate moments, and continues drinking. For months. To an observer, an Exaholic will not listen to reason, continues making self-destructive choices, and then complains about the outcome. But inside of them, a deep and difficult emotional process is occurring: the process of severing their primary attachment. Challenge yourself to reconnect with the pain, madness, and obsessive longing you experienced when it was your turn to go through this, keep your heart open, and have patience for their healing.

If you're the one suffering now, I want you to know that this entire book was written with empathy for you, because I have lived through it too, just like everyone else. I remember what it was like: how obsessed I was with my Ex, all the stupid things I did in effort to reconnect with him, and how bad it made me feel about myself.

Here's my story:

"Does he still love me? Heads yes, tails no."

The quarter spun in the air and landed to show its mute answer: Heads. Yes. Relief.

"Does he wish we were back together? Heads yes, tails no."

Tails. Anxiety tightening like a fist in my chest.

"Okay, two out of three." Flip.

It was Christmastime. I know this, because I remember sitting on my pink-carpeted bedroom in a red jacquard two-piece outfit with a ridiculous lace collar, prepared to go to church with my parents as I obsessively flipped my quarter. We'd broken up in September, but James was still all I could think about. I was living in a nightmare from which I could not wake up or escape. Breathless with anxiety, abandoned, rejected, and obsessed by unanswerable questions, I was so desperate to understand what had happened that I compulsively sought to make meaning from the random flips of a quarter. It was all I had.

This is not how it started. Two years previously, I'd been okay. I'd been doing the honest work of a teenager—peeling away layers of stumbling self-consciousness through every interaction with my friends, and trying on a new, confident identity every time I put on my stonewashed denim jacket and sprayed up my hair. I'd pulled further away from my parents every time the screen door slapped behind me and I ran out to the putt-putt-putting Volkswagen bug full of friends in front of my house in the morning.

Then one day in this midst of this garden-variety adolescent budding, James appeared. I don't know when he started at my school, but he had not always been there, like the other kids I'd known since kindergarten. Suddenly there was an intense presence behind my right shoulder in typing class. (To this day, the single most useful class I've ever taken.) He told me what an amazing typist I was. I noticed how expertly the keys clacked under my flying fingers. He laughed at my awkward witticisms. I realized, for the first time, that I *was* pretty funny. He watched whatever I did, and I began to feel extremely interesting.

I felt more alive in his presence, like a better version of myself. His interest made me worth something. I had been chosen. And everything *he* did seemed perfect and endearing. Even when he was angry or erratic, it was because he was so sensitive and passionate. He wanted only to be with me, alone. Which was perfect, since he was the most fascinating and important person in the world. The smoky, crowded green bug sped past the bottom of my street every morning now, as James picked me up in his silver sedan. We crawled into a cozy world of two. We fused into a unit. I was no longer an entity, but rather part of "James-n-Lisa." Some primal urge to mate had been satisfied. I had bonded. Seasons floated by.

At some point, our respective parents became concerned about the intensity of our attachment, thinking we were too young for this kind of relationship. (And of course they were right.) He was sent to France for the summer. We talked as often as possible while he was away, his voice crackling through the French pay phone that he had to plug francs in periodically to keep running. I did not know what to do with myself during the millennia between phone calls, so I began spending time with the girl across the street, Laura. She was short and blond and intense. She drove fast and talked faster, and was funny in a cruel way that broadcast her social power. Her wisecracks and bulls-eye jabs quickly organized other teenagers into a fawning hierarchy around her. That summer I became her accessory.

We often snuck out together at night, drifting her dark car to the bottom of the hill before starting the engine and making our escape into the subversive night world that only exists for teenagers. At sailing camp I watched in awe as she unzipped our tent, intent on a nighttime excursion to make out with Dave, the cutest counselor. She brought me to parties and introduced me to important people, and I held her long hair back while she threw up liquefied green Jell-O® shots. It was fun.

Then James came back from France. I was excited to resume our fused life. But things were different. As August turned into September and the trees turned gold, there was a cooling in the new space between us. He turned up the car radio when I talked. My jokes now elicited eye rolls instead of amusement. I didn't know what had changed. I paid extra attention to my hair, my clothes. I tried to figure out what I'd done. I felt careful and tentative around him. One day, we were lying on his bed together and he was extremely quiet. On impulse, not believing it was true, I asked him the unthinkable—if he wanted to break up. It felt like I was asking him something ludicrous like, "Do you want to get a unicorn tattoo on your face?" I was shocked when he let out a long relieved breath and said, "Yes." In hindsight he was probably lying there, trying to figure out how to tell me, until I said the words for him.

The moment he said "Yes," my whole body felt cold, and I felt fear crystalize the room around me. I couldn't breathe. *Could this be happening? What just happened?* I reached out for him. He didn't want to hug me anymore. My right to touch him was over. We were no longer together.

I went home, driving slowly, my ancient, tawny-gold Datsun wobbling down the road with every sob. It felt like my heart was dissolving and pouring out of my face in a flood of tears and mucous. I threw myself on my bed. I wailed. I screamed. My mother stood in the door, wanting to comfort me. I screamed at her too. I felt broken. Destroyed. In the days, weeks, and months that followed, he was all I could think about. Even though we were not together, he was still my constant companion, in my mind. I replayed our conversations in my head. I traced back the lines of our interactions to see if I could figure out what had changed. How could his love for me have been so intense, so certain, and then gone? Why? What had I done? How could it have changed? Had it ever been real at all?

The trauma of rejection was visceral: The best, most important, and most perfect person in the world had been attracted to me, come closer, fell in love with me, chosen me, looked deeply into my soul ... and then changed his mind. James was the first person who had really gotten to know me. I trustingly gave him my heart. It had been returned, unwanted. I felt like a bruised apple that looked good at first. Then he had taken a bite out of me, examined me more closely, and dropped me back into the bin. Rejected. Not good enough. It was as humiliating as it was painful.

I didn't know what to do. I sobbed, inarticulately, on Laura's sexy waterbed as she watched with hard eyes. When she said in a sharp, cheery voice, "Well I guess it's over. Time to move on." I was so surprised that I stopped crying. How could she trivialize this? Did she not understand that source of all love and joy in my life had just rejected me? She seemed irritated with me and the intensity of my pain. She told me it was time to go home because dinner was ready. I was confused by her callousness.

Until I saw the silver sedan parked in her driveway a couple of days later.

Something inside me broke that day. From that moment on, I couldn't sleep. I couldn't eat. I couldn't speak without my voice cracking into tears. I felt like my guts had been scooped out and replaced with broken glass. I walked the halls of my high school enveloped in a repellant fog of aching vulnerability. I had lost my boyfriend to not just my best friend, but to the most socially powerful girl in my school. A career politician is less sensitive to falling political power than a teenager, and Laura's many friends set their gaze firmly on distant objects over my shoulder as we passed in the hall. James-n-Laura were the fun new power couple, surrounded by a lively bouquet of fans. I slid past them, trying not to notice the victorious glances in my direction.

Nights were the worst. Every night, I sat alone in the dark square of my window, listening to music that was even darker, waiting for a new horrible thing to happen. I saw James's nocturnal visits to Laura's house, across the street. I saw him slip into Laura's bedroom, conveniently located just behind the sliding glass door on the ground level (her parents sleeping in ignorance, three stories above). Everything I saw made me feel worse. Every new bit of information about them exploded inside me like an emotional grenade. But I couldn't stop watching. Having more information about them felt like picking an itchy scab: painful, destructive, and irresistible. I was frantic to know, and always in worse pain once I did. I was helpless to stop hurting myself through the bits of information I compulsively gathered, every new morsel blooming into nightmare scenes in my mind's eye. When my compulsion to know was blocked by reality, I found ways around it. I consulted psychics. I flipped my quarter.

I thought it couldn't get any worse. I was wrong.

James started calling me again. At first I was overwhelmed with relief. My nightmare was ending. I would be vindicated, and valuable again. Perhaps I was not worthless and unwanted after all. When he explained that I'd have to sneak out to meet him, so that Laura wouldn't find out, I felt an entirely new emotion—a uniquely terrible blend of resentment, humiliation, and excitement. He wanted to meet me in odd locations: under a bridge, or at the empty ballpark at night. I knew I was being used, but my addiction to him possessed me entirely. I didn't care. I would meet him wherever he wanted. The shattered wineglass of my self-esteem held back together, briefly, while his eyes glittered with interest, only to fall apart every time his receding red taillights left me alone in the dark again. With each rendezvous, the fragile, broken glass of my self-worth was gradually pulverized to dust.

My need for his acceptance and attention was stronger than my dignity. The temporary high I had in his presence was the only time I felt normal, that life was worth living at all. I knew that I was pathetic, the same way that any addict must feel—scrabbling through the carpet, desperate to recover the lost flecks of hallucinatory paradise that they know are destroying their life. Like every addict, I bargained, convincing myself that I was in control of the situation and that I could still win: I could make him fall in love with me again. I kept his secrets and felt the cold comfort of revenge as I watched him and Laura hold hands down the hall in the daytime. At the end, I hated myself as much as I hated them.

It was around this time that my parents finally brought me to see a shrink. This was my first experience, and I was hopeful that she could save me. She was youthful, with curly hair in a banana clip, with the stiff nebula of fluffy bangs arranged into a cupcake on her forehead that was so prized by my peers. I told her what was happening to me as best I could. I told her that my boyfriend and best friend across the street were together now. I attempted to convey my emotional truth: "I am dying. Help me." She apparently heard me say, "It's just normal teenage drama. I'm fine," so she smiled kindly, gave me a relationship book, and said that I should get more exercise. I obediently drove to the track but sat in my car, paralyzed by heavy sadness, and watched normal people jog. I knew that there was no help for me.

I needed new friends. So I pretended to be okay with other people who I knew were adrift and not already part of a tight pack—other loners who might give me a chance. But it's nearly impossible to be normal enough to form new friendships while it feels like a New York rat is gnawing its way out of your stomach. The pain is so intense that it eclipses all other emotion. You don't know what you should be feeling so you smile when other people smile, and nod your head when they're talking even though you have no idea what's going on until it's time to force a laugh again.

The truth is, even our closest friends have a limited capacity to deal with our being a total and complete wreck. Our relationships are transactional, to a degree. Our friends like us because we are there for them, we are interested in them, we are fun to be with, and we bring value to their lives. We are enjoyed when we are easy, interesting, supportive, and self-sufficient. Gutted, needy shells of obsessive pain and self-loathing are just not great companions.

The kindest, closest, most patient friends during that time were ones who had gone through their own breakups. They were on the other

Exaholics Breaking Your Addiction to an Ex Love

side of the darkness, and had done the work of healing that still lay ahead of me. They were eager for me to feel better, so they helpfully shared what they had learned, and were entirely correct and well intentioned when they said things like:

"You have to love yourself first."

"He wasn't good enough for you."

"You have to move on and let it go."

I had no idea what they were talking about or how to accomplish what they were encouraging me to do. The black, uncharted chasm between my destruction and my healing was just too wide. So I just agreed with whatever they said, feeling grateful that they were talking to me at all, and resolved to stop sharing my shameful, pathetic feelings.

I tried to take their advice. I went on dates. I joined the swim team. I read the book the soulless shrink gave me. I filled out college applications. I ran, breathing out the mantra, "Let it go. Let it go. Let it go." But what I really wanted was to travel back in time. To the world that was real, when I was the girl in the silver sedan. The world where I was loved by James, before he became a cold stranger. Before he decided that I wasn't worth loving after all. Before I was rejected and abused by the person who tricked me into believing that he loved me. Before I lost myself.

People who are not currently Exaholics don't understand that you cannot let it go. That as you dutifully run, you're flooded by memories of the time you drove together past the park you're now running through, and what the light of that day looked like, and what you were wearing, and what he said, and the way he looked at you, and whether he is looking at her that way right now. You run through the nightmare you cannot wake up from, and through a reality that you cannot escape. Your only solace is the silent voice that will non-judgmentally allow you to feel what you feel and patiently answer your unanswerable questions.

"Is he with Her right now?" Flip. Heads.

"Is he thinking about the diamond ring he gave me last Christmas?"
Flip. Tails.

"Does he ever feel like I feel?" Flip. Tails.

This is my story, but it's also your story. It's everyone's story. It doesn't matter what stage of life, what the circumstances are, how old you are, or anything else: When you have a profound romantic attachment to another person who suddenly changes from being the source of your love and comfort to the source of intense pain, it is deeply traumatic.

Our stories are all different, but they have common elements: The addictive process through which we fall in love, the primal experience of bonding, our tendency to isolate ourselves into a magic bubble of two, the panic and despair we feel when our attachment is threatened, the sickening slash of rejection or betrayal, our compulsion to obsess, how lonely it feels to be lost in the pain of grief, how helpless we feel to get over it, and the complete annihilation of our self-esteem in the process.

I'd like to tell you that by virtue of some insight or specific practice I was healed from my pain, and that I'm going to share the secret of my salvation with you, too. But the truth is, healing is a process. It took me years to recover completely from the trauma of my breakup, but I had no help or support—only platitudes and invalidation. I had to muddle through it on my own.

I learned a lot along the path of my own healing. Then I learned more in counseling school, and still more working as a therapist in private practice, and even more through my work with Exaholics. I've walked back into the fire to meet countless people burning in the hell of their emotional pain and obsession, and walked back out with them again. And now I am here with you.

Let's get started.

3

ADDICTED TO A
TOXIC RELATIONSHIP

"You're spellbound . . . You have no choice."

—SIOUXSIE SIOUX, "SPELLBOUND"

PEOPLE CHUCKLE SOMETIMES WHEN I USE THE TERM
"EXAHOLIC" IN CASUAL CONVERSATION.

"Oh that's clever," they say, "Like an alcoholic except you're
addicted to an Ex! Haha! That's so cute!" Other times they roll their
eyes and say, "What, you mean like someone thinks they're addicted
to a person? Pfft."

Depending on how much time and energy I have at the moment,
I usually smile and nod and then change the subject. But sometimes,
especially if I'm caffeinated, I will burst forth in all my righteous
turbo-nerd glory to earnestly explain how love is necessary for our
survival, how people are actually biologically hard-wired to become
bonded to each other, how falling in love is an addictive process, and
how ejecting someone from a relationship is essentially like forcing
an addict to go cold turkey, except worse.

Until my listener smiles and nods and changes the subject and I
realize I've done the conversational equivalent of pointing a fire hose at

their face, soaking them in new ideas that simply do not fit our cultural norms about what relationships are, or the significance of ending them.

The actual experience of what happens to people in the aftermath of a lost, cherished relationship has been minimized and misunderstood. Hardly anyone understands what's really happening to people when vital relationships are severed or threatened, and why becoming completely unhinged is normal. The reality—that throbbing, messy, inconvenient, and emotional mayhem is *supposed* to happen when emotional bonds are broken—has been whitewashed. The neat and acceptable story that we've all been served and encouraged to swallow instead, goes like this:

You meet someone, you have a lot in common, and you enjoy their company. Maybe you fall in love. You start building a life together. Sometimes it works out, and sometimes one or both of you decides that it's not a good match after all. In that case, you should pack up your stuff, literally and emotionally, and vacate the premises promptly. You're allotted a grace period of few days to possibly a few weeks for self-pity, eating too much ice cream, doing stupid things while you're drunk, and crying to your friends. Then it's time to pull it together—decide you're better off without them, get your teeth whitened, and saddle back up. That's what reasonable people do. Doing this speedily and with a minimum of drama is virtuous. Protracted months of whining and moping are frowned upon.

That all sounds fine on the surface, except that it is not actually what happens when someone is losing a cherished relationship. Yes, sometimes at least one person has already emotionally detached to the point where they can actually follow the "normal" script. But this is comparatively rare.

What is much more normal is that people go absolutely bananas when their primary attachment is breaking. This is true even when they are the ones doing the leaving. They obsess and think constantly about their Ex—where they are, what they're thinking, or how they're feeling. Even if, intellectually, they know the relationship needs to be over, they still crave the love of their Ex, desperately. They can't sleep, they're an anxious wreck, and they can't focus on anything else. Nothing else brings satisfaction or enjoyment. They ruminate, often replaying memories and trying to figure out which of their personal flaws or mistakes was the deal breaker. They catastrophize, feeling certain that they will never see love the same way again. They seek information about their Ex—stalking social media pages, pumping mutual friends for information, and haunting likely Ex-sighting habitats like Captain Ahab obsessively cruising the Pacific in search of the diabolical white whale. This can last for many months. Sometimes years.

Clearly, not "normal."

The beliefs around what should be happening during a breakup are also reinforced by well-meaning friends and family encouraging you to "move on," "let it go," and "find someone better." Friends and family become increasingly impatient with you when you can't break free from the purgatory of obsessive pain you're trapped in. And god help you if you get back together with your Ex, friends' sympathetic smiles harden into brittle judgment, and you're on your own next time you're disappointed by the relationship.

So what happens, of course, is that you start to believe that something is wrong with you for feeling the way you do. Then, not only is your heart broken, your self-esteem skewered, you are alienated from others, and you feel like you're going crazy—but you also get tricked into believing that you are unusually weak, pathetic, emotionally fragile, or fundamentally damaged because you are so helplessly hung up on this person. Lost love is the arrow that pierced your heart, but as you lay, crumpled and sobbing on the ground, it's shame gleefully driving a steamroller over you. Slowly.

Why is there such a stark contrast between our beliefs about what "should" happen during a breakup and what actually happens for people in 95 percent of breakups?

1. We are collectively uncomfortable with vulnerability
2. Emotional amnesia
3. We do not fully grasp what love actually does to us

Let's tackle the first reason first: there is not much space for vulnerability in our culture. We value strength, stoicism, and independence. Everyone who plunges into the depths of despair tries to swim to the other side and haul themselves out into some semblance of okay-ness as fast as they can. If it takes climbing up a flimsy ladder built from banana-nut muffins, a crazy-busy schedule, escapist adventures, fruity cocktails, and compulsive Cross Fit . . . that's okay. Society tells us that whatever you have to do to get it back together is fine—just do it quick.

Together, we've embraced the idea that pain and vulnerability are shameful, and no one wants to be "that person" who cannot move on. So we hide, stuff, minimize, and disown our pain, and attempt to distance ourselves from the truth of our devastation as quickly as possible. We feel like something is wrong with us when we are genuinely inconsolable, that we're unusually weak or pathetic. So the shameful reality of what actually happens to us in breakups is hidden, like a high school suicide attempt. We don't talk about it. Or if we do, we gloss over the finer details and instead emphasize the part about how it "made us stonger."

People also suffer from emotional amnesia. Like a mother who has only the vaguest recollection of the screaming agony of child-birth when she thinks back to it ten years later, we legitimately forget pain. This is particularly true if the painful experience led to something positive. (And the ending of relationships usually does, eventually. Most people do move on, grow as a result of the painful teachings of their failed relationships, and eventually find love again.)

While everyone who has suffered the loss of a cherished rela-tionship descends into the hell you are now experiencing, those who are on the other side have healed from it. Even the most tortured love does fade. Pain does end. Most people do move on to love again, oftentimes in better and more fulfilling relationships.

They went through a healing process. They learned from the experience. They care about you and want you to feel better too, so they rush the punch line: "It's all going to be okay, and the sooner you let go, the quicker you'll heal."

But when they tell you this, they leave out the part about how they were Exaholics once too. Yes, they got over the relationship, but it actually took them many months of obsessive agonizing to do it. Maybe they legitimately forgot that it was a long, slow, and difficult process. Or perhaps they also succumbed to our collective discomfort with vulnerability, and their shame makes it hard for them to talk about how bad it really was for them and how long it took them to heal. Glossing-over the details ensues.

However, the real reason that both you and everyone you know is still buying into the idea that being in crazed, protracted pain and despair over a breakup is problematic is that there is very little understanding of how vitally important love is to your existence, what it does to you, or how it actually works. When you fall in love, you undergo an addictive process that emotionally welds you to another person. When that love is broken, it is deeply and profoundly traumatic on levels that are so primal and so deep that they are difficult to fully appreciate.

Until you have had the honor of sitting with many Exaholics and bearing witness to their stories.

You cannot non-judgmentally listen to someone helplessly churning in agony, anxiety, craving, obsession, madness, and shame, who wants to be rid of their attachment to a person but feels helpless against their impulses to maintain contact, and leave the conversation believing that they are struggling with anything other than a grave and unwanted addiction. The truth I have learned is that getting addicted to the wrong person can be one of the most harrowing and soul-flaying experiences a person can live through. It can ruin a life just as thoroughly as having a profound addiction to a substance, but be more confusing and difficult to recover from.

You begin to understand just how deeply the hooks of addiction have been sunk into an Exaholic when you understand how desperate they are to be rid of their unhealthy attachment to another person, and the degree to which it is damaging them.

A typical Exaholic often feels mistreated by their beloved. They have often been stuck in an unsatisfying relationship with a person who is not able to meet their needs or love them in the way they wanted to be loved. After putting up with this treatment and trying everything they know to salvage the relationship, oftentimes sacrificing their feelings, comfort, and other relationships in the process, they were either rejected or disappointed again and again.

It turns into a statement of their worth—to be rejected or abused after how hard they've tried, and how much they've given must mean that they aren't good enough to love. (Which usually makes them try harder.) Most Exaholics are thoroughly beaten down even before the relationship rattles out its last breath.

The relationship is formally over when their lover rejects them with finality or does something so unacceptable that even the Exaholic cannot continue to tolerate it. But it never ends when it's over. The end is just the beginning.

Because even if the Exaholic was the one that did the breaking up, they don't *want* the relationship to be over. They want it to be *better*. And it feels like their partner doesn't love them enough to try harder, or to love them well. It feels like they are being abandoned, and that sends them into a frantic, obsessive protest and despair that possesses them entirely.

Exaholics are angry. They are hurt. They are sad. But they have a terrible, gnawing craving to be back with their Ex—no matter how bad it was. They understand that they should move on. They want to, desperately, but they can't.

Exhibit A:

Exaholic-on-My-Therapy-Couch: [head in hands] "Oh my God, I miss her so much."

Me: "What part do you miss? You told me that she was hostile and critical of you most of the time."

EOMTC: "Yeah, she was really pretty horrible. But I still miss her. It wasn't always horrible."

Me: "She got pregnant with the guy she cheated on you with. She got drunk and wrecked your car. Your kids hate her. She hates them."

EOMTC: "Well . . . yeah. She was actually a pretty crappy girlfriend. But I can't stop thinking about her. If she called me I'd take her back in a second. I don't want to be with her anymore, not really, I know the relationship sucked, but how do I stop wanting her back???"

This is obviously an extreme example. Not all Exaholics are attached to people who are this terrible. (Though some are stuck on people that are much worse.) Most of the time, relationships are a mixed bag: more subtly frustrating and more ambiguous. Some parts were really good. Some parts were hard but tolerable. You genuinely miss them, even though the relationship frustrated you. That's part of what makes it so hard to let go.

I can, and routinely do, spend weeks or months combing back through the tragic trajectory of a failed relationship with Exaholics. We talk about how, truthfully, the relationship was unsatisfying in many ways. The person they are stuck on is literally unavailable (as in, married to someone else), emotionally abusive, emotionally unavailable, irresponsible, manipulative, selfish, narcissistic, dishonest, or simply a bad match in terms of personality, character, values, hopes, dreams, and life goals. We dissect moments of betrayal and heartache. Evidence piles up, tipping the intellectual scale in favor of letting it go.

Exaholics are able to openly acknowledge how crappy many parts of the relationship really were for them. They are fully aware of how they have suffered, put their lives on hold, missed opportunities, and endured misfortunes because of this relationship. They understand why their friends wanted to cheer, throw parties, and shoot themselves out of cannons in celebration when the relationship ended. They are able to talk about what they would really like to have in a relationship, and how *that was not it.*

But it does not matter. They crave only one person: their Ex. Even if 80 percent of the relationship was difficult and unsatisfying, they focus on the 20 percent of the time when they felt loved and enchanted by their Ex's positive characteristics.

If feels like nothing but the love of their Ex can touch the pain. Nothing else soothes the ache. Nothing else stops the insane obsession and the longing. Their craving for reconnection feels unstoppable, like a force of nature.

Unmanaged, the cravings, obsessions, and emotional turmoil can be very serious, and with far-ranging consequences. When people are in the throes of a raging Ex addiction, jobs are lost, schools are flunked out of, other relationships are strained to the point of breaking, and health declines. At their most tragic, people trapped in obsessive grief can develop more serious mental health issues, including substance abuse problems, major depression or anxiety, and even become violent or suicidal. But all Exaholics share one thing in common: feeling like they cannot move forward.

Exaholics are stuck in an attachment to a person who no longer exists: the person who once loved them back. They languish in a purgatory of pain and longing, as days, weeks, months, and years of their lives drip away. New opportunities for love, fun, meaning, and fulfillment slide past them, as they sit, alone, with visions of an old lover flickering in their mind's eye. And those are the lucky ones.

The Exaholics who suffer the most are those who yo-yo in and out of a quasi-relationship that one of them needed to put down a long time ago. For years, even decades, they can cycle through the hope of change, the euphoria of honeymoon reunions, the familiarity of old frustrations, the sinking disappointments, and the agony of the next betrayal/rejection/or seriously-for-real-this-time-deal-breaker. Then they are alone again, obsessing and agonizing, until the next "How R U?" text flashes their silent phone back to life, and they saddle up for the next spin around the sad rodeo, only to be bucked off again a few months or years later.

A year before he died, I sat with Tom as he continued to obsess over Sarah. He'd left his wife and children for her several years previously. Their affair had sparked a passion deep inside him, like nothing he'd ever known. They laughed a lot. Their sexual connection was intense. As destructive and crushing as the relationship had ultimately been for him, he was still addicted to the way she made him feel: euphoric. Then devastated. Then euphoric again.

Sarah was pretty but mercurial. She would get upset and break up with him frequently, for reasons that mystified him and left him despondent. The fabric of their relationship was pleasure. They had a lot of fun together: motorcycle trips, music festivals, and margaritas were their thing. But even during the good times, he disapproved of her self-centered parenting and he hated her free-spending ways. His friends disliked her. His daughters hated her. Even so, he stayed by her side, even when she was found guilty of shoplifting. At least, until another fight left him alone in a restaurant after she walked out on him again. Tom's face got red as he talked about his frustrations, but his brown eyes welled up with tears at the thought of being without her forever.

During the breakups he and I weathered together, he couldn't bear to erase her number, unfriend her on Facebook®, or block her emails. The idea of being Capital-D Done and cutting the electronic cords filled him with fear. If he cut her off completely, he wouldn't get the inevitable "Thinking about you today, baby" text that would flood him with hope, and reel him back in to her arms for another few months of bliss. The total loss of her was unthinkable. He simply couldn't be without her. He fantasized about her while they were apart, and the pain in his heart eased every time they reconnected for another hopeful cycle of honeymoon love.

But when they reunited, the actual experience of being with Sarah was much more difficult than his idealized daydreams of her. While Tom lived for their intoxicating "peak moments," you can only spend so much time riding a motorcycle, cresting waves of sexual ecstasy, dancing at a concert, or having drinks and dessert. Sooner or later someone has to pay the tab, take out the trash, solve a problem, or decide what to cook the kids for dinner. And that's when the inevitable friction would start. Harsh sparks of judgment from a clash of values would quickly flare into anger and incinerate the good feelings that were the basis of the relationship.

When things got hard, Sarah would again reject Tom and refuse his calls, leaving him slumped miserably on my couch, pining for her. He couldn't eat. He couldn't sleep. He started smoking again. Ever the reasonable therapist, I suggested that maybe this relationship wasn't really good for him—that as much as he liked her, as intoxicatingly pleasurable as the good times were, it wasn't enough. It wasn't a whole relationship that had a solid, stable, and healthy attachment to support the romance.

We talked about the addictive nature of this relationship, and Tom could understand it intellectually when I said things like, "Doing cocaine is lots of fun too, but just because it feels good doesn't mean it's good for you." He could see the parallels. But he was simply hooked. He felt euphoric when they were together. He felt a craving for her when they were apart. The fact that this particular partnership was the relational equivalent to eating ice cream for breakfast, lunch, and dinner didn't matter. He just wanted to feel it again.

And so it is with all addictions. Here is the definition of an addiction:

1. (Insert name of vice here) changes your mood.

2. Engaging in _____ stimulates your reward system.

3. _____ causes negative consequences for your life.

4. Despite being aware of the negative consequences, you can't stop.

The alcoholic drinks to change his mood: to celebrate, console, unwind, and feel free and loose. The gambler pulls the handle to feel the surge of excitement and the intermittent thrill of victory. The lover desires to be with their irreplaceable other for the comfort, pleasure, and joy of the experience.

All these pleasures powerfully stimulate a neurological reward center deep in your brain that floods you with feelings of euphoria. This part of your brain, evolutionarily speaking, precedes the development of parts responsible for rational decisions, language, and thought. It seems that we descended from animals that were built to crave pleasure—particularly pleasures that are connected with our survival drives (or pleasures that trick our brains into believing that). This is the physiological engine of addiction that drives our compulsions for "more." It overrides pain, fear, and values. It can motivate pigeons to peck for reward-laden pellets until they drop from exhaustion, and shivering, skeletal addicts to exchange the last remnant of their human dignity to experience it again.

In groundbreaking research, evolutionary biologist Dr. Helen Fisher identified subjects who reported being in love and collected MRI data of their brains. Sure enough, she found that when people were exposed to images of their beloved, their reward centers lit up with pleasure. Her research suggests that romantic love stimulates the same addictive neurological pathways as opiates and amphetamines. We crave love chemically.

When you consider that above all else (from an evolutionary perspective), the survival of our species has required us to pair-bond, reproduce, and remain committed enough to successfully raise babies together, having physiological brain structures that support "addiction" to intense feelings of love make perfect sense.

Taking pleasure in proximity and having an irrational devotion to an irreplaceable other that overrides pain, fear, and logical thought is necessary if we view the power of love in the context of survival. Think of a prehistoric man carrying a limp deer home through thigh-high snow to feed the vulnerable woman and children waiting for him. Without the emotional bonds that connect them to each other, what else would motivate him to keep going through so much exhasution, danger, and pain? Without the original craving for one specific person, people wouldn't stick together long enough to form this attachment—the deeper bond that remains after romantic love fades.

One interesting theory is that this pair-bonding process was the original function of the brain's reward system. More modern addictive substances and diversions may actually be hijacking the ancient neurological highway of pleasure craving that romantic love has ridden on since the beginning of time. While our pleasure system can be recruited for the pursuit of dark vices involving syringes and crack pipes, it's true purpose may be to drive us toward the pleasure we experience when we're with our irreplaceable other. It's there to pull us toward the healthy attachment that sustains marriages, families, and enduring partnerships that create an ideal society. It's there to push us towards True Love: the most powerful, most positive, and most noble of all human experiences.

Unless, of course, you fall in love with ("get addicted to") the wrong person—someone who rejects you, who is not compatible with you, or whose personality/values/judgment you'd find off-putting were it not for the surge of endorphins you feel in their presence and the horrific craving you feel in their absence.

Even if you know in your head that the relationship is wrong, when you're separated from your beloved your reward center still craves closeness with them. When you're cut off from your irreplaceable other, the obsessions start and the compulsion to connect with them can be overpowering. If you've ever gone through a bad breakup, you know that "relationship withdrawal" is a uniquely horrible experience. It consumes your mind, you can't eat, you can't sleep, and you burn with anxiety that only reconnection with your lover can soothe.

Sadly, this is what happened to Tom. Of all the Exaholics I've worked with, his preoccupation with Sarah was one of the most toxic. Certainly the most tragic. We circled the drain together many times: rejection, obsession and craving, reunion, honeymoon, mounting frustration, rejection. And each time, through our work together, the threads binding him to her stretched thinner as his awareness of his unhealthy dependence grew. He became more aware of the negative consequences his addiction to her was creating, and more able to see the relationship for the unhealthy roller coaster ride it was.

But for Tom, clarity about Sarah and freedom from his addiction came too late. He started losing weight and complaining of odd pains in his stomach, and by the time he finally went to the doctor, he was diagnosed with late-stage pancreatic cancer, with a dismal chance of survival. Sarah accompanied him to one doctor's appointment and then bailed for good, mumbling something about how "she just couldn't stand to see him like this." Clearly, the thrill was gone. She abandoned him to face the procedures, the chemo, the surgery, and the recovery alone.

Only then did he see the truth of his addiction for the hollow reality it was: the pursuit of fleeting feelings, and a deeply unhealthy fixation on the wrong person. He'd left the security of his marriage and family to dance in a mirage of excitement that crumbled to dust in his hands when he reached out for real support. Like Coleridge waking from his fever-dream about a pleasure-dome, Tom finally came to his senses only to find that he was alone in a desert without the True Love of attachment and commitment—from Sarah, at least.

So he went home. Because thankfully for him, the True Love of his ex-wife and children had endured through the years of his obsessive intoxication. Their True Love, the unbreakable bond of a merciful family, was the nourishing, stable connection of support that was there for Tom at the end of his life.

In his final days, Tom was finally healed of his unhealthy attachment to Sarah. He found forgiveness and redemption when he came to understand and appreciate what True Love really is: the quiet, unselfish service to the well-being of another that endures long after the sparkles of romantic love fade. It's not always fun or exciting. It's not terribly addictive. But it is there at three a.m. to mop up vomit and to shelter you at the end of your life when you have nowhere else to go. Only True Love has the courage to walk beside you into death, and maybe even meet you again on the other side.

True Love is never an addiction, because it's not actually a feeling at all—but a values-based choice.

Tom's addiction to Sarah destroyed his life. He might have died of cancer regardless, but the last decade of his life was largely spent in misery, punctuated by brief moments of euphoria. Tom wasted his final years chasing the dragon of love. His addiction blew apart his family. It damaged his relationships with his children. It kept him hanging in limbo, waiting and hoping for an impossible outcome. It severely compromized his ability to be happy and well.

It's easy to hear Tom's story and get moralistic about it. "Well he shouldn't have cheated on his wife," you might think, huffily. Or, "Sheesh—what an idiot. Clearly that woman was bad news." Its easy to look at these situations from the outside and have judgment about them, in the same way it is easy to look at (or be) an Exaholic and see someone who is irrationally stuck on an unavailable or unhealthy person, despite not wanting to be.

It seems crazy until you have the rest of the information about how important love actually is, how it works, and what it does to us. Only then will Tom's story—and yours—start to make sense.

PART 2
WHY YOU ARE STUCK ON YOUR EX

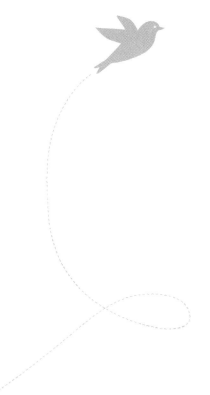

4

BUILT TO LOVE

"We are born to need each other."

—DR. SUSAN JOHNSON,
IF YOU ARE AN EXAHOLIC, YOU FEEL STUCK.

You want to move on but you simply cannot stop caring about your Ex. You feel helpless to stop the pain, the longing, and the craving you have for them—even when you know that the relationship is over and that it should be over.

Exaholics often feel ashamed of this reality. They hate the fact that they still care so deeply about someone who has rejected them or who mistreated them to the point where they had to do the rejecting. They feel like something must be wrong with them for continuing to ache for and crave the presence of their phantom lover. They genuinely feel that they must be uniquely miserable and broken people who are unworthy of love because they should be able to get over it. The word "pathetic" flies around a lot in my sessions with Exaholics. It's how they make sense of their apparent helplessness to stop their despair and pain over their lost love.

I need to tell you something really, really important:

There is nothing wrong with you for feeling the way you do.

Your body and mind was built to do exactly what it is doing right now: develop and maintain powerfully strong attachments to others.

The fact that you are in so much pain, that you are traumatized by rejection, and ache so deeply for this loss is evidence that you are a normal, healthy person. You were built to bond. You are hurting because you were built to hurt when your bond to a cherished person is broken. The pain you are experiencing is part of a natural, biological process. Everyone who loses their primary attachment suffers deeply.

The truth is, we all depend on love for our literal survival, to a degree that is difficult to fully appreciate. In our collective journey through time we have lost our understanding of how powerful and important love is. We have forgotten that love is a basic drive that we seek from the moment of birth, and a basic need that is vital to our existence. As a byproduct of that amnesia, your reactions of pain, grief, and torment at losing love are viewed as problematic by everyone—including you.

The problem is not that you are hurting. The problem is that we have collectively forgotten what a primary need love truly is. And you are being judged—both by yourself and others—for having an absolutely normal human experience.

LOVE: A FORGOTTEN NEED

The ones who came before us understood love. The well-worn, prehistoric Venus figurines, ancient stone carvings of lovers wrapped around each other for all eternity, moments of tenderness frozen in fresco, and liquid poetry that still rolls off the tongue after thousands of years all carry a message of love through the millennia.

> "Let him kiss me with the kisses of his mouth:
> for thy love is sweeter than wine."
> —Song of Solomon 1:2

But as the Age of Reason spun its gilded arches and turrets up into the sky of ideas and technology, it lost sight of the earthy foundation on which humanity was built: love. Philosophers, academics, and scientists minimized its importance, preferring to look elsewhere to understand one another and ourselves.

When scientific exploration exploded on the scene a few centuries ago, excited researchers started dashing around measuring things, squinting through telescopes, and breathlessly explaining how everything works—stars, plants, electricity, machines, and our bodies. The scientific method works brilliantly when applied to most aspects of the natural world. If you can see it through a microscope, or measure it, or calculate its properties, or observe it conform predictably to a theory, it's considered worthy of study.

However, our inner experience is much harder to quantify and accurately explain. Probably because of its vexing nature, for a long time psychology was overlooked by hard science. For centuries, matters of the heart were tackled primarily by theologians or philosophers. Psychology was considered a branch of philosophy until the late nineteenth century. Human psychological processes were therefore vulnerable to being explained by either supernatural factors or grandiose "theories" that were largely based on the opinions of influential charismatic types rather than actual research.

Consequently, our understanding of how people work psychologically was first founded on mysticism and speculation: dream analysis, Jungian archetypes, and Father Freud's suggestively cocked cigars were all we had to go on. Even today at it's most rigorous scientific best, psychology is still largely a "soft science" primarily based on normal distributions and bell curves, with pesky statistical outliers and subjective experiences mucking up the data. This tendency toward vagueness makes psychological research suspicious to hard science. That, combined with its history of mysticism, makes researchers in psychology a bit defensive. Their fragile, academic prowess is threatened when they start drawing conclusions from things so nebulous as feelings.

Because of this, until fairly recently, "love" was thought of as gum-cracking, fluffy stuff in the academic circles of psychology—the domain of poets and teenagers, and absolutely irrelevant to medical and psychological researchers and "real" scientists. For most of the twentieth century, love wasn't just considered irrelevant to relationships or human functioning, it simply wasn't considered at all.

Freud and his disciples dismissed love as a distracting byproduct of repressed sexual urges, and a confounding phenomenon that must be analyzed away, lest it create neuroticism. The chain-smoking behaviorists of the 1950s thought of loving feelings as being a result of the reinforcement of pleasurable gratifications. The cognitive camp didn't think of love at all, preferring to believe that people simply made a series of rational decisions leading them down a straight and logical path of social conventions and stable family life.

Well into the 1980s and beyond, even marriage and family therapists conceptualized relationships as functioning on a set of unspoken mutual agreements, defined by power struggles, hierarchies, and the replaying of old dramas from the family of origin. The words, "But I love him," elicited eye rolls from therapists and researchers, rather than an attempt at understanding. To this day, well-meaning pediatricians advise parents to let their babies "cry it out" so as not to encourage unhealthy dependence.

As a result, our culture lost sight of what love really was, what it actually does to us and for us, and what happens to us when we lose it. At least, until fairly recently.

It's only been over the last few decades some brave pioneers have hauled love research back out from the dumpster behind the university and started exploring it with open minds. In doing so, their science is putting love back where it belongs: in the center of our understanding of people—who we are, how we work, and what we need. As it turns out, love is among the most powerful and essential parts of the human experience. We literally require love for our survival.

A Theory of Attachment

This radical shift in thinking began in the 1950s, when the work of a psychiatrist named John Bowlby began to circulate. In the 1930s, Bowlby was a young doctor working in a psychiatric hospital with orphaned children. He began to notice a pattern of disordered functioning in kids who had been deprived of the love of a family.

He saw that kids raised without loving bonds did not do well. He observed that some children seemed nearly non-human in their emotional disconnection and apparent disregard of other people. They stole or became violent without any empathy for the feelings of those that they hurt. They appeared numb to their own feelings, as well as those of others.

Exaholics Breaking Your Addiction to an Ex Love

Other children seemed frantic to connect with people, not discriminating between people they knew and strangers. They clung to whoever was nearby, professing their love to people they just met. They could not tolerate being alone, even for a moment. They were also prone to mysterious rages and intensely manipulative and controlling behavior designed to make other people gratify their emotional needs.

Bowlby had an idea that the deprivation of love these orphans endured changed something important about the way they functioned.

He then spent many years observing how children and parents naturally interact with each other in cultures all over the world—as well as the consequences to children who do not have those normal, early interactions. He noticed that babies and young children who came from warm, loving homes had things in common: trust, easygoing temperaments, good relationships with others, higher intelligence, and better health in contrast to abused, neglected, or orphaned kids.

He noticed that, like all mammals, babies and young children become extremely distressed when they are separated from their parents. Across all cultures, normal babies vigorously protest separation and frantically attempt to reconnect with their parents when their connection is threatened. He also saw that babies and young children who were abandoned eventually gave up the fight of attempting to reconnect and sank into a depressive despair.

John Bowlby saw that babies who had their physical needs met but did not have an emotional connection with a caregiver, often stopped growing and wasted away. He provided mountains of observational evidence to support his ideas, including heartbreaking films of toddlers in anguish at a hospital where the policy at the time was to strictly limit parents to one weekly visit with their children.

Old, odd stories began to make sense when seen through the lens of Bowlby's theory. At some point, someone dusted off the account of Frederick II, a thirteenth century Roman emperor, who accidentally and unknowingly undertook one of the first experiments in human attachment theory. Frederick II wanted to find out what the "natural" language of people was. So he decided to take a group of infants and have them raised by foster wet-nurses who were instructed not to speak or interact with them at all. Then he'd be able to find out whether their natural language was Greek, Hebrew, or Latin. However, he never found out: all the babies died.

The pieces were coming together. For decades prior, doctors and psychologists had been genuinely mystified by a phenomenon called "Failure to Thrive" in very well-cared-for babies and young children. The best science available in the early twentieth century advised that the best way to care for orphaned infants was in hygienic nurseries where they would be protected from germs. This was achieved through a sterile environment and by keeping human interaction to a minimum. Despite being fed and kept warm and clean, these babies died in droves.

Bowlby wove these observational strands together into his theory. His premise was that human infants and children literally require love, close contact, and connection with people who love them and are affectionate toward them in order to develop normally, both cognitively and emotionally. An absence of love and affection is life-threatening to young children.

He speculated that, because this need is so fundamental, both mothers and babies are hard-wired to form an instinctive and powerful emotional bond with each other. This bond makes babies seek their mothers for security and shelter in times of distress. It makes babies crave closeness with their mothers and become very upset when separated. It drives mothers to be inseparable from their babies. He called it "The Theory of Attachment."

Although observable phenomena fit his theory, in Bowlby's own era his Attachment Theory was ridiculed and put down. The cool psychoanalysts cattily bashed the notion that anything as earthy and physical as maternal affection could be more important than subconscious or symbolic sexual urges. Behaviorists argued that "love" was simply a thing that happened when basic needs were gratified. In the neat equations of the cognitive psychologists, love did not compute as well as logic.

But a few people paid attention. Bowlby's theory felt right to them. It made sense. They talked about it, thought about it, and in the 1950s and '60s, researchers began experimenting with his ideas.

LOVE AND ATTACHMENT IN HUMAN DEVELOPMENT

In the 1950s, Harry Harlow began testing Bowlby's ideas about Attachment Theory versus the Gratification Theory of behaviorists with baby monkeys. His team offered orphaned infant monkeys a wire mother replica fitted with bottle "breasts" to nurse, or a plush fluffy mother replica with no milk. Hungry baby monkeys would creep to the cold breasts to nurse, but cling to the fluffy mommy monkeys for comfort when fearful or stressed. Being rewarded with milk was not the key to bonding. Check minus for the behaviorists.

Harlow also found that the presence of even a surrogate mother allowed baby monkeys to manage stress, explore their environment, and assert themselves. Without it, they would cower and suck their thumbs for comfort. Baby monkeys totally deprived of maternal love and connection grew up to be hostile, violent, and incapable of functioning normally in monkey society in patterns that echoed those of Bowlby's orphans. Harlow's experimentation with monkeys supported Bowlby's ideas that love and connection was crucial to emotional and social development.

In a long term, longitudinal study beginning in 1969, Mary Ainsworth was able to predict outcomes for human infants based on the quality of their early attachments with their mothers. She correctly predicted that infants with warm, stable, and responsive moms would develop a secure attachment to them. She further anticipated that these babies would grow into confident children, able to make friends, and generally feel good about themselves and the world around them. Over subsequent years of tracking they conformed to her expectations. Securely attached babies had better outcomes in every area of their life, including better social and romantic relationships, a sense of confidence and personal empowerment, academic achievement, better health, and more financial success.

She also correctly, and tragically, correlated infants with emotionally unavailable or harsh parents with the development of avoidant attachment styles as infants and predicted that these tendencies would persist into later childhood. She also demonstrated through observed outcomes that these "avoidant" kids trended toward delinquency, substance abuse, and antisocial personality traits as they grew older. She foresaw that infants with distracted or erratic parents would develop an anxious attachment style and be more likely to grow into children and adults who were hungry for attention, struggled with self-esteem and anxiety, had trouble making friends, and tended to need high levels of reassurance in their romantic relationships.

Her undeniable findings were a showstopper. As her results were publicized, other factions began to incorporate the primacy of attachment into their understanding of people. Before the psychoanalysts flew screeching back to their covens, the Jungian analysts vanished in a puff of purple smoke, the fuzzy family therapists resumed their dramatic enactments, and the behaviorists returned to the rats in their buzzing fluorescent labs, they all broke off a piece of the Attachment Theory communion wafer. Amen. Since then, virtually every flavor of psychology has accepted that love and attachment are vital to early childhood development and human functioning.

ATTACHMENT AND HUMAN DEVELOPMENT

Over subsequent decades of research into attachment and neuropsychology, it has been well established that mammalian brains—from rats to puppies to humans—require physical and emotional contact with others in order to develop normally. Human infants in particular have an intense need for attention and interaction in the first years of life in order to develop normally, both cognitively and emotionally.

For example, babies come out of the womb hard-wired to look at faces, and are especially drawn to eyes. The brains of human babies develop through mirror interactions involving attentive caregivers spending hours face-to-face, smiling, cooing, and reflecting emotions back to them. Through the faces of their caregivers, babies learn about themselves. Similarly babies acquire language through hours of pleasant babbling conversations with their parents pointing out objects and talking to them.

Secure attachment is also vital to cognitive development. Babies and toddlers use their parents as safe harbors in an uncertain world. They look to their mother's face before reacting to ambiguous situations in order to understand how they should feel. The more confident they are that their parents are available, the more they will take risks, explore, and conduct the messy experiments necessary to understand physical reality and grow their brains. Fearful toddlers who feel alone in the world do not explore nearly as much as those who are securely attached; neurological development is negatively impacted as a result.

Attachment plays an important role in the physical health of babies and small children. For example, infants are physiologically regulated through proximity to their mothers. Their breathing, heart rate, and body temperature are stabilized and optimized when they are in close physical contact with their mothers. This is true both for humans and many other baby mammals.

Furthermore, young babies cannot yet regulate themselves nor soothe themselves emotionally. They most borrow the emotional regulation system of their parents before theirs develops. This requires a patient, present, comforting parent available to cuddle, shush, and soothe on demand. Over time, an echo of a calm parent's emotional core resonates in a child, providing an inner sense of safety, security, and confidence. Being able to "borrow" a calm adult's emotional regulation system allows children to develop the capacity to calm themselves down, too. Being connected to a safe and caring adult also allows children to internalize and incorporate a calm, reassuring inner voice. Through experiencing consistent love, children develop a positive expectation of themselves and others that they will carry into the world, and into all of their subsequent relationships.

How Secure Attachment Develops

Secure attachment is built through thousands of seemingly insignificant daily interactions that communicate care and responsiveness. Babies develop secure attachment to an adult when that person shows a baby accurate empathy, meaning that they understand what the child wants or needs, and then provide it. The adult must be highly attuned to a baby in order to do this, picking a baby up when they want to be picked up, and putting them down when they communicate they've had enough. They understand when a baby is hungry and respond by feeding them, not by getting angry with them or changing their diaper.

Babies cry because they cannot chase after their mothers, they can only seek responsiveness by communicating their distress. This is especially true when they feel pain or are nervous or afraid. They cling to their parents and insist on togetherness, they treat separation like a threat to their lives.

Their cries are their begging for reconnection and love. They say, "Are you there? Are you coming back? Please take care of me, I need you!" And as any new mother knows, hearing a baby's cry connects with something deep inside her. Nothing can get in the way of a connected mother whose baby needs her. She seeks them out, craving closeness too. Her emotional wiring for attachment is just as strong as her baby's—it needs to be. They are bonded together in a dance of attachment.

In short: Human babies need to be absolutely slathered with love, affection, and attention for many years in order to develop normally. As every parent knows, parenting a baby well requires an enormous amount of time and energy.

What would compel parents to focus so intently on this needy little being, sacrificing their own needs and feelings in order to care for the baby? Why would anyone prioritize cuddling the baby, gazing into their eyes for hours, singing to them, and carrying them around everywhere over everything else? Love.

Love is a basic human need. For infants, love literally means the difference between life and death. The love showered upon infants and young children provides the foundation of intelligence, as well as physical, emotional, and mental health.

LOVE AND ATTACHMENT IN ADULTS

Our need for love doesn't stop at the threshold of adulthood. In fact, in some ways, as we mature our need for love only becomes stronger. Our understanding of love, attachment, and bonding began with infants and children. But in the late 1980s, marriage and family therapist Dr. Susan Johnson considered the possibility that our need for love and attachment is just as powerful in adulthood as it is in childhood.

Until that point, the concept that love might be an important part of adult relationships was not entertained by marriage counselors. Instead, couples therapists spun elaborate theories in efforts to explain their client's distressed relationships. (As in, "This makes you so angry because he subconsciously reminds you of your father.") Couples therapists instructed couples to speak in calm tones and "use 'I' statements." Couples in counseling dutifully negotiated household chores and went on date nights, but the long-term success rates of marriage counseling were pretty dismal. Even when people were coached into behaving well, they were still aching, anxious, and resentful in the absence of a secure attachment with their partners.

Dr. Johnson looked past the presenting problems of the couples in front of her ("We can't communicate," or "She doesn't follow through," or "He's always mad at me") to see the heart of the matter: disrupted, insecure attachments. She correlated the patterns of anger and withdrawal she saw in the couples she was working with to the protest and despair response that all mammals display when blocked from connection to their attachment figures.

She saw that adults have emotional needs for comfort, security, and reassurance just as children do. Where children are dependent, adults are interdependent on each other. Adult bonds are maintained through intimate conversations, sexual experiences, supporting each other's hopes and dreams, physical closeness, working together toward mutually important goals, and sharing the joys and frustrations of life together.

While it's not as obvious as the screeching need of babies, adults have profound needs for secure attachment that has now been well documented in research. Dozens of studies have shown that people with satisfying relationships—particularly a strong intimate relationship—tend to report higher levels of subjective happiness, have fewer chronic health problems, and live longer. Conversely, a lack of primary social support is correlated with higher rates of anxiety and depression, later-life cognitive decline, an increased risk of heart disease, and earlier mortality.

Self-sufficiency is a myth. Our ability to be happy and well is largely dependent upon our ability to find people who help soothe and support us, and then staying connected to them. There is strong evidence to support that adults physically coregulate each other, similarly to mothers and infants. This means that our physical wellness, including heart rate, breathing, immune system, sleeping patterns, and emotional regulation are all strengthened and smoothed out by our proximity to someone with whom we feel safe and connected.

In 2008, researchers David Sbarra and Cindy Hazan found that, just like tiny babies depend on their mother's breathing, mood state, and biological rhythms to regulate their emotional and physical wellness, adults do too. Being closely connected coregulates you, or matches you to your partner's rhythms and functioning, and separation dysregulates you—creating erratic emotional and physiological functioning. For example, adults separated from their partners show disrupted sleeping and eating patterns, they have less stable heart rhythms, are more easily upset, and more difficult to calm down. Myron Hofer's 1987 work showed that the regulatory impact of our relationships is hidden most of the time. It's only when attachments are disrupted, and people become dysregulated, that we see the true physical power of an attachment bond.

Having a healthy and secure primary relationship is also vital to emotional functioning in adults. Our connection to our number-one person becomes our emotional home base—our soft place to fall. As adults, we are soothed when our partners are there for us emotionally in times of distress. We feel connected when our feelings are honored and validated. We feel deeply connected to our partners when they communicate, "You are important to me" through their actions. We reach out to our beloved in times of fear, emotional pain, or in efforts to reconnect when distance creeps into the relationship. All of these small daily moments of touching base help us restore our equilibrium. And just like babies, when the dance of attachment is disrupted, we protest.

Sometimes, when our secure attachments feel threatened, our protests come in the form of gentle, vulnerable bids for reconnection that are easy for our partners to respond to: "I miss you. Let's go to bed early tonight." But because primal fears and anxieties flare in moments when our attachment bond is threatened, they often take on harsh tones: "Where the hell were you? I've been waiting here by myself all night!" The "protest" adults engage in often sounds like criticism. We can even become hostile and berate our partners, in efforts to make them understand how not okay we are, and attempt to regain their love and responsiveness.

When these efforts to reconnect and obtain reassurance and responsiveness are met with rejection or apparent indifference, we continue to protest and pursue—often becoming angrier and more extreme in our efforts to communicate our distress. The offending partner's secure attachment is disrupted as well, as their formerly safe person has suddenly and mysteriously become a hostile and critical source of fear instead of comfort. Predictably, they withdraw in self-protection, which further frightens and inflames their pursuing partner.

Dr. Johnson saw her pursuing partners protestation as the adult version of the howling that babies engage in under the same circumstances—but spinning out into arguments that threatened attachment further and created feelings of fear, rejection, and despair in the withdrawing partner.

By tying the emotional needs of adults back to Bowlby's Attachment Theory, Dr. Johnson created a method of couples counseling called Emotionally Focused Couples Therapy that helps couples learn how to understand each other accurately and understand when a seemingly hostile or cold response is an attempt to communicate protest, fear, or despair. By helping couples repair their secure attachments with each other, she helped them rebuild their relationships.

In doing so, she revolutionized the field of marriage and family therapy by bringing love back into the conversation. Years of subsequent research has shown that helping couples restore their strong bonds is much more effective and longer lasting than other more "rational" and behavioristic approaches to couples counseling. Once again, John Bowlby's theories about love and attachment were vindicated.

Broken Bonds

As you well know, not all relationships can be mended. Sometimes couples cannot find emotional safety and contentment with each other no matter how hard they both want to. Sometimes trust is broken beyond repair. Other times romantic attraction to a new person tears a formerly secure attachment apart. But at the core of it, relationships end when one person feels hopeless that the other person can ever be the person they want and need them to be.

Whether you have been rejected, or whether you are the one who has determined that your lover will never be the emotionally safe and responsive person you need them to be does not matter. The primal fear that broken bonds trigger seethe inside of you, out of control.

Your ancient attachment machinery grinds into life in these moments when your bonds are breaking. When you are suffering from a ruptured attachment your body is under an immense amount of physiological stress and strain, increasing both your heart rate and ambient stress hormone levels. You are experiencing an involuntary protest response. Every fiber of your being, every shred of your attention if focused like a laser on your partner, their absence, and how you could reconnect with them. If you don't, despair ensues.

People going through the protest phase of a breakup often experience a great deal of shame for how absolutely unhinged they feel. They feel like they are going crazy and that something is terribly wrong with them for feeling as out of control and inconsolable as they do. That you feel this way is not because of a moral shortcoming or personality flaws. It is because you are human. You feel the way that all humans who have bonded to another person respond to unwanted loss and separation: you are profoundly traumatized.

Dr. Brené Brown said it best, in her article on happiness and perfection, "A deep sense of love and belonging is an irreducible need of all people. We are biologically, cognitively, physically, and spiritually wired to love, to be loved, and to belong. When those needs are not met we don't function as we are meant to. We break. We fall apart. We numb. We ache. We hurt others. We get sick."

You were built to love and to be loved. The fact is that from the moment you took your first breath on this earth you were seeking to bond with another human who loved you. The all-consuming pain and despair that you're experiencing when those bonds are broken feels like an unstoppable force of nature . . . *because it is*.

5

THE NATURE OF LOVE

"Romantic love is not an emotion, it's a drive."

—DR. HELEN FISHER

IF THERE IS ONE STATEMENT THAT SUMS UP
THE ENTIRE EXAHOLIC EXPERIENCE, IT IS THIS:
"I KNOW, INTELLECTUALLY, THAT I NEED TO MOVE ON.
BUT I FEEL LIKE I CAN'T."

Most people, in the aftermath of a failed relationship, feel two ways about it at the same time: they know it's over, but they don't *feel* like it's over. It's incredibly frustrating to feel that there are two distinct parts of you, pulling you in different directions. One part, the healthy rational part, knows what you should do: move on. The other part of you feels like it is a slave to love, maddeningly, irrationally obsessed with your Ex. And the obsessed part is winning.

Love possesses us seemingly against our will, and makes us do things that we would never do otherwise. Sometimes this works out well. Sometimes it does not.

If we are fortunate, we will fall in love and become ferociously bonded to a good person who can love us well in return. In these positive situations, love brings out the very best in us, prompting us to live lives of both meaning and heroism as we selflessly devote ourselves to the people we cherish. Men and women all over the world spend their lives happily sacrificing everything they have to throw their children over the wall and into a better future. Obedience to healthy, wholesome, and reciprocated love can lead us to a life full of compassion, generosity, emotional security, grace, and connection with others. It creates healthy children and strong partnerships and is the foundation of a life worth living.

However, as you know too well, the force of love doesn't always lead us into the light. It can also lead us astray. Love can strike like lightning, unpredictably, sometimes attaching us to unhealthy or unavailable people. Love can chain us to relationships that we know are not good for us. Love can make us do terrible things in efforts to win the love of someone who we may never be able to please. Love can drive us to the brink of obsessive madness, wasting years of our lives longing for someone who cannot love us back.

Whether it's positive or diabolical, when love is alive inside of you, you feel powerless to do anything but obey it. You crave contact with your lover. You ache to be with them again. You feel torn apart, even frantic, at the thought of being apart from them forever. These feelings make you do things that you would never do otherwise. They eclipse your better judgment and roar past the part of you that wishes you could just move on. You wish you could change the way you feel, but you can't.

Why does love have such an incredible power over you? Over all of us? Why can it possess us to the point that it overwhelms our will, self-control, and rational minds? Why does it sometimes go so terribly wrong?

For decades, therapists such as myself have sat with our clients as they suffered and wrestled with these questions. We've had a general understanding of the sticky, seemingly addictive bonds of relationships—particularly in light of Attachment Theory. But as we therapists listen to the stories of our clients unspool, often the best we can do is grope around in the dark with them as they attempt to make sense of what's happening. It can be hard to understand the biological mechanisms powering their experiences, and the larger patterns and processes at work in their unique tales of heartbreak and love. As we listen to their one-of-a-kind stories, we sense a familiar pattern, but without knowing *why*. (Or, more important, what needs to happen for healing to occur.) It was only when Dr. Helen Fisher came striding in to turn the lights on with her research on the nature of love that we could finally see what we've been fondling and speculating about all these years.

Dr. Fisher has taken the study of love to the next level, dragging it into the twenty-first century. An evolutionary biologist, she has reminded us of not just the evolutionary necessity of love, but also taught us how love actually works. She traced the etiology of love through its predictable course of lust, romantic love, and attachment, and then essentially put the process under a microscope (or rather, a functional MRI). She conducted a series of experiments in which she measured the brain activity of people in love (newly in love, in long-term relationships, and also rejected lovers) through functional magnetic resonance imaging (fMRI), and was able to pinpoint the areas of the brain and neurological processes at work in our experience of love and loss. Much of what we understand about the physiologically addictive process of love, the fact that it is a survival drive, and the impact of those realities on people's lives, stems from her groundbreaking research.

LOVE: A FORCE OF NATURE

Here's her first point: Nature really, really needs you to fall in love and attach to other people.

In 1994, Dr. Fisher published her work, "The Nature of Romantic Love," in which she reminded us that, from an evolutionary perspective, love is vital to every aspect our very existence. Since we emerged as a species about 100,000 years ago, we humans have had serious challenges to overcome. We are soft and weak compared to the predators that surrounded us in nature—even compared to our great ape cousins. We have no fangs or claws, or even a pelt to keep us warm. All we have are our brains . . . and each other.

Evolutionarily speaking, humans simply do not survive as individuals. The success of our species is largely due to our collective nature. One person with a spear can't easily take down an elephant or bear. But together we have conquered an entire planet. Since the

Dreamtime, when we shuffled out of Africa and across the mountains and steppes of Eurasia, we did it together. In loyal clans and tribes we hunted with each other and for each other, we took care of one another's children, we defended one another. We put our brains together. Our societies became stratified, and strengthened in the process. It is only by virtue of our collective social systems, and the fact that not everyone needs to directly produce food, that our art, science, and technology has advanced to the point it is today. We need one another.

But even more vital than our need to bond with a tribe or clan, is our need to bond with a partner—a mate. The ultimate purpose of any animal is to reproduce. That's the bottom line of survival as a species—to keep at least one kid alive long enough so that they too can pass along the family genes. Here humans are at another disadvantage: Human infants are entirely dependent and vulnerable for a very long time compared to other mammals. In order to develop our magnificent minds, human babies require the opportunity to explore, learn, and grow in a protected environment for much longer than other animals do. This creates significant problems unless there are stable attachments supporting both the baby and their parent.

In the few months that baby monkeys are dependent, they can cling to their mother's flat backs. But our survival required us to stand up. To see farther. To migrate. And that meant that human mothers had to carry their babies with them . . . and for a long damn time. From a biological perspective, a woman with a baby or small child is incredibly vulnerable: She cannot defend herself or provide for herself as easily with a baby in her arms. Evolutionarily, a human woman has needed a mate (or a village) who is devoted to her and her children. Having a mate to love her and care for her and their child massively ups the odds that that child will make it to adulthood. And of course, that child needs to be adored full-time by at least one primary caregiver in order to give them the tender responsive care and safety they need to become healthy adults. At least from an evolutionary and historical perspective, a parent needs someone to care about them and help them in order for them to meet the needs of a child in turn.

Whether you look at it from a clan level, couple level, or parent/child level, love—the force that bonds us to each other—is as essential to our survival as any of our other primary survival requirements, like food, water, and warmth.

Because love is so vital to every aspect of our reproductive success, we have love-inducing machinery hard-wired in our brains. In fact there are old, deep, and specific structures and neural systems in our brains that are built for this very purpose, ready and waiting to flare into action like a light switch in a house waiting to be flipped on. Except that when the light of romantic love begins to glow, it is very, very difficult to turn it off again. And from the perspective of nature, this process of bonding is crucial. Our ability to form stable, unbreakable attachments to a mate is key to our survival. This is a good thing.

Unless you're an Exaholic. Unless you are stuck on someone who can't love you back. Unless you're attached to a painful and unsatisfying relationship. Unless you are desperate to let go and move on but feel trapped in the past. Then it's bad.

I don't know about you, but for me, understanding how things work helps me feel more in control and empowered. When I understand why something is happening, it helps me rise above the immediate experience and see the longer view. I stop thrashing around in my feelings and feel calmer when I know that what I'm going through is a *thing*, and especially if that thing is normal. It gives me hope.

That's what I'd like to offer you in this chapter—insight and understanding into what's going on with you. I especially want you to understand why you feel like you have some kind of split personality, with your head telling you one thing and your heart telling you another. For this reason, I am going to teach you what love is, how it operates, and why it creates such a powerful hold over you.

To understand what's going on inside you, you need a basic understanding of your brain.

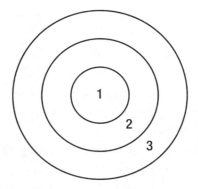

1. Brainstem
2. Midbrain or Limbic Brain
3. Neocortex

YOUR BRAIN 101

Our brains evolved over millennia, through countless survival victories. When our forebears had neurological traits that made them more adaptable to their environments, their offspring were more likely to survive into adulthood and have successful children of their own. As species evolved and progressed, more advanced neurological structures were built on the platforms of those of preceding generations. We humans have inherited the latest model of brain: the three-layer deluxe edition.

BRAIN STEM

The deepest, oldest layer of your brain is built on a reptilian chassis and drive train and is the command center controlling your automatic bodily functions like breathing, maintaining your body temperature, reflexes, movement, and blinking. We share this layer of brain in common with reptiles. This core area of our brain is in charge of our survival drives like hunger, thirst, safety, lust, rage, and fear. That's about it. As far as can be said for brains, they're pretty simple machines.

Consequently, there is not much happening emotionally inside of a lizard. They don't really have feelings in the way we think of feelings. Reptiles have drives. Survival drives are powerful motivations that an animal is simply compelled to obey, like finding water, having sex, eating something, protecting or attacking when under threat, and finding warmth.

When you recoil in involuntary fear before you've even registered what exactly has scared you, your reptilian-era brain is doing its job. When you are thirsty or very cold, you become single-minded

Exaholics Breaking Your Addiction to an Ex Love

in your determination to drink water or find shelter: You are obeying a commandment issuing forth from the reptilian part of your brain that is either going to keep you alive or die trying.

Reptiles are generally indifferent to their young or other living creatures, unless they are interested in eating them or mating with them. As you know, reptiles lay eggs. Very few species of reptiles stick around to see what happens to their babies.

Mammals, however, are different. Mammals give birth to live young who are entirely dependent on the milk of their mothers for their survival. That means that mammalian babies require mothers who bond with their offspring and care for them intensively in their first days and weeks of helplessness. Furthermore, just like you, mammals of all species (as well as many birds) are selective about whom they choose to mate or pair-bond with, and many have evolved to form pods, packs, and herds—all deeply invested in keeping their partners and families close to them.

Limbic Brain

As eons passed and the brains of ancient creatures evolved in the great fuzzy, milk-dripping factory of the mammalian age, they gained a second layer of brain called the midbrain or the limbic brain. This is the part of your brain that feels emotions. It makes you, like all mammals, socially aware and able to pick up nuances of emotional expression in order to develop and maintain relationships with other animals. Your emotions flare and fade in your limbic system, which also consists of structures allowing you to understand and respond to emotions in others. This part of your brain helps you pick up on social cues, particularly those having to do with emotional communications. Your limbic brain is the seat of your primal emotions and motivational attachment drives: to care for babies, to fall in love, and to attach to a tribe.

In contrast to most other species of mammals (that basically just have limbic engines of emotions, memory, and social motivations built on a frame of primary survival drives), humans got tricked out with a highly advanced communications and guidance system called the neocortex. This is the newest and outermost layer of your brain.

NEOCORTEX

Your neocortex is the part of your brain that really makes you human. It imagines. It is able to think ahead, make decisions, and anticipate consequences. Your neocortex can think abstractly about things that don't even exist yet, and then figure out how to build them. Your neocortex is the part of your brain responsible for language and for communicating your abstract ideas to other people. It doesn't feel, but it thinks about what you're feeling in order to make sense of your experience and decide what to do. We call these features executive functioning skills.

Let's think about our neocortexes for a minute. (Our neocortexes enjoy thinking about themselves.) Even though your neocortex is a state-of-the-art communications and guidance system exclusive to one of earth's most successful species, it has limitations. Although it has a very high opinion of itself, the truth is, it was built over much older, and quite frankly, more powerful brain systems. For all its logic and imagination, your neocortex is relatively powerless against the emotional intensity of your limbic system or the primal drives of your reptilian brain. Most of the time, it doesn't even understand them. It stands, bewildered, trying to make logical sense out of feelings that are not rational, reasonable, or linear: they simply exist. Your neocortex doesn't really know what to do with that.

Imagine a pleasant, mild-mannered person standing in the middle of a drunken, raging brawl, attempting to get everyone's attention by clearing his throat politely and saying reasonable things, and getting increasingly confused as to why no one is listening. That's basically your neocortex trying to manage a limbic emotional storm or fierce and single-minded reptilian drives. It simply gets swept away by the power of the older, deeper parts of your brain that are much more intense and ferocious. Your reptilian brain stem and midbrain are not verbal, they are not visionary, nor are they rational, but they pulse and pound inside of you, creating feelings and urges that you must obey. They are the drumbeats of your survival.

That's why we are all so often frustrated with ourselves for doing the opposite of what we know we should. Your neocortex decides you should lose twenty pounds, clicks around on shopping websites dreaming of your new slim wardrobe, creates motivation charts, and plans menus for the week . . . and then some primal lust for salty fat gets triggered and you eat a whole bag of Ruffles®. Pow: Your reptilian brain just punched your neocortex in the face and took what it wanted.

POSSESSED BY LOVE

The forces of love are much more basic and powerful than your transient cravings for potato chips. Love is a primary drive. It is older than humanity itself, first awakening in our mammalian ancestors as they nuzzled their newborn babies to suckle. The parts of your brain that are involved with love exist at the intersection of your reptilian and limbic brains. The drive for love goes very, very deep. This explains why people will routinely forgo food, sleep, and basic safety in service of love for each other. The power of intense love is humbling to experience.

For example, in the hallucinatory months after our son was born, I was completely swept away by what I can only describe as a primal mothering instinct. Generally fairly easygoing and flexible, I suddenly felt crazed. I felt addicted to my baby. All I wanted to do was be with him and I became intensely agitated if I felt prevented from taking care of him for even a moment. I felt like I would have gone through a brick wall with my teeth to get to him if he needed me. Nothing else mattered.

One time, a few weeks after he was born, my husband and I were in the car, and our son started crying because he was hungry. I insisted that we pull over immediately—*like immediately*—so I could feed him, and flew into a rage when my husband reasonably suggested we wait until we got to our home, less than ten minutes away. I felt so furious that I wanted to bite him if he didn't stop the car right then. (I didn't.) But I felt absolutely enraged and possessed by the deepest, most profound mixture of primal anxiety, anger, and love I'd ever experienced.

Rationally, I knew that I was being completely unreasonable, weird, and controlling but I couldn't help it. Later, I tried to explain this sudden, radical shift in my entire way of being to my confused and alarmed husband. I heard myself saying, "This is how a mother baboon must feel about her baby monkey. This ferocious love is the energy that has kept infants alive for millennia." And as I said those words, it dawned on me that I had been experiencing commandments coming from a very old, very deep, and very powerful part of myself that simply blew away anything coming from my "normal" (neocortex) mind.

Just like my body had all kinds of dormant reproductive machinery that involuntarily fired into action to produce my miraculous little baby, powerful structures in my limbic brain were also recruited into his service without my knowledge or consent. When they roared to life I was entirely possessed by love. Absolutely nothing else mattered at all. Not my need for sleep, food, productive activity, or being civil toward my husband. If my baby was hungry, I just had to feed him right that very second.

It makes sense. From an evolutionary and biological perspective the scarily intense love I felt for my baby was as essential to his survival in the months after his birth as my uterus had been before he was born. Love was a tidal wave of inarticulate emotion. I had to obey it, no matter what my neocortex and the rest of polite society wanted me to do.

We think of our minds as being the seat of our self-awareness. The mind we know is the mind that thinks. But there is more to us. There are older, deeper parts of our brains that are not self-conscious. They simply *are*. We aren't aware of them until they hijack our subjective experiences to serve certain purposes. When they do, they are often much more powerful than the part of your mind you think of as being "you." You must obey.

Love Is a Drive

Romantic love is just as involuntary, powerful, and essential as mother-love. It may be even more so, as the intense cravings for union that go along with romantic love are often what makes babies happen in the first place. Romantic love has also been known to even eclipse the mothering instinct (often tragically). As far as your brain and body are concerned, if you do not fall in love, you are going to die in the most absolute sense from a biological perspective:

Exaholics Breaking Your Addiction to an Ex Love

without passing on your genes. Therefore the structures that exist inside of you, making you a slave to love, are immensely more powerful than mere emotions. They are survival drives—primal forces inside of us that have existed much longer than humanity itself.

A drive is not a feeling, but an intense motivational state. If you were freezing in sub-zero temperatures, nothing would stop you from frantically seeking shelter until you achieved warmth. That is a drive. Romantic love is such a fundamental part of the human pair-bonding and mating process that it is a drive too: It's not a mood state, but rather a motivational state.

Here's the deal: Falling in love happens at a much deeper level of your brain than your thinking brain. It has nothing to do with the good intentions of your neocortex. Neurologically, love happens at the intersection of your reptilian and limbic brains. It is old. It is deep. And it is very, very powerful.

This is why you feel like you are going crazy right now. Your drive to maintain connection with your cherished person simply feels more powerful than your neocortex, and it is nearly impossible to control. As an Exaholic, I'm sure you are well aware of these crazy-feeling limbic-level impulses at work in your own life right now. Your neocortex is still there, but its voice gets lost in the primal howl of your limbic brain when you are confronted by fear, loss, and rejection.

When you fall in love, it sets your limbic system ablaze. You go through a process that essentially addicts you to another person on a primal level, in parts of your brain that are much deeper and older than your Johnny-come-lately neocortex. This isn't your fault and it doesn't mean that anything is wrong with you. This is what you were built to do. But it's why you feel so powerless to control the feelings that you have for your Ex.

Your neocortex can still tell you, rationally, that the relationship is over. It can produce lots of evidence as to why this person is not good for you. It is standing by, wringing its hands, whining about how normal people should behave every time you compulsively check your Ex's Facebook page again. But it doesn't really matter. Even with your neocortex shrieking at you to behave yourself, it feels like you simply must obey your drives.

Nature knows what it's doing. From the moment you met your Ex, a chain reaction of events began deep in your reptilian and limbic brain without your conscious knowledge or consent. Your body and mind went through a series of emotional and biochemical experiences that bonded you to your Ex, through a highly addictive process: the process of falling in love.

FALLING IN LOVE

Just like birds-of-paradise strut around with their swanky dances, enticing each other to come closer, we have a similarly instinctive and involuntary process through which we fall in love and become deeply bonded to each other. Becoming a couple is a process that weaves together the three elements of mammalian pair-bonding: lust, romantic love, and attachment. These experiences recruit separate yet interrelated parts of your reptilian and limbic brain, igniting them in an addictive process that welds you emotionally to another person.

LUST

In adults, the first stage of bonding is often lust. Lust is the simple urge to have sex. Lust is not specific to any particular person, just whoever is nearby and good enough. Functional magnetic resonance imaging (fMRI) scans on the brains of people in love have determined that the area of the brain associated with feelings of lust resides in a very old and deep part of your limbic brain. This is a part of your brain that we share with other animals, including rabbits, flamingos, and horny goats. When it is active, an ancient part of our brain is issuing a commandment to copulate—and the sooner the better.

Imagine a young man surveying a crowded bar on a Saturday night, scanning the room for women of the right age and shape who appear to be available. There are a number of prospects, and whomever he connects with first will likely have his undivided attention for the moment. But there is no special bond, no attachment. When lust is driving the bus, the girl at the bar is replaceable—her value is based on her immediate availability as much as her general attractiveness.

Lust is perking his ears and making him pay attention to women he might be with. As he thinks about sex, he's aroused and highly attuned to possible possibilities. Lust can be an end in itself or it can be the sexual spark that ignites a romantic relationship.

ROMANTIC LOVE

If lust is a greedy rascal wearing beer goggles at Mardi Gras, romantic love is a Casanova strumming a guitar outside your window, a troubadour singing love songs written just for you. While lust is indiscriminate—simply seeking sex—romantic love is a fixation on one particular person. Romantic love has been described as "being on fire" for a beloved person. It is a total and absolute focus on a cherished and irreplaceable other.

Romantic love starts when one special person begins to glow with a certain energy and starts to seem uniquely special and important. The first clue that romantic love is starting to bloom? You start thinking about the special person when they are not around. People often describe these thoughts as "intrusive," meaning that they are involuntary and seem to come out of nowhere.

Simple lust drives our young man at the bar to talk to different women. But as he chats up one, he notices that there is something about her. He can't quite put his finger on it, but she is touching something inside of him: the way she smiles, the sound of her voice, or something she says. All of a sudden, she begins to stand out from the crowd. He finds himself thinking about her the next day. As he gets dressed the next morning, he wonders what she would think of the shirt he's putting on. He has little conversations with her in his head while he's at work. He goes back to the same bar the following weekend, hoping to speak with her again. He looks past the other women, searching only for her. When he sees her, he feels electrified: feelings of nervousness, anxiety, excitement, and longing whirl inside him all at the same time. Romantic attraction has awakened. He asks her out a few times and she quickly becomes all he can think about. In short order, being with her is the only thing he wants to do. She has won his heart.

Romantic love is an intense drive for emotional connection with one irreplaceable other. When you're in love, you want as much contact with your cherished person as possible. When you are close to your beloved, you may feel euphoria and intense joy. When you're separated from them, you may feel a longing and craving to be together again. They feel like they're with you even when they're not. It's like they occupy a space inside of you. They're all you can think of, all you want, and all you need. You might even say that being in love feels addictive.

Romantic love is nature's way of locking you onto a good mate and wrapping you both up in bonds of enchantment that hold you together. Nature is creating a desire for connection that transcends sex. She is attempting to create a sacred nest of love into which a child may be born, ready and waiting to be lavished with the overflowing love of their mutually devoted parents.

You don't do anything to make this happen. It just happens. When you find the person who, for whatever reason, has this affect on you, you fall in love. It is not a rational decision. Some researchers think that we all have imprints or love maps based on our childhood experiences of being in relationships. But when a person comes along who tickles our lust under the chin and prods our romantic drive awake, ancient mating machinery grinds into life without our permission or intention. When it does, the drive to connect eclipses pretty much everything else that we think, feel, or care about.

Romantic attraction starts for all kinds of reasons. Lust can drive you to have drunken sex with an anonymous stranger and then wake up in the morning next to the most fascinating person in the world. Sometimes simple anxiety is the spark that lights the fuse of love—people are more likely to develop a romantic attraction to another person in an emotionally turbulent or frightening situation. Sometimes falling in love is as basic as proximity combined with convenient timing—an alarm goes off, waking up our primal mating drive, and we turn to whatever available person is nearby at the moment. Sometimes, moments of mutual appreciation in a friendship breathe oxygen on embers that begin crackling into a cozy, romantic fire. And, of course, sometimes we develop wild attractions to deeply troubled but charismatic people who will only make us miserable in the end.

For better or for worse, in most species of mammals, including humans, the overwhelmingly intense and exciting phase of romantic love is fairly brief. It lasts only moments in most rodents, days to weeks among elephants, and a few months among certain species of foxes and penguins. International marriage and divorce statistics reveal that couples are far more likely to get divorced at the three-, four-, or five-year mark of a marriage than any other time. This dovetails precisely with the general amount of time it takes for intense romantic love to fade into healthy attachment: about four years. Almost exactly the same amount of time it requires to get pregnant and raise an infant into a sturdy, independent, self-feeding preschooler.

The intense flash of romantic love does not last very long, but it's not the end of a relationship. Rather, it can be the beginning of a much deeper and longer-lasting connection. Romantic love can ignite coals of attachment that smolder warmly for decades.

ATTACHMENT

Attachment can be thought of as a calm, deep, and profoundly secure love that only comes from trust created over time. Attachment is the bond between long-term lovers, the ties that keep families together, and the usually indestructible force that keeps parents devoted to their children.

Attachment is the connection that's developing between two people behind the scenes while the flames of romantic passion are roaring. After the intense, unsustainable fire of romantic love dies down, secure attachment is like the warm embers that live on eternally, binding us together for a lifetime of affection, caring, and tranquility. Ideally, romantic love bonds us to people who will make good long-term partners: loyal, kind, and compatible.

Imagine that our couple at the bar were a good fit, in terms of their values, personalities, hopes, and dreams. They loved each other and were both stable and emotionally available partners. They fell passionately in love, dated for a couple of years, got married, bought a house, and had some kids.

Maybe they aren't on fire for each other anymore years down the road, but they still enjoy each other's company and fall asleep spooning at night. They are a social unit, they are best friends, and they share a life together. They are each other's number-one person, turning to each other for comfort in times of stress and to celebrate life's joys with each other in happy moments. They have bonded deeply, becoming intertwined and dependent on each other emotionally, financially, and materially.

The forces of nature have done their job: sniffing each other out through lust, driving them together in the searing heat of romantic love, and creating permanent bonds through attachment.

Lust, Love, and Attachment

Although they are related, lust, love, and attachment operate in separate parts of your brain and can act independently. You can have intense feelings of lust for different people while you're intensely in love with someone else. You can be securely attached in a long-term relationship to a person you cherish and yet fall passionately in love with a different person.

Of the three, the drive for romantic love is the strongest. It is stronger than that of lust. If a purely sexual overture is rejected, we shrug and move on. But when we are fixated with a passionate craving for the most singularly unique person in the universe, romantic rejection can drive us to the brink of suicide.

The drive for romantic love is also stronger than our drive for attachment. While we think of attachment as being the apex of a relationship—the stable, lasting bonds of a family—the drive for long-term attachment is a relatively new and mostly a human/primate experience. In contrast, because it happens in a deeper and older part of our brains, the drive toward romantic love is a more aggressive and biologically more powerful drive than that of attachment. Romantic attraction is an obsessive, magnetic fascination with a prospective mate that trumps familiar affection. When romantic love flames to life, it creates such a strong drive that it can (and sadly, sometimes does) tear families apart when one of the partners is swept up in the intoxication of an intense new romantic attraction.

These ancient systems of lust, love, and attachment can work both separately or in concert, lighting up complementary areas of your brain like a pinball machine in the process. The symphony they create when they all work together is the sublime experience we think of as love. Love is a biologically rooted experience that exists beyond the influence of consciousness and outside of the direct control of your bossy neocortex. It is not verbal. But the commands love issues from the irrational, primitive, and dark nooks and crannies of your brain can possess you entirely, without your permission or intention. Love has a life of its own. Love is a drive.

At the core of love is a powerfully motivating drive to be connected to your beloved: if you achieve the goal of union, you feel bliss. If anything gets in the way of that, you are consumed with a single-minded focus and determination to reconnect again, any way you can. Love is activated through an addictive process that sinks hooks into your soul, fusing your attachment to another person.

If you become bonded to a positive person who can love you back, all is well.

If not, you will suffer.

6

ADDICTED TO LOVE

"Love includes obsessive behaviors and can ruin lives,
just as substance abuse does."

—DR. LUCY BROWN

IN THE ANCIENT WORLD, BEFORE WE COULD RACE
MOTORCYCLES, SNORT COCAINE, OR THROW OURSELVES
OUT OF AIRPLANES FOR SPORT, IT WAS THE INTOXICATING
EXPERIENCE OF FALLING IN LOVE THAT BROUGHT PEOPLE TO
THE HIGHEST HEIGHTS OF EUPHORIA. FALLING IN LOVE FEELS
LIKE THE EPITOME OF MAGIC ON EARTH—THE MOST BANAL
MOMENTS ARE ELEVATED TO SUPREME IMPORTANCE WHEN
THEY CONCERN YOUR LOVER. LOVE IS THE ULTIMATE DRUG.
WHEN YOU ARE IN LOVE, EVERYTHING IS SUFFUSED WITH
A SPECIAL GLOW OF MEANING AND JOY.

Falling in love is the natural process of becoming addicted to
another person. As we discussed in the last chapter, when you are
pulled through the involuntary, normal, and usually healthy process
of falling in love, very old, rudimentary parts of your brain shove your
neocortex aside and take the wheel. You are then guided through
a specific set of neurological experiences that sink the hooks of
love into you on levels so deep they are beyond both language and
comprehension. This is largely achieved through altered states of
consciousness that occur when we fall in love.

Your Brain on Love

As mysterious and magical as your brain is—an elaborate system to run your body, make you feel things, solve complicated problems, and spin out enchanting visions—it is also quite mechanical. It works in part by generating substances called neurotransmitters, which are chemical messengers that our bodies and minds react to, making us think, feel, and act in different ways.

When romantic love shows up, it starts fiddling with the dials. Instead of the steady drips and squirts of neurotransmitters elicited by normal life experiences, when we fall in love our brains are drenched in a flood of the neurotransmitter dopamine. Love gleefully opens the floodgates of this natural substance while simultaneously cutting off your supply of serotonin. In doing so, falling in love creates a chemical experience that has a great deal in common with using patently addictive substances like cocaine. Like cocaine, love makes your neurological reward system quiver with pleasure and crave more contact with the object of your affection.

We know this because of research exploring the neurological activity of people in love. In 2008, Dr. Helen Fisher and a team of researchers compared the brain activity of participants when they looked at photographs of their beloved vs. another person known to them. They found that when participants looked at pictures of their lover, they had intense activity in the parts of their brain associated with pleasurable rewards and goal-directed behavior— the ventral tangential area and the caudate nucleus accumbens. These are key players in your drive to seek out rewarding, pleasurable behavior. These are the parts of your brain that are implicated in addictions.

Researchers have explored brain activity in cocaine addicts and found activity in the same brain regions of people in love. While they vary slightly—different sides of the same brain regions are implicated—there is a great overlap of classic reward areas involved in sexual arousal, love and attachment, and drug addiction. Both of these areas lie deep in the limbic brain. When they are activated, they bathe your brain in dopamine. Dopamine has a very specific impact on people; it is a stimulant. In fact, stimulant drugs work *because* they flood your brain with dopamine, and in doing so, gratify the reward and motivation areas of your brain.

As improbable as it may be to consider, falling in romantic love has a great deal in common with using cocaine. When love cranks up the dopamine dial, you begin to feel euphoric, giddily happy, and full of energy, similar to the effect of caffeine, cocaine, or Ritalin®. Additionally, you begin to feel more intensely emotional, restless, and excited. You feel like you don't need to sleep or eat as much. And you become intensely fixated on the source of your pleasure, and crave, crave, crave more.

From the moment you first started to fall in love with your Ex, sizzles of dopamine began stroking your central reward area, waking it up, turning it on, causing intense emotional pleasure (and pain) in their presence, and craving one thing—emotional union with your beloved. And you got hooked.

The other thing falling in love does to your brain chemistry is drop your serotonin levels. Serotonin is the neurotransmitter largely responsible for feelings of peace, satisfaction, and well-being. As romantic love increases dopamine, it also reduces serotonin. When serotonin drops, you feel anxious, agitated, restless, and have a tendency to be obsessive, compulsive, and impulsive.

One interesting study found that people who are in love are similar to people with Obsessive Compulsive Disorder in that they both have much lower concentrations of platelet serotonin transporters than subjects who were neither in love nor had an OCD diagnosis. The decrease in serotonin associated with romantic love is likely responsible for both the obsessive thinking and the impulsivity associated with it.

This love-cocktail of neurotransmitters—high dopamine and low serotonin—does a few things to you. First of all, it gives you a sort of "love high." When you're in love, you feel incredibly energized, restless, and euphoric. When you get a sign that the person you are enchanted with loves you in return, it brings feelings of joy and intense happiness. Pleasure somehow feels more vivid. You may become entirely focused on your lover, to the point where you might even feel distracted or have a hard time sleeping. You think about them obsessively, and often to the exclusion of things that had previously been important to you. You become single-minded in your desire to be with them, connect with them, and you become bonded to them. People in early stages of love, particularly when faced with obstacles to connection, also tend to be angst-ridden, anxious, intensely emotional, and inclined to behave impulsively.

The new lover, infused with dopamine and deficient in serotonin, daydreams at work. They fantasize about their next encounter with their beloved, planning trips and outings when they should be working. They experience a surge of giddy excitement with every call or text from the object of their ~~infection~~ affection. The absence of contact or any indication that their lover is pulling away sends them into an emotional tailspin. They want to stay up all night, talking and making love. They'll drop everything, including work, hobbies, and other relationships for a chance to be with their cherished person. They may become impulsive, calling randomly, showing up with flowers, spending too much money on dates. They internalize their lover, replaying conversations in their mind or thinking about things they want to share. As these things happen, ancient areas in the limbic brain sparkle and writhe in dopamine-soaked delight and the hooks are dug in deeply.

As relationships stabilize and become more familiar, the surges of dopamine begin to fade. (Perhaps you build up a tolerance.) The addictive zinging in your reward center bathing your brain in dopamine and making you feel the butterflies of angst and excitement are replaced by increased activity in parts of the brain responsible for manufacturing opiate-like serotonin, vasopressin, and oxytocin. These are the "cuddle hormones" that make birds nest, keep mothers mesmerized for hours by the faces of their babies, and compel you and your beloved to spend your weekends reorganizing your garage and going furniture shopping together.

As the churning, apprehensive excitement of romantic love fades and attachment slinks in, it gently wafts the neurological equivalent of opium—oxytocin—into the opiate receptors of your brain. Orgasms, physical contact, time together, and moments of emotional connection repeatedly infuse you with nature's original smack. As jittery, thrilling romantic love is replaced by the luminous tranquility of stable attachment, it feels like the only thing in the world that matters is that you are together. You gravitate toward your person, the source of your safety, your comfort, and your solace. Being wrapped in the arms of your beloved feels like your safe harbor in a crazy world. Your contact is your fix.

As attachment deepens, serotonin levels rise. As they do, they bring feelings of peace, confidence, and satisfaction. As attachment grows, serotonin builds, and feelings of stability and calm replace the frantic intensity of early stages of love. Serotonin dampens the exciting, obsessive energy of dopamine and life settles back down again. Sexual intensity may fade along with passionate feelings. Just like Prozac® (which also dramatically increases ambient serotonin levels) is notorious for throwing cold water on libido, secure attachment combined with familiarity often has an anti-erotic effect.

The irony for many couples is that as their relationship becomes safer and emotionally secure, their sexual desire fades. Some couples think that the feeling, "We love each other but we're not in love with each other," indicates a problem, but this is simply the lifecycle of a normal relationship. Lust, romantic love, and attachment are different things. Couples savvy to the neurological underpinnings of love can keep romance and eroticism alive in their relationships deliberately, but that is the subject of a different book. (A great book on this subject is *Mating in Captivity* by Esther Perel.)

The attachment phase of a relationship is characterized by tranquility when you're in each other's presence. Brain image scans of people in long-term relationships reveal that, neurologically, people in deeply attached relationships have more in common with heroin addicts than cocaine addicts. The neurotransmitters involved in attachment—vasopressin and oxytocin—actually bind to opiate receptors in your brain. Life brings you your daily dose of connection. Car rides, quiet dinners, and trips to Costco® feed the monkey.

And when the stability and closeness of the relationship you depend on is taken away from you, you go into withdrawal just as fierce as any other groveling addict. You crave and you obsess. You do the social equivalent of smashing windows and yanking out car stereos in order to get your next fix: showing up intrusively, behaving erratically, stalking online, and calling repeatedly. And even when you swear off the sauce, you relapse.

Love: The Ultimate Drug

The trajectory of romantic relationships follows that of other addictions. It starts out casually. While garden-variety lust may first focus your eyes on an attractive person, the first symptom that romantic love is starting to happen is the presence of two things:

1. Anxiety (which lovers prefer to think of as "butterflies")
2. Intrusive thoughts about the person

Unlike snorting cocaine or base-jumping, both of which require a certain degree of premeditation, anxiety and intrusive thoughts about an attractive person simply happen. The biggest risk factor for developing a crush is proximity. If you don't want to get addicted to a person who elicits fluttery feelings and daydreams inside you (and who may be an unsuitable partner for various reasons) it's best to stay away from them—literally.

If you choose to continue spending time around an increasingly fascinating person, your love-seeking brain will unleash a cluster of cognitive, emotional, and behavioral experiences. These alter your state of consciousness and make you think, feel, and act in ways that may be uncharacteristic for you when you're not under the influence of love.

Cognitions

The key feature of the experience of falling in love is having intrusive thoughts about your beloved, meaning you think about them all the time. Intrusive thinking is the hallmark characteristic of romantic love. What are they doing? When will we see them again? What are they thinking about? Even when you are not together, you are having imaginary conversations with them in your mind. It seems like the only thing that can stop the obsessions and bring us peace is to be with them and have their love confirmed. Some researchers have found that people who score highly on measures designed to rate feelings of romantic love report thinking about their sweetheart more than 85 percent of the time.

You begin to focus your attention on this special and important individual, seeking them out, trying to be near them, paying special attention to them. You are absorbed with them entirely when they are around, and, in particular, on their positive characteristics.

Just like people under the influence of cocaine may believe grandiose things that are not objectively true (*I'm the best dancer in this whole club!*), romantic love brings cognitive distortions too. Your view of the world changes when you're in love. Your lover seems more special, important, and amazing than anyone else. You inflate and cherish their positive qualities, magnifying them until they are the only truth that matters. Potential problems are minimized, disregarded, or explained away, and you shrug off any potentially troubling aspects of their character. As the dreamlike euphoria of early love wraps around you, oftentimes lovers believe that their connection is unique—different than anything that's ever existed before. You both may exalt the relationship itself, genuinely feeling that it is closer and more special than anyone else's. It often feels like being in a dream.

BEHAVIORS

Because love is biologically tied to your goal-directed motivation drive, being in love brings with it a variety of goal-oriented behaviors, all focused on connection with your one and only. In other words, you put lots of time and energy into winning the love and affection of your beloved. You call, give gifts, and may put great effort into being kind or thoughtful. You may go to heroic, and sometimes irrational, lengths to be with them.

You turn away from other things that were once important to you, instead preferring the pleasurable intensity of time with your adored. Like an addict hocking his television, you too pour your social, emotional, and sometimes financial resources into sustaining your delightful new habit—your relationship. This is good and normal, in the context of a healthy and mutually loving and respectful relationship.

Lovers often feel quite possessive of the objects of their affection and react negatively if it seems like any other person may be threatening their union or swaying their sweetheart's attention. They may become agitated, demanding, or controlling if they feel fearful that someone or something else is blocking access to their lover. It's not that uncommon for people to do desperate or sometimes even dangerous things in efforts to get around obstacles that prevent union with their beloved. When the drive for love is burning brightly, we may do foolish and impulsive things to connect with the person we're craving.

Union with a lover becomes the most important thing, and entire lives become oriented around connection. Hobbies, commitments, and other relationships are often neglected and sometimes even abandoned entirely. A love-drunk person might skip out on school or work responsibilities, blowing off the things they need to do in favor of spending more time with the object of their desire. It's very common for people in love to let go of other relationships, preferring to spend time exclusively with their lover. They may withdraw from friendships, leaving even their best friends feeling disregarded and uncared for. A person under the influence of love may flat-out reject anyone who expresses concern or doubt about their lover, choosing the lover over even long-term caring relationships with formerly cherished family members.

People in love have a tendency to become impulsive and lose control over the things that they say and do. A person in love might spend money on things they cannot afford in efforts to be with or impress their lovers, like plane tickets, expensive dinners, hotels, and gifts. People in the grips of intense, infatuated love may even abandon their other attachments, like their family, or in extreme cases, even their children. Tragically, some people who are married or in long-term attached partnerships and fall in love with another will abandon their partners and families in favor of their intoxicating new infatuation.

EMOTIONS

Romantic love brings with it a very specific physiological state, one that is heightened and intense and that people often describe as being on a euphoric drug. The lover is likely to feel highly energized, to the point where they may have less need for sleep. They might feel hyperactive, like Tom Cruise jumping onto Oprah's couch. They are likely to feel a pit in their stomach or knots in their stomach when thinking about or in proximity to their beloved. Romantics refer to this as "having butterflies." (Party-pooper psychologists just call it anxiety.)

But being in love is more than happy or thrilling feelings. It can also bring irritability, intense mood swings, and deep despair when you feel blocked from being with your lover. The emotional intensity of love can be hard to bear. The obsessive, single-minded focus and the unquenchable craving for union with your lover is just as intense as the craving of an addict for their substance of choice.

Emotionally, lovers may sway all over the place, feeling anxiety, despair, euphoria, and elation all in the same day—and all depending on the kind of reaction they get from their beloved. They feel strongly motivated to win the affection of their lover, and their emotions swing wildly from one extreme to another, depending on the signals they get back in return.

More than anything, the lover wants to feel emotionally connected to the one he or she adores and to feel that adoration reciprocated. The love-stricken person may feel intense sexual desire for his beloved, but it is not the number one priority—emotional union is. Most people in love deny that "Sex is the most important thing," they simply cherish the other person and want desperately to be close to them.

As relationships deepen and the roots of attachment begin to take hold, lovers start to feel emotionally dependent on each other. They become each other's "number one person" with whom they want to spend time with above all others. When away from their irreplaceable other they may feel anxious or have trouble sleeping. They feel emotionally joined and often have a deep sense of empathy and compassion for their beloved. These feelings may be so intense that people say things like they would die for their irreplaceable other.

The emotional power of deep attachment is quiet and unobtrusive; an afternoon spent raking leaves together is different than the intoxicating first months of a new relationship. However, when attachment bonds are threatened or broken, the panic and despair it brings can be life shattering.

Our species needs these fundamental survival systems—craving and seeking this sensation of euphoric, transcendent connection and experiencing intense pain upon separation—in order to survive. We need to come together, fall in love, reproduce, and bond into a family unit that can care for our children together. We need to love our little babies so much that we lavish them with affection, attention, and responsiveness 24/7. Because love and attachment are based on survival systems, the underlying physiological and neurological structures involved are very elaborate, they are redundant, they recruit areas in many parts of the brain, and they are extremely difficult to control by force of will.

When viewed from an evolutionary perspective, having powerful and enduring attachments is a good thing. The forces of nature are working perfectly.

However, as you know too well, there is a very dark side to this natural addictive process. The same brain systems that pull us helplessly toward healthy love and connection are the very ones that can get helplessly attached to dark things—substances that trick us into feeling joy, contentment, and safety or that link us to people who may abuse and mistreat us.

Black Hat Love

When your natural, addictive process toward sex, love, and attachment becomes activated, it can have either positive or negative consequences. If you become bonded to a positive person who can love you back, all is well. If not, you will experience a great deal of pain when the person you adore is not able or willing to love you well in return. Unfortunately, the most addictive kinds of relationships are often the ones that are the most pathological and unhealthy.

The key experiences of romantic love—anxiety and intrusive thinking—are heightened by adversity, obstacles, and uncertainty. Every grand coquette uses this romantic jiu-jitsu to their advantage, knowing that when love is blocked or rejected it makes our feelings of passion and longing more intense. When you feel more anxious and preoccupied with the state of your relationship, worried that your love is not reciprocated or fearful that your connection is being threatened by something, dopamine surges, serotonin drops, and you feel love much more vividly.

So, ironically, when you are romantically attracted to someone who gives you mixed signals, who is charming, passionate, and exciting sometimes, but who also tends to be selfish, who is demanding, who gets upset and threatens to reject you, or who is inconsistent in their affections, it raises your anxiety—and your passion. Both anger and fear are tightly entwined with the neurological underpinnings of love. The relationships that are the most frustrating and tumultuous are therefore often the most fascinating and irresistible to us.

This common phenomenon is caused by the protest response that flares in moments of distress: we become elevated in response to threats of abandonment. This is because dopamine surges in the context of anxiety and uncertainty. As it does, we are profoundly affected, becoming hyper-vigilant and on-edge about the state of our connection. Our heart rate goes up, we feel agitated, restless, emotional, and absolutely fixated on our beloved. At these moments, our physiological drive to connect gets stronger, not weaker. The stress response we experience in the face of abandonment mimics the biological "love cocktail" we sip when in love: heavy on the dopamine, light on the serotonin, with an adrenalin garnish. It's galvanizing and crazy-making: When we are in unstable, insecure, and/or dangerous relationships, our drives for connection are burning most brightly and we are consumed in an inferno of desire and longing.

This is one reason why illicit affairs often feel so uniquely intoxicating and magical. They are fraught with obstacles, adversity, and uncertainty. Relationships that begin as affairs create a perfect storm of anxiety and romantic frustration that unleash passion of a magnitude that rarely occurs in a secure, predictable partnership. Similarly, attractions to people who are not emotionally safe or emotionally available may elicit feelings of feverish desire that stable, consistently present partners can never incite. The intensity of the experience that people have in these unhealthy contexts may lead them to believe that the relationships themselves are much more special, important, and meaningful than anything else they have experienced. Until, of course, the situation stabilizes, the flurry of dopamine settles, and a once-feverish lover finds themselves helplessly attached to a person who may not be a satisfying or desirable long-term partner.

When people confuse feelings of intense romantic craving and obsession for healthy, real-deal love, they may find themselves repeatedly frustrated and heartbroken by ultimately toxic relationships. Sadly, people seeking the intensity of passionate love without understanding that it is heightened by fear and uncertainty (and that the final destination of any relationship is secure, stable attachment) often dismiss generous, emotionally available, and thoughtful partners due to "lack of chemistry." Healthy relationships simply don't inflame crazed passions the way that unstable ones do. They are not as addictive.

Many of the most deeply addicted Exaholics I've worked with were hooked through the gills by profoundly toxic relationships. However, any cherished relationship that leads you to feel romantically in love and/or emotionally bonded is, by nature, addictive—and powerfully so. It's easy to smirk at the thought of romantic relationships as being a real addiction, until you consider the fact that the neurological hardware and reward systems responsible for the experience of love is precisely what people are stimulating when they develop recognized, pathological addictions.

LOVE: THE MOTHER OF ALL ADDICTIONS

Dr. Lucy Brown of Albert Einstein College of Medicine has postulated a theory that the natural physiology of the systems in our brains that drive us toward lust, love, and attachment are the same ones that get activated when people abuse substances. It's increasingly understood that addictive disorders such as drug and alcohol abuse and "soft addictions" like gambling and sex are recruiting our survival physiology—the innate, overwhelmingly powerful drive we have to connect and bond—to create crippling addictions. Brown says, "Available evidence strongly suggests that substance abuse neurophysiology may be based on survival mechanisms and their mesolimbic reward systems associated with sex, romantic love, and attachment."

Stimulant drugs such as cocaine artificially simulate the euphoric feelings we experience when we fall in love. Opiates synthetically replicate the tranquility, peace, and safety we feel when we securely attach to someone who loves us. In other words, addictive disorders are addictive because they are hijacking the systems that nature built to drive us toward each other. They artificially—and powerfully—stimulate the neural networks that create the feelings of euphoria, pleasure, and peace we feel when we fall in love. Some researchers postulate that this is the reason why addictive drugs have such a spellbinding effect on us: They are momentarily gratifying our basic needs for connection and love.

In normal, healthy relationships, people turn to each other for comfort in times of stress, anxiety, and fear. Secure attachment and having connections are the way that people bear emotional trauma. Research shows that the presence of secure attachment eases both physical and emotional pain. (Remember, attachment stimulates nature's opiates.) It has been said that humans can bear any trauma, if able to grieve and recover in the arms of someone who loves them. Secure attachment is how we regulate ourselves emotionally.

In the absence of (or confusion about) the real thing, people turn to artificial substitutes. Since the time of the ancient Greeks, it was known that mixing opium in the wine of the battle-scarred troops would soothe the emotional trauma inflicted in even the worse massacres of war. Soldiers could lose an entire platoon and yet remain placid, as long as they had the arm of Nepenthes around their shoulder. Substances that ease physical pain soothe emotional pain as well, like love does.

It is also well known that many of the people who become the most thoroughly and desperately addicted to substances are often trauma survivors or had attachment disorders in childhood that metastasized into personality disorders in adulthood. People who have been terrorized, abandoned, or who failed to form secure attachments in childhood often turn to substances to help regulate otherwise out-of-control and overwhelming negative emotions. In the absence of secure attachments it feels like they cannot survive or function without the comfort of drugs to soothe their emotional pain.

Progressive thinkers in the field of addiction, like Johann Hari, postulate that the underlying causes of addictions are deficits in social connections and secure attachment. Addictions researcher Philip Flores agrees, noting, "Without normal attachment, emotional regulation is compromised and individuals are vulnerable to addictive compulsions."

Because the need to attach to loving people is so essential, the people most vulnerable to developing profound addictions to substances are those who do not have meaningfully bonds to emotionally safe people. Instead, they bond with the tranquility of heroin, the euphoric romance of cocaine, the coziness of getting slurry drunk, or the anxious thrill that gambling or anonymous sex delivers. In these cases, addicts are unknowingly stimulating their bonding and attachment systems, recreationally. (And at great cost to both themselves and society.)

In his 2015 piece "The Likely Cause of Addiction Has Been Discovered, and It Is Not What You Think," Hari cites studies conducted in the 1970s by Dr. Bruce Alexander in which rats are heavily exposed to opiates for a period of months, which thoroughly addicts them on a physiological level. The junkie rats were then put into one of two conditions: a spartan, lonely cage, or a happy, fun cage full of toys and lots of opportunity for social interaction. Just like 95 percent of opiate addicted American GI's returning home from Vietnam—back to their comfortable homes and loving relationships—the rats transferred to the happy, healthy cages quickly became disinterested in heroin. Hari concludes, like Alexander before him, that, "the opposite of addiction is not sobriety. It is human connection."

Love is the mother of all addictions. Any other substances that we think of as being addictive are only pale imposters to what we truly crave (and need) in our hearts, brains, and bodies: meaningful union with other people.

The most successful drug and alcohol treatment approaches, therefore, are those that understand the natural need to bond and actively work to help people in recovery build meaningful relationships with others. In doing so, they help addicts detach their reliance on substances and reattach it where it belongs: to other people.

Through mending broken bonds with friends and family, establishing relationships with supportive groups of fellow recovering addicts, and by having a positive and productive role in a community, addicts may be healed. In contrast, harshly punitive, moralistic, or pull-yourself-up-by-the-bootstraps treatment approaches that create more shame, psychological distance, and social isolation will often only deepen an addict's attachment to the reliable, unconditional "love" of an ultimately destructive substance.

THE TRAGEDY OF EXAHOLICS

When people get hooked on a substance or experience that triggers the reward systems and attachment machinery that nature designed for your survival in unnaturally intense ways, it overwhelms their ability to control themselves. Sadly, artificial stimulation of the euphoria of love or the comfort of attachment can eclipse the real thing.

Alcoholics walk into the bar knowing full well they are not going home that night.

Gamblers giddy with guilty hope clean out the last of their kid's college fund at the casino.

Meth addicts drive past the social services office for the supervised visit with their kids to their dealer's house instead.

Exaholics feel like slaves to their frantic, raging, despairing, single-minded craving for emotional connection with their Ex. They churn with anxiety in the blue light of their laptops, knowing that whatever they are about to see on their Ex's Facebook page will devastate them for days, but they cannot stop themselves from looking. They have trouble focusing on, much less emotionally connecting with, friends, family, children, or potential new and healthy lovers. They lie awake all night, ruminating. They drive by homes and offices, craning their necks to see the familiar car in the parking lot. They may engage in stalking or illegally break into private email, bank, or phone accounts. They beg for more chances or allow themselves to be abused by their Exes. They hate themselves for what they do, but they do it anyway.

The compulsions and cravings of an Exaholic are often so intense and out-of-control they can feel frightening. At these moments, illusions of control and choice are stripped away and we're able to see the panic, obsession, and unstoppable hunger for connection for the bald addiction that it is.

Unfortunately, the potentially severe and crippling addiction Exaholics struggle with is not recognized as such. There are good reasons for this. First of all, bonding to another person is a natural and healthy experience. While abusing alcohol or other drugs is always patently destructive, falling in love can be the best thing that ever happened to someone. Falling in love is not a disease, it's a cause for celebration. It's only when people experience unrequited love or rejection that their addiction becomes a problem.

Furthermore, the addictive process of falling in love is biologically mild compared to the galvanizing intensity with which illegal drugs stimulate your system. Needing to recover from a bad breakup is not the same as becoming profoundly addicted to alcohol, cocaine, or heroin. Recovering from a substance-abuse problem has far-reaching physical, emotional, psychological, and social consequences that make recovering from a failed relationship seem like a trip to Disneyland.

And yet, there are important similarities.

Unfortunately, most addiction counselors, mental-health counselors, nor the general public conceptualize people struggling in the aftermath of a failed relationship as having a biologically rooted addiction. Even if they did agree that relationships can have addictive qualities, they would never elevate the experiences of Exaholics as being as "real" as people struggling with substance-abuse problems. At best, recovering from an unwanted relationship loss is conceptualized as an adjustment disorder or as someone having difficulty coping with life transitions. (Both of which supports shame, in that they imply the person is having an unusually hard time getting over it.)

While other addicts have the support of their anonymous meetings, caring therapists, intervention by family and friends, and our sympathies for their struggle, Exaholics get invalidating advice and impatience:

"You have to let it go."

"There are lots of fish in the sea."

"Have you tried online dating?"

We would never dream of looking into the sweaty, gray face of a heroin addict shaking in withdrawal, and say, "You need to move on." We have compassion for their undeniable suffering and try to help them through it. But our society does exactly that when it ridicules, minimizes, or shames Exaholics for their experiences.

The terrible irony, of course, is that of all addicts, Exaholics are the ones struggling at the ground-zero of the most fundamental, survival driven, and biologically based addiction of all—they are addicted to love. Furthermore, not only are they going through the intense withdrawal of a primal addiction, they are simultaneously suffering from one of the deepest and most basic traumas a human being can experience: disconnection. On top of that, Exaholics may be coping with the loss of access to their home or children, the loss of once-meaningful or pleasurable activities, and social isolation. They are going through withdrawal, trauma, and decimated lives all at the same time—exactly the opposite of what they need to be healthy and well.

But in my opinion, the true tragedy is that in their darkest hour, at the time they are in most need of support or compassion, they are often made to feel ashamed for not being okay.

I believe it is time for us to understand the magnitude of suffering and pain people experience in the aftermath of a relationship loss in a more realistic way. As opposed to us each taking our turn of suffering in shameful silence as we bear the agony of unwanted separation, we can begin to understand and appreciate these losses for what they really are: profound traumas to fundamental and addictive survival systems. Exaholics experiencing the devastation of losing a primary attachment need support, patience, empathy, tolerance, and guidance in their recovery, just like other addicts, even though they don't have a disease. They're just suffering through the dark side of human bonding—which is intense. And real.

The first step in developing compassion for the plight of Exaholics is recognizing what an unwanted relationship loss actually does to us. Understanding what is a normal and expected reaction to the loss of a primary relationship will help Exaholics fight crippling shame. Having their experience be taken seriously opens the door to their receiving patience, compassion, support, and inclusion from others. Most important, my sincere hope is that understanding what has been happening inside of you helps you develop compassion, tolerance, and patience with yourself as you embark on the journey of healing.

PART 3
PROTEST AND DESPAIR

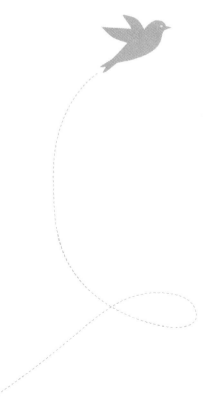

7

WHEN LOVE IS LOST

"When he moved out, I felt like a crazed animal.
I was hyperventilating."

—EXAHOLIC

AS ROMANTIC RELATIONSHIPS EVOLVE AND YOU CIRCLE
THROUGH THE ANCIENT, SPIRAL DANCE OF LUST, LOVE,
AND ATTACHMENT, YOU BECOME PSYCHOLOGICALLY AND
EMOTIONALLY INTERTWINED WITH YOUR BELOVED.
THE BONDS OF GALVANIZING ROMANTIC FIXATION AND DEEP
ATTACHMENT WRAP AROUND YOU, EMOTIONALLY WELDING
YOU TO YOUR ONE AND ONLY. AS THIS BEAUTIFUL, NATURAL
PROCESS OCCURS YOU DON'T REALIZE THAT WHAT IS REALLY
HAPPENING IS THAT YOU ARE—IN A VERY LITERAL WAY—
BECOMING ADDICTED TO YOUR MOST SPECIAL PERSON.
THIS IS NOT A NEGATIVE THING, BUT RATHER THE NORMAL
AND HEALTHY PROCESS OF HUMAN PAIR-BONDING.

Until, of course, your primary attachment is threatened or lost.
And then you go bananas.

Threatened Attachments

Even before a breakup happens, most people who care deeply about a relationship that is failing are really not okay for a long time before the relationship is officially over. Their emotional trauma begins weeks, months, or even years before, as they struggle with the stress of an insecure and unstable primary attachment.

Your limbic brain senses emotions and degrees of connection like a bloodhound reads the colors of scents on the forest floor. You know that something feels different about your relationship even if you don't know what it is yet. It just feels like you don't have your partner's attention anymore. They are not coming toward you, seeking you, but rather, pulling away. Perhaps they are irritated and impatient with you most of the time. Or else, the way they behave may not match what they say: they may be telling you they love you, but you don't feel it. Instead, you feel uneasy, as your finely attuned limbic system sniffs the space between you like a wary wolf.

From the subtle currents of communication that exist without language, your limbic brain understands that you are in one of the most terrible dangers a human can experience: disconnection. Your anxiety flares.

Your neocortex, as usual, has no idea what's happening yet. It tries to find evidence to make sense of your inarticulate emotional experiences, getting stuck on rational details like what exactly was said, or whether a task had been completed as promised. It attempts to wrestle validation out of your lover like an overly prepared young trial lawyer with charts, video clips, and color photographs. (*Is it not true sir, that on the evening of August seventeenth you were on the corner of Elm and Main wearing a blue ball cap when . . .*) Great fighting ensues.

Other times, when the gulf of disconnection is slowly yawning, your neocortex chastises you for being irrational. You feel apprehensive, but when you look at your relationship things are objectively fine—nothing has really changed yet. You feel uneasy, but you're told rational and plausible things by your lover. When your limbic brain brings you information that does not make sense to your neocortex, it often loses. Feelings are briskly rationalized and shooed away like an anxious animal whining inexplicably in the moments before the earthquake hits.

When the earthquake finally does hit—even though things haven't felt right for a long time—you may still have no idea what happened to your once-blissful love.

Why Relationships Fail

I have never met an Exaholic who is not obsessed with this one question: "Why did this happen?" Much of the snooping and researching that Exaholics do is in efforts to gain insight into the mind of their Ex, and figure out what went wrong. *Was it a midlife crisis? Were they having an affair? Was I not good enough? Was I too needy? Was I not attractive? Are they a narcissist? Am I a narcissist?* The endless, unanswerable questions will torment you. Even if you do have the opportunity to ask your Ex directly, you may not trust their answer. You might not trust my answer either, but I will share the insight I have gained from sitting across from many Exes and Exaholics (as well as distressed couples) in the counseling room, in hopes that my experience helps you make sense of what just happened.

Relationships end for many reasons. Sometimes, particularly in more casual arrangements, one person is simply less interested than the other. Or sometimes, it ends for incredibly superficial reasons: "Her legs were too pale." "His nose whistles." "Her lips are always chapped." "Her arms are too big." "He doesn't make enough money." These are all things I have actually heard from people sitting in front of me with straight faces. Regardless of the trivial reason they attempt to pin it on, one person is just not feeling it. It's important to remember that just because you are in the same relationship doesn't mean you are having the same experience. We all tend to project our feelings on other people, assuming that others feel the way that we do. But truthfully, one person can be awash in romantic infatuation with another person who simply doesn't feel the same way.

The most merciful outcome in these situations is that the less-caring partner is brave enough to cut things off sooner rather than later. Unfortunately, sometimes these relationships (or more accurately termed, "situation-ships") can linger on the shelf long after their expiration date. As they molder, the more committed partner becomes increasingly anxious and despondent as their love goes unappreciated and unrequited. They may accept scraps of attention in the form of booty calls or friends-with-benefits arrangements, decimating their self-esteem in the process and sometimes descending into full-blown craving, obsession, and longing. These situations end when the less-into-it partner finally feels guilty enough to pull the plug, finds someone they are more interested in, or when the Exaholic finally hits their bottom and decides to end things on their own terms and take their power back.

However, formerly happy and connected relationships where both people love each other and are deeply committed fail too. When once-solid relationships begin to fall apart, there is often a dance of rupturing attachment that both people engage in long before they finally break up. Whether the fights are about parenting, household tasks, sex, whether or not you're spending enough time together, or the tone someone is taking, the core is always the same: you feel that your partner does not care enough to do the things that would make you feel emotionally safe and loved by them. Your once secure attachment has become insecure.

When a romantic attachment starts to feel less secure, most relationships begin to polarize into a pursue/withdraw pattern. In other words, one partner chases and the other pulls away. The pursuer experiences the other as unavailable or unresponsive and attempts to seek contact and reconnect with increasing intensity. The withdrawer experiences the pursuer as emotionally unsafe and withdraws both physically and emotionally (which heightens the pursuer's anxiety). Without intervention, this cycle usually intensifies over time. Each spin around the cycle stretches the attachment ever further, until eventually, it can break.

Pursuit

When a relationship begins to feel unstable or disconnected it creates feelings of anxiety for both partners. Anxiety always results in safety seeking, and if you're a pursuer, you will try to seek reassurance from your partner that everything is okay. But vulnerable feelings of longing and anxiety are difficult to translate into language under the best of circumstances. Unfortunately, perhaps because the parts of our brains responsible for love, anger, and fear are so tightly intertwined, anxiety often gives an angry edge to your voice as you seek to reconnect. Feelings of loneliness, worry, or rejection often come out as angry barking: "You were in the garage all day! I have to do everything around here! You don't give a crap about me!"

The harder you try to make them understand your feelings the more forceful and hostile your communication becomes. It is not uncommon for livid pursuers to do extremely dramatic or aggressive things in efforts to get through to their partners. Unbeknownst to you, this creates feelings of fear and anxiety in your partner, leading them to clamp down ever tighter in self-defense. Eventually it's like screaming at a clam. Or worse, a clam with legs that scuttles away from you, seeming not to care about your feelings at all as they seek to escape the tirade.

WITHDRAWAL

If you are in the other position of a wobbly relationship—the withdrawer—you feel anxious too, but for different reasons. You probably feel attacked and vilified by your partner. You may perceive them as becoming increasingly irrational, demanding, and unpredictable. It seems like your partner is always angry with you, and for ridiculous reasons. At the core, you likely experience a great deal of shame for never feeling like you can please them or make them happy. You survive the onslaught of their disappointment and accusations by hunkering down like a cat in a hailstorm, becoming smaller, more defensive, less communicative, and more tentative in everything you do.

Sometimes when you feel attacked, you hit your breaking point and yell back. You feel so victimized by your partner's harassment that it is almost impossible to see them as anxious and hurting and you may get quite mean. When withdrawers have been in self-protection mode for a long time, they may genuinely experience their partner as being a terrible person who is out to get them—and feel entirely justified in treating them with shocking callousness in return. It's easy to forget that they are hurting underneath the anger. You don't realize that your self-protection feels to them like emotional abandonment or even emotional cruelty. Your withdrawal throws kerosene on the fire of their fear and rage. The times that you become hostile in return only adds to their evidence that you don't care.

DAMAGE DONE

These pursue/withdraw patterns are most obvious in the midst of a fight. Once couples calm down, they can often repair their bond by expressing vulnerability and responsiveness to each other. This goes a long way in repairing the emotional safety and secure attachment of a relationship. However, every time your partner experiences you as either hostile and accusatory or withdrawn and uncaring, it harms the basic trust in your relationship and the security of your attachment is damaged.

If pursue/withdraw interactions start to become the norm in your relationship and effective repairing is not done in the interim, even the good parts of your relationship will begin to erode. When that happens, your entire relationship starts to feel different, even when you're not actually fighting. As time wears on, people begin to perceive their partners as being fundamentally flawed and simply unable to be the person they want or need them to be. They feel hopeless that things will change and may entertain escape fantasies. Sometimes they develop emotional attachments to others.

Finally, just before the end, fighting often stops entirely. Your once-feisty lover's hurt and anger with you has been replaced with the cold silence of contempt. They have given up on you, and nothing you do or say can make them believe in you again. When withdrawers are done with you, they simply stop engaging altogether. They are gone, even on the rare occasions when they are actually home. Eventually, someone finally says the magic words or throws down the gauntlet of an ultimatum that the other declines to pick up.

It's unusual that someone is entirely blindsided by a breakup or betrayal. You can almost always feel it coming before you understand what is happening. But sometimes relationships do end without any warning at all. You genuinely think and feel that everything is okay, right up until the very end. Whether a relationship disintegrates slowly or flashes out of existence, the early experience of a lost attachment is the same: protest.

THE AFTERMATH OF A BREAKUP

In the midst of a betrayal, rejection, and unwanted separation, even the most generally pleasant and psychologically sturdy among us will find ourselves shrieking at the top of our lungs, throwing dishes, screeching off dramatically in cars, and feeling inconsolably sad for days and weeks on end. The most ordinarily reasonable and rational person can descend into obsessive madness when cut off from their primary attachment: stalking social media accounts, checking phone records, and rehearsing the conversations they hope to have in orchestrated "surprise" encounters. As the frantic flopping of protest fades to grim despair, even the most naturally optimistic and resilient person may believe that they will forever be chained to the slavish love they have for their Ex and never be able to love another.

Separation distress is considered to be the strongest indication of the existence of an attachment. The true power of an attachment often goes hidden, especially in long-term attachments. Even in the most boring, TV-watching, box-store shopping, sexless, and seemingly desiccated relationships, attachment can be profound. It's only when the attachment is threatened or broken that people begin to understand how deep their attachment goes. Many times people realize, too late, that their annoying, boring, or inconsiderate partner was incredibly important to them.

And then they freak out.

Every person I have ever talked to in the fresh aftermath of a lost cherished relationship describes the same experience: feeling devastated about the loss, being obsessed with thoughts of their lover, feeling an overwhelming desire to reconnect, doing compulsive things in efforts to maintain proximity with their Ex, and feeling absolutely helpless to stop those feelings—even when they really want to and know they should. It's even more terrible and confusing when their relationship seemed satisfying and meaningful.

All humans capable of forming attachments are terribly impacted by the horrible feelings that rejection creates, and nearly everyone goes through it. In their exploration of breakups, Roy Baumeister, Sarah Wotman, and Andrea Stillwell found that 93 percent of all college students in their sample had been rejected by someone they loved intensely. (95 percent had at one time been the rejecters.) People going through a breakup commonly feel shock, anxiety, and loneliness; they experience changes in eating and sleeping patterns; they crave contact, obsess about their lover, and experience severe emotional distress. This constellation of experiences is what the protest response looks like in adults.

Anyone who has ever experienced an unwanted separation understands what protest feels like: intense restlessness and single-minded focus on reconnection. The frantic, panicky feelings are overwhelming. Having any indication that your lover cares, even the tiniest bit, becomes the most important thing in the world. Vigilant scanning for glimpses and signs of your beloved, obsessive thoughts, and efforts to get information about them: these are all parts of the normal mammalian protest response. Human infants search and wail. Puppies frantically scrabble and whine. You have powerful urges to contact the other person for flimsy reasons, like wanting to return personal items in person or having final conversations "for closure." It's all an intense desire to reconnect, even briefly.

It is simply the human experience of lost love.

It's also incredibly traumatizing.

Many people describe the moment they realized their relationship was ending as having an unreal quality to it, like a nightmare—similar to how victims of a violent crime or horrific accident describe their traumatic experiences. In these first moments when you are confronted with rejection or abandonment, everything in your body surges into survival mode. Your heart is beating rapidly. It may feel like you can't breathe. You might be shaking and crying. You probably feel overwhelmed with emotion and may not be able to speak at all.

For humans, like most other mammals, abandonment is a primary trauma. When you lose your cherished person, your body, mind, and emotions experience it as a direct threat to your survival and fundamental well-being. When loss is happening (or even threatened) excitatory neurotransmitters like dopamine and norepinephrine soar, creating intense agitation and emotionality. When enduring the trauma of abandonment, you may be flooded with anxiety that can border on panic or terror.

PROTEST AND DESPAIR

When you take any infant mammal away from its mother, it goes crazy. It exhibits the universal mammalian reaction to separation: it protests. It whines, barks, cries, and tries frantically to get back to its mother. Babies scream and cry when they are away from their mommies, desperate to reconnect with their safe person. They might become angry with their caregiver for leaving them, clearly communicating with their distress that separation or lack of responsiveness is not okay, in efforts to reinforce the need for connection. This phase of separation is known as the protest response.

From an evolutionary perspective, protest makes perfect sense. When baby mammals are separated from the caregiver they rely upon entirely, their life depends on their ability to call for help, search for, and reconnect with their mothers. Despite our illusions of independence, the attachment needs of adult humans are really just a few notches below those of infants. The loss of our most important connection sends us into a similarly panicked frenzy for reunion.

Even if you are the one initiating the breakup, in the moment that you separate from the person to whom you have been so strongly attached you are still likely to have an intense emotional reaction. The emotions associated with a threatened primary attachment feel less like sadness and more like a threat to your very existence. People can often feel intense fear, panic, anger, and an overwhelming desire to reconnect when their primary attachment is breaking. This primal experience can be very confusing for people, particularly if they are the ones initiating the breakup. The fear and anxiety they feel at the moment of separation can make them think that maybe they should stay in the relationship after all. (Even if the relationship is very unhealthy for them.)

The drive to reestablish contact is so strong that it can feel absolutely overwhelming and impossible to resist. This is why people call even when they know they shouldn't, drive past houses, stalk Facebook pages, and arrange for unexpected encounters, even when the object of their affection no longer wants anything to do with them.

Humans seek and search for reconnection. This can take the form of repeated texts, calls, emails, letters, or surprise encounters. The frantic and devastated pleas for reconnection that jilted lovers express are simply a more complex version of a baby's screams or puppy's whine and frantic scratching at the gate: we are desperate for reconnection. You, with your iPhone® and well-stocked grocery store, may be under the impression that you are different from a baby monkey, but the way your brain and body works when your primary attachment is severed is exactly the same.

Our protest response is emotional, behavioral, and psychological, but it is also very physical. As Thomas Lewis, Fari Amini, and Richard Lannon describe in their marvelous book, *A General Theory of Love*, when we are galvanized by the protest response it impacts us on every level of our being. We have increased agitation and motor activity; we are physiologically restless. Our heart rate and blood pressure are up and our bodies flood with stress hormones like adrenalin and cortisol. These hormones make us very alert and vigilant for any signs of our lover. Agitating, elevating dopamine floods our brains, and we become singularly focused in our minds. We can't sleep. We obsess. We cry. We try to talk to our rejecting partner. Sometimes we yell and scream in efforts to communicate our pain. We search for them everywhere: in person, on the phone, online.

If a separation endures, all mammals—human babies and adults included—will enter a state of despair. Like protest, despair has very distinct characteristics and is a coherent physiological and psychological state. Despair begins as frantic efforts to reconnect collapse, single-mined hope is replaced with hopelessness and a new certainty that the beloved is not coming back. Human babies and small children too, will become listless and depressed. As their protest response fades into certainty of aloneness, they fail to thrive and can waste away.

This protest and despair response does not go away when we grow up. You were built to bond. When that connection is severed, ancient and primal systems inside of you scream in protest. The intense distress and miserable depression that envelops you when you are disconnected from your cherished person is hardwired inside of you throughout your life.

WITHDRAWAL

Researchers have attempted to measure and quantify the madness of romantic rejection and loss. fMRI scans of heartbroken people revealed neurological activity very similar to people in the early stages of love. In particular, participants displayed intense activity in parts of the brain associated with reward and motivation, such as their ventral tangential area and nucleus accumbens. Again, the same areas that other researchers have associated with craving in drug addicts. These findings support the idea that the protest response is akin to being in withdrawal from an intense, primary addiction: love.

As we've discussed, romantic love is experienced through the same reward and motivation systems that illicit drugs hijack when you get high and falling in love is similar to having a fierce substance addiction. Using—also known as having contact with your adored person— has been flooding your reward centers with euphoric, energizing dopamine. If your relationship has been longer and more enduring, the attachment bonding process has also been stroking your opiate receptors into tranquility. When you take the ultimate drug of love away, everything inside of you blazes into a fury of craving and need.

A person addicted to a substance will have unique physiological symptoms when they abruptly come off of it because of the way their body has become accustomed to it. However, all addicts in withdrawal share common elements: intense cravings to use again, obsessions about using, and having compulsions to use that feel outside of their control.

Just like lovers in the early stages of a relationship describe symptoms consistent with being addicted, the experience of jilted lovers is highly consistent with symptoms of withdrawal to addictive substances. Withdrawal, or being prevented from access to a substance that you are addicted to, is characterized by cravings, obsessions, irritability, single-minded efforts to obtain your substance of choice (to the exclusion of all else), and feelings of shame and self-loathing for not being able to stop. All of which are reflected in the thoughts, feelings, and behaviors of a heartbroken lover.

Furthermore, the fact that fMRI scans revealed that the reward centers of despairing lovers lit up intensely when exposed to photographs of Exes suggests that brokenhearted people are highly rewarded by contact with their sweethearts. This implies that you can still feel the "high" of early-stage love when viewing photos or mentally envisioning your beloved, even when you are estranged from them. The relationship between visual contact and reward may partially explain the overwhelming obsessions, cravings, and compulsions to contact an Ex lover that torment most Exaholics.

What research data points to is something extremely important: that loss triggers intense feelings of love. The fear, stress, uncertainty, and panic of a broken attachment replicate the neurological and biochemical experience of early-stage romantic love: high dopamine, low serotonin, and flashes of adrenalin. That means that even if you'd been feeling somewhat ambivalent about your relationship before it ended—or even contemptuous of and frustrated by your partner—when you lose them, you will go into withdrawal and therefore experience highly intense feelings of love and craving to be with them again. This explains one of the reasons why even difficult relationships are so sticky: a person who experienced their partner as disappointing, irritating, or boring will often feel overwhelmed with fear and longing as soon as they head for the door.

Whether we call it "protest" or "withdrawal" the experience is the same: you become single-minded in your efforts to get your fix. In this case, the "fix" is knowing that you are loved by and connected to your beloved. The obsessive thoughts and behaviors that this need triggers can ruin lives, just as thoroughly as substance abuse does.

OBSESSION
Obsession fuels love. Early-stage love is characterized by obsessions that percolate excited feelings and daydreams about your lover.

Similarly, a bad breakup is defined by dark obsessions that spin out into nightmarish anxieties. The biochemical state of romantic love that erupts inside you when an attachment is broken causes you to obsess.

One important thing to understand about obsessions after a breakup is that because losing an attachment triggers the biological, physiological experience of love, your thoughts about your Ex are much more likely to be focused on all of their positive qualities. No matter how dissatisfying your relationship actually was, when your attachment is severed, it injects you with the love drug. This means that under the influence of the love cocktail of neurotransmitters fizzing and sputtering in your brain, you will once again begin to idealize your lover, downplay their flaws, and focus on the wonderful parts of your relationship.

Frustratingly, this idealization of them will occur even if your rational neocortex is screaming at you that your Ex is a sociopath and that you should hate them for all the horrible things they've done to you. This can feel extremely confusing. People often say things like, "My head tells me one thing, but my heart tells me another." I'd like you to consider the possibility that the reason for this split is that your limbic brain is jonesing for its fix, not that your heart is telling you that Ex really is the love of your life. This is biology, not a Lifetime movie. This might sound harsh, but I want you to understand that when you're having this experience you are in an altered state of consciousness. As such, you may not be able to trust your feelings in this specific context.

Nonetheless, when your relationship is lost and the trauma of broken attachment has thrown gasoline on the fire of your romantic fixation, your Ex may be only thing you can think about. You see your lover in your mind's eye, and at every moment think about what they might be doing, where they are, and who they are with. You replay scenes in your mind, imagine conversations with them, and fantasize about future outcomes. This is your mind's way of maintaining your addiction. Even if you are not with them physically, their living in your mind maintains your connection to them. Every fantasy interaction you have in your head lights up your reward centers and keeps your addiction alive. In the absence of actual contact, your thoughts about your Ex are the fix that keeps your limbic brain on the hook.

I know that sounds odd, but it's true. Having mental representations of attachment figures are how we hold each other close and they are a huge part of the healthy bonding process. Psychologists call this internalizing an attachment figure. Research shows that thinking about a lover and replaying memories reactivates the same physiological processes that actual interactions do. Obsessing about them is connecting with them, on a limbic-brain level. (Your limbic brain is not great at differentiating between the things your neocortex envisions, and the things that are actually in front of you.)

In addition to grinding away on memories and imagining new interactions, you may also spend many, many hours trying to figure out what happened. You might think about small moments that happened in the past: things that were done, or said, or unsaid. You attempt to unravel unconscious motivations in an effort to find explanations for why their love withered. You dissect memories in an autopsy that might reveal the cause of death—hoping for clues about how to bring the love of your cherished person back to life again. Replaying events, attempting to find toeholds of control, and finding a coherent story are all your brain's way of trying to work through the trauma.

Often, people attempting to make sense of what just happened will compulsively seek information that helps them understand their experience.

INFORMATION GATHERING

If you can't communicate with your lover or have actual contact with them, gathering information about them is another way to keep your beloved close to you, emotionally. Through your surveillance, you attempt to gain insight into their state of mind, and also try to make sense of what happened. You may watch their social media pages for evidence of where they've been, who they're with, and how they're feeling. You try to interpret small clues and nuances from things they post about how they feel. Are they sad? Do they care? Do they still love you? You may even personalize their online activity, interpreting posts and pictures as efforts to communicate with you. Watching

Exaholics Breaking Your Addiction to an Ex Love

Facebook pages or Twitter™ accounts may become obsessive as you monitor, hypervigilantly, every action.

You may pump friends and even acquaintances for information, asking if they've seen your Ex, and if they have, asking for more and more specific information. Who were they with? How did they seem? Where were they going? What were they wearing? All clues to help you understand how they might be feeling and whether they could be coming home to you. At its worst, obsessive information gathering can become outrageously inappropriate to the point of becoming criminal—hacking into email accounts, bank accounts, and phone records in order to satisfy your need for information.

CRAVING

Many people who have lost a cherished relationship have an intense desire to reconnect with their beloved. In their craving for connection, they may project their own feelings of longing onto their Ex and assume that their lost lover feels similarly. They fantasize about their Ex realizing how much they love them and want to get back together again. Their most sincere wish is that their Ex will come to their senses and that the madness will end. They will be wanted again, and their self-esteem will be restored. They want to get their old life back and restore the right order of the world. Then they could go home, emotionally or literally. They spend a lot of time thinking about how wonderful it would be to reunite and feel determined to do so.

For the record, I am all for love. I will go to the mat in support of any of my clients who want to see if they can repair or resurrect their relationships and I have helped many of them do just that. Sometimes reunion is possible, and couples can and do weather hard times and go on to have much happier and healthier relationships than ever before. But sometimes it's just not possible. In these cases, part of my job as the therapist to Exaholics in the grips of craving is to puncture their inflated fantasies about how awesome and perfect their relationship will be once they are back together again with the sharp needle of logic. It is easy for me, as a bystander, to remind them of what a frustrating, disappointing, and hurtful emotional desert their relationship actually was at the end because I am not under the influence of romantic love. But my intentions are good—when people are able to soberly acknowledge the reality of their relationship, sometimes their romantic fantasies lose some of their power.

If what I'm saying feels true for you, it may be helpful to take a step back and observe yourself, reminding yourself that you are in withdrawal and under the influence of romantic love. This may help keep you from getting tricked into believing that your relationship was better than it actually was. The fact that you're having an intense, almost physical desire to reconnect with your Ex may be evidence that you are experiencing withdrawal as much as it is that you are missing them.

Your cravings may be so strong that they are leading you to believe that you really do want to talk to, spend time with, or get back together with your Ex. Part of the healing process can be finding out whether repair and change is actually possible. So when your cravings for reconnection are intense and your neocortex is rationally on board with the plan to try (or gets kidnapped by your limbic brain), you may find yourself doing compulsive or impulsive things in attempts to engage with your Ex.

COMPULSIONS

Compulsions happen when your obsessions turn into behaviors. They often start when you begin to believe that if you could just talk to your Ex, they might realize what a huge mistake they are making. They might remember that what you had together was so special. The love they had for you could wake back up, and then you could be together again. So you do everything you can to re-engage them.

You might devise complex schemes to regain any kind of meaningful contact with your beloved. You may linger at your old haunts, hoping for an opportunity to talk to them. You might go where you know they will be and act surprised to run into them. You may attempt to return items personally, for an opportunity to speak to your Ex. You may insist on having final conversations and lengthy explanations in person, for the purposes of "closure." If your flimsy excuses for contact are rejected, you might even show up at their home or work demanding that they talk to you. At worst, compulsions for contact may devolve into outright stalking—driving past an Ex's home or work, or waiting for them to leave or return so that you can confront them.

Your need to know what is happening, and the urge to reconnect with them is so powerful it can even make you do things you know you shouldn't. You may call over and over. You may send a flurry of texts. You may share intimate feelings with them, even when the likely outcome is rejection. You demand their time and attention. You might scream with hurt and rage, inarticulately trying to convey how deeply you need their love and connection. You may beg for another chance. You go to them hoping you will get your needs met. You may even sleep with them, or give them money. You do everything you can to win them back. You approach every encounter hoping to feel better, but you usually feel worse once they've left you again. Some people even hurt themselves in efforts to communicate to their lover how profound their pain is and motivate their Exes into loving responses. Vincent van Gogh, packaging his bloody ear with trembling hands, was an Exaholic performance artist as well as a painter.

If you are able to get the attention of your lover, a variety of things could happen. You might plead with them or make demands of them for explanations or another chance. You might attempt to seduce them or manipulate them into re-engaging with you. You may accuse them or attack them angrily. You might try to win them back with love offerings or warmth.

If bids for connection fail, demands can disintegrate into threats—even violence.

LOVE AND HATE

Interestingly, even when people are very angry with their rejecting partner, their brain scans still give evidence of much of the same activity as romantically attracted people. This implies that as intense as your hatred toward your Ex might be, it doesn't necessarily extinguish your feelings of love. In fact, researchers Ellis and Malamuth found that even when you are in the depths of red rage toward your rejecting lover, you can still have powerfully strong feelings of romantic love for them at the same time.

While you would think that intense hate might cancel out feelings of love, the truth is, love and hate are close neighbors, neurologically speaking, occupying nearly the same small patch of real estate in your brain. They fuel each other. In practice, love and hate tend to go hand in hand—which may be why your partner can incite rage and irritation in you the way that no one else can. The true opposite of love isn't hate at all, but indifference.

As you well know, heartbroken lovers are anything but indifferent.

INTENSE EMOTIONAL PAIN

The pain of a breakup is breathtaking. It is all-consuming. It hurts you in places so deep you didn't even know they existed until your lover's leaving set them on fire. The torment can overpower every other part of you, including your rational mind, your ability to function at your job, your basic needs for food and sleep, and sometimes even the will to live. The power of this experience is shocking and oftentimes frightening.

This pain is not in your head, either. A 2011 research study led by Ethan Kross from the University of Michigan explored the impact of rejection on physical pain. Using fMRI brain image scans, he found that when participants looked at photographs of their Exes and thought about being rejected, the pain-sensing areas of their brains became active. This means that rejection shares neurological aspects in common with physical pain. The emotional pain Exaholics live with every day can be both intense and inescapable.

One of the worst aspects is that every single thing seems to trigger a painful memory. Everything from waking up in an empty bed to the absence of texts at lunch to the smell of their shampoo elicits another sharp pang of loss. It doesn't matter whether they broke it off or you did. You still miss them, profoundly.

PHYSICAL SYMPTOMS

As discussed in previous chapters, studies have found that people in long-term relationships tend to impact each other physiologically. Stable relationships create a sense of security and co-regulation that has physical implications. When that security is disrupted, it takes a physical toll.

Abrupt disconnection from a long-term lover creates changes in sleeping and eating patterns, affects your immune system, and triggers a stress response. It can even create changes in measurable cardiac activity. In the fresh aftermath of a relationship loss people have a higher risk of dying, particularly of heart attacks.

Exaholics therefore often feel physical symptoms in the days, weeks, and months after their love is lost. They complain of stomachaches, heartburn, and headaches. They can't eat or else they binge. They have trouble sleeping or sleep too much. They live with a hollow ache in their gut and slivers of anxiety needling their chest.

Though the physical and emotional experiences associated with a lost relationship are terrible, many Exaholics have an even harder time with the way their thinking changes after a breakup—particularly the way they think about themselves.

Loss of Self-Esteem

Breakups are so fundamentally traumatizing and damaging to your self-esteem because of the rejection at the core of the experience. If you are heartbroken, it means that you really loved them. You believed that they loved you. You gave yourself to them and trusted them to love you back. When they couldn't, or wouldn't, it feels like a statement about your worth. If you had been better, sexier, more fun, more accomplished, less difficult, or more lovable, you would have been enough for them. They would have loved you better. Instead, they hurt you, mistreated you, or simply rejected you.

Even if they didn't leave you for another person, it still feels horrifying to think that they would rather take their chances and be alone than continue to be with you. That you meant so little to them, or were so unsatisfying to be with that they'd walk away from you or abuse the love you had to offer.

When the one person you totally opened up to—the one who really, really loved you and the one who knew you the best—changes their mind about you, it changes the way you feel about yourself. Any self-confidence you had is shattered when you are dropped by your beloved. When you lose value in the eyes of the person you adored, you lose value in your own eyes too.

Coping with this primary rejection is devastating, but it doesn't stop there.

In the throes of protesting our abandonment or rejection, we can all do embarrassing, humiliating, and even dangerous things. Even though we know better, even though we know we are acting crazy, our drive to reconnect is too strong. It overpowers our rational mind. The need to reunite, in the form of contact or information, is so basic and primal that we feel absolutely helpless in the face of it.

The pain of rejection and abandonment is traumatizing enough. But when you become absolutely unhinged in the protest phase of loss, it can feel like you are losing yourself. People who are at the mercy of their raging panic often feel like they are losing their minds. They do things impulsively that they know they should not and frequently feel humiliation and shame for their behavior.

They use words to describe themselves like "pathetic" and "weak." Self-esteem takes a huge blow when your beloved rejects you. But when you start doing things that you know are inappropriate or unhelpful but feel like you can't stop, it strips away another layer of your self-esteem. You begin to feel like there really is something wrong with you.

Then shame sets in.

SHAME

I like Brené Brown's (paraphrased) explanation of shame the best: Shame is believing that you are bad. Shame is the experience of feeling flawed, broken, or unlovable. Shame is the sadistic bully that lives in your head, telling you that you are an ugly, fat, stupid, boring, crazy failure who no one could ever possibly love. For too many Exaholics, when their Ex moves out, shame moves in.

Shame can make you second-guess yourself, shut down emotionally from other people, and avoid new opportunities. Because shame is telling you that you suck, you are a broken weirdo, no one likes you, and you're going to make a fool of yourself if you try, it can build a wall around you. If you get tricked into believing what shame is telling you, and it sinks its talons into you too deeply, black roots of depression can take hold.

The gnawing anxiety of rejection and the grief of your many losses eat away at you, but the helplessness to stop the pain and the shame you feel are the truly scary parts of a breakup. Your inability to escape the pain feeds your shame. The fact that you cannot will yourself to crawl out of the pain and get it together, combined with the belief that you could stop this if you were a better, "normal" person, seems to be evidence for the fact that you really are pathetic and unworthy of love. "No wonder this relationship didn't work out," shame sneers in your ear.

This sadistic triad of pain, helplessness, and shame that most people experience during a breakup is the one-two-three knockout punch that can leave a gaping black hole where your sense of self used to be. These three are so terribly effective at making you feel worthless because they poke their bony, salty fingers into the primary wound of rejection, which is the idea that "I'm not good enough to love."

You replay all of your failures and shortcomings before, during, and after the relationship, spiraling deeper into self-loathing. Instead of being able to comfort yourself and cope with the loss, you criticize yourself mercilessly for being such a stupid, foolish loser. Your self-esteem, already crushed by your Ex, then macerated by helpless pain, finally gets steamrolled by shame.

SOCIAL AND OTHER LOSSES

In the midst of your inner torment, the outside reality of your life may be in shambles as well. You lose so much when a relationship ends. Your entire life, as you've known it, might be different after a breakup. When you lost your lover it is likely that you lost your emotional home base, your social partner, and your best friend. There is no one to talk to or sit next to on the couch in the evenings. Your day-to-day reality has changed. The person that you relied on for emotional support and companionship is physically gone. Even if it has been a long time since you actually experienced emotional support from them, you still feel the loss.

Your other friendships may be strained as well. Attempts to spend time with friends you knew as a couple may be awkward. You are decimated by pain and may be in the grips of a feverish compulsion to know everything about your Ex, making interactions uncomfortable for everyone. The loyalties of your friends may be divided. Or perhaps most of the people in your social circle were closer to your Ex than to you, making you suddenly aware of loneliness in a life that had once seemed well-populated.

Additionally, if for you breaking up involved moving out, you may have lost your access to your home, trading your comfortable dwelling for an anonymous, depressing apartment. You might not feel able to go to the same places that you did when you were a couple, for fear of being flooded by painful memories or having a traumatizing run-in with your Ex.

Losing your relationship may make you feel like you have lost your entire life.

RELATIONSHIP LOSS AND MENTAL HEALTH

In the days, weeks, and months following a major relationship loss, it is not uncommon at all for people to experience symptoms of depression and anxiety. If the symptoms began in direct response to the loss it's called "Adjustment Disorder." But it still just feels like being anxious and/or depressed.

People in the first phase of loss, the protest phase, often describe feeling anxious. They're often jittery, sleepless, and obsessed. They worry; they cast about in their minds and often hook catastrophic thoughts. Worst-case scenarios feel true. They also tend to make global attributions based on their current experience: "This relationship ended, therefore I am unlovable and going to be alone for the rest of my life." The fears feel real and cause people going through breakups an enormous amount of pain.

People in the second phase of loss, the despair stage, often experience symptoms similar to those of depression: fatigue, social isolation, low mood, and changes in cognition (toward shame or hopelessness) are common. The fact that animals experience depressive symptoms too suggests that the second, despairing phase of loss is a biologically based reaction to loss. This depressive response is akin to the sickness response that most animals go through when highly stressed or ill (withdrawing, low energy, etc.) Researchers speculate that this serves an important function, in that feeling like withdrawing from life helps both people and animals recuperate and recover from both physical and emotional trauma.

Nonetheless, the heavy sadness and isolation of despair may trigger an actual depressive episode, particularly in people who are vulnerable to it. With depression comes feelings of hopelessness, helplessness, shame, low energy, a desire to isolate, and a great deal of sadness.

Gender Differences

Men and women often deal with the aftermath of rejection differently. In heterosexual relationships, men are often more dependent on their romantic partners for social connection, companionship, and emotional support. This may be due to females, in general, having stronger ties to friends, family, and other social supports than men. Therefore when men are rejected they may not cope well, often turning to alcohol, drugs, or other various exercises in self-destruction than to supportive friends or family. Men are also more likely to stalk or violently attack female partners after a relationship loss, as well as commit suicide.

Women who have been rejected describe feeling more deeply depressed than men do. They often report feelings of helplessness or hopelessness after a relationship ends. They are more likely to show outward signs of distress like crying, losing weight, having changes in their sleeping patterns, feeling unable to concentrate, and having problems with their memory.

While women may talk more, and more openly, about their lost relationships with their friends and family, these discussions may not always be helpful, particularly if a woman is made to feel shame or invalidation for her feelings. However, more recent research shows that talking about a relationship is not unhealthy and in fact it may be an important part of the healing process. Grace Larsen of Northwestern University found that when people have the opportunity to talk about their experiences it seems to help them reorganize their sense of identity and create a new, healthier narrative. People who have opportunities to talk about their experiences may therefore recover more quickly.

Relapse

Like any addiction, a fixation on one particular person can be very difficult to break. Once a fire has ignited inside of you and burned brightly for one magical person, it does not take much to breathe the glowing coals back to fiery life. Months, even years after a breakup, a chance run-in with an Ex can trigger all the old desires and longings.

Often, Exaholics in recovery are triggered by seeing certain people, being in particular places, or hearing songs that remind them of their Ex. Such exposures can bring about a new round of craving and obsessive thinking, and even trigger a new flurry of writing, calling, and lurking around in efforts to reconnect with their lost love.

Even after you have resolved to be done and have broken off contact with your Ex, a chance encounter may reel you back in. It's not uncommon to go back and forth in a quasi-relationship with your Ex for a long time: not quite together, but not really apart. You're still talking and sleeping together, but you feel emotionally unfulfilled. Allow me to put my marriage counselor hat on for a second to say this: Unless you two get serious about addressing the problems that drove you apart in the first place, simply getting back together again after a period of time is not likely to create a better future outcome for either of you.

You Are Normal

The truth is, love is enormously important to all of us. When we bond, we do so on levels that go so deep we are not fully aware of them until the relationship ends. We need secure attachments to survive, as well as be healthy and well. To despair and be fundamentally traumatized when love is lost is therefore not just natural, but expected. This is nothing to be ashamed of. You are experiencing the deepest, most fundamental kind of loss a human being can experience: the loss of love. It affects your body, mind, and feelings on a biological level. To feel like you are losing it is normal. You can't control it. You can't make it stop. No one can. You're just doing what nature built you to do.

It surprises many Exaholics to hear that the experiences I've described here are all normal. As terrible as this has been for you, I want you to know that everything you are going through is perfectly normal and expected in the aftermath of a traumatic breakup. Feeling out of control, obsessed, and decimated by self-flagellation and shame is simply the human experience of being rejected by someone who was very important to you. I hope that knowing how normal and common this is helps you feel the tiniest bit better.

8

Types of Loss

*"I built my whole life around this relationship.
When it was gone, everything collapsed."*

—Exaholic

WHILE THE EXPERIENCE OF PROTEST AND DESPAIR AFTER
THE LOSS OF A CHERISHED RELATIONSHIP IS UNIVERSAL,
ALL THE INDIVIDUAL STORIES ARE UNIQUE. YOUR
RELATIONSHIP WAS ONE OF A KIND. NOTHING EXACTLY
LIKE IT HAS EVER EXISTED BEFORE OR WILL AGAIN.

At the same time, you may have things in common with other
people who traveled a similar path to yours. Circumstances do matter.
The breakup of a teenager, as searing and devastating as it may be, is
different than the collapse of a twenty-year marriage or the dissolution
of a partnership that has been the sacred nest for children. Being the
"other" in a failed affair is entirely different from losing a marriage to
infidelity. All have unique challenges and growth opportunities.

Young Love

In the case of young lovers—teens and college-age young adults—
losing a primary relationship can feel like a nuclear bomb going off in
the center of their lives. When younger people fall in love, they tend
to do so with ferocious intensity. They also have a tendency to become

immersed in a relationship to the exclusion of all else. Shakespeare cast Romeo and Juliet as teens for a reason: the level of intensity and irrationality that adolescents in love are capable of are legendary. There are many reasons for this.

Our brains, believe it or not, don't finish developing into maturity until we are in our mid-twenties. Until then, our executive functioning abilities are still developing. A twenty-two-year-old adult, legally able to vote, drink beer, and serve in the military, is still very much an adolescent from a psychological and emotional perspective. Because their ability to plan ahead, anticipate consequences, and regulate their emotions is still developing, adolescents tend to be impulsive and reckless under the best of circumstances. The ability to manage themselves and envision future outcomes is born from past experience that adolescents have not yet acquired. When they fall in love, they do so with abandon.

Adolescents are full of vigorous, brand-new hormones that inflame lust. They are also on a hair-trigger for falling in love. When love cranks open the floodgates and a sparkling waterfall of dopamine washes through them for the first time, it can feel to them like they were cracked wide open. When adolescents and young adults fall under the spellbinding influence of love, they are often carried away by a flood of intoxicating dopamine, excitement, and idealization. Their love is brand new and unlike anything else in their subjective experience. Their attraction to each other blazes like the hot white tip of an acetylene torch, melting the boundaries between self and other, and fusing them together psychologically, emotionally, and socially.

Even without being spellbound by love, adolescents gravitate toward fantasy and idealism: there is a reason why the young adult section of your local bookstore is packed full of supernatural tales involving wizards, vampires, and gifted children with psychic abilities. They have not yet let go of the magical possibilities of childhood and are prone to viewing their incandescent new relationship with the same guileless hope with which they consume other fantasies. When magical thinking, idealism, and trust are applied (thickly) to another teenager, their irreplaceable other glows with an importance that transcends that of anything else: parents, other friends, and themselves.

Sexuality is also an enormous factor in young relationships. The physical intensity of orgasms and the novelty of exploring the pleasure that bodies were built for are inherently bonding. Physical union blurs the boundaries between self and other. Vulnerable adolescents, in addition to getting biochemically swept away by the intoxication of dopamine and compulsive agitation of reduced serotonin, also bond powerfully through the oxytocin released through transcendental sexual experiences.

Psychologically, the work of adolescence and young adulthood is trying on different identities, and then discarding them. Every incarnation of the self adds another layer of self-awareness, self-confidence, and a new taste of the world. The summertime athlete will morph into a brooding artist by wintertime, only to emerge as an impassioned activist for social justice by spring. Diving into the pool of experience completely and with abandon is what defines adolescence, psychologically. When this tendency is applied to relationships, it results in kids doing a cannonball into the deep end of infatuation, creating feelings of love and attachment that are so strong they overtake them entirely.

Another reason why young people are so deeply affected by romantic relationships is that young lovers also don't have the solid sense of themselves that older lovers do. Their interests and preferences are still developing. They are uncertain of themselves, and prone to insecure anxieties under the best of circumstances. Everyone who falls in love inflates the positive qualities of their lover —the most cynical middle-aged attorney will sincerely make excuses for a new flame. The sweethearts of adolescents become demigods, deities that they emulate, worship, and follow. Music, clothing, interests, the trappings of the social tribe that their adored currently holds membership in, all become necessary for an adolescent in love. Anything (or anyone) that is frowned upon by their lover is quickly shoved away, including other friends and family members. Anyone who tries to warn the young lover or protect them from the inevitable end will become the enemy. Obstacles to overcome together only join the young couple more fiercely to each other.

Adolescents and young adults also bond so tightly because they are emotionally and developmentally (even if not consciously aware of it) seeking the safety of a new primary attachment. The normal scuffles over control that teens and parents have are necessary catalysts for independence. When a young person emotionally and psychologically begins to detach from their parents, there is a new dependence on other people for a sense of security, identity, and belonging. Sometimes this fierce bonding occurs with friends. Sometimes, it is with a lover. In the case of the latter, the attachment and importance of the beloved often eclipses everyone and everything else in their lives, becoming their new primary attachment—a position formerly held by a parent.

Emotionally, college-age people often feel adrift in the world. They are struggling to compile a life. They are in the space in between: no longer a child entirely taken care of by a family but not yet a self-sufficient adult. It can be a difficult and disorienting time. Young adults will often lock on to groups—fraternities or sororities—or passionate new interests to provide them with a sense of identity and purpose. But when young lovers find each other and form a new home base in the fragility and uncertainty of just starting out, they can cling to each other like two people adrift in an ocean. This tendency can be even stronger if one or both people did not feel that their needs were emotionally met by their parents. Their lover becomes their chosen family, their best friend, and the person who may right the wrongs done to them, finally providing the love and care they've been craving their whole lives.

On the blank canvas of a brand-new reality, young couples sketch out a life. Firsts are shared: first apartment, first futon, first graduation, first "real" job, first car accident, first successes, and first failures. All of these are major bonding moments where couples turn to each other for comfort, support, and guidance. New friends are made in the context of social partnership. The "I" previously known dissolves into "we" and all aspects of the new life being built may be shared.

The primary problem with relationships that begin in adolescence and young adulthood is that by definition, they often should end. Young people need to molt. By experiencing and then shedding identities, self-awareness and clarity about values are forged.

Immersing themselves in an interest, relationship, style, or religion, and then discarding the once-vital aspect of their being like a snake shedding its skin is the process of growth in adolescence and young adulthood. This process is also how they develop insight about what kind of partner they need. Becoming glued to one person during this important developmental phase can, for some people, be limiting. Other couples who come together in adolescence or young adulthood and do stay together for the long haul will, eventually, need to make space for each other to change, grow, and explore within the relationship. If that important work doesn't happen, sooner or later the relationship will usually either wither or explode.

People grow at different rates. People in the same relationship often experience it differently. The illusion of union is just that: an illusion. Two separate individuals inhabit the emotional space of any relationship. But in young relationships, more than any other, people tend to fuse together emotionally, becoming highly reactive to each other. For that reason, adolescent relationships tend to be chaotic and explosive. When one person begins to lose interest, move away psychologically, or shift their emotional energy into other interests, it often unleashes enormous amounts of pain, despair, rage, panic, and frantic efforts to reconnect on the part of the partner that feels left or abandoned. At these moments, young people are flooded by anxious, agitated dopamine, experience sharp drops in serotonin, and go into a frenzy of withdrawal as their secure attachment fails them.

Young relationships are therefore incredibly addicting, and the aftermath of a failed relationship in this stage of life—though normal—is exquisitely traumatic. Adolescents and young adults have vulnerabilities that older people often don't. Because they tend to idealize, trust, and glorify their partners to such an extreme degree, when they are rejected it often becomes a statement of their inherent worthlessness as a person. This can be so extreme that it feels like a condemnation from God himself. They have bonded so tightly and so absolutely to their irreplaceable other that it is a loss on the order of being thrown out by your parents. Because young people invest so much of their already sparse lives into a relationship, when it goes it takes everything and everyone with it.

Many times, other relationships are neglected by young adults in favor of their romantic addiction. They build their new lives around their partners. The only friends they may have are those they share in common. When the relationship fails, so does their social support system. If their parental relationship is rocky, as is often the case with individuating adolescents, they usually only have other kids to turn to in their time of gravest need. Other adolescents have, understandably, absolutely no idea how to help or comfort their friends as they struggle with the enormity of the loss, grief, panic, fear, despair, and obsessive craving of a failed relationship. They can offer invalidating encouragement ("You'll find someone new") or shame-inducing advice ("You just have to get over it and move on"). When their Exaholic friend remains stuck in obsessive despair, other teens and young twenty-somethings quickly become impatient and move on to friends who are, quite frankly, more fun.

Another undeniably difficult aspect to these relationships is that when they end, teens and young adults may have much less control over their lives than older people do. For example, they may be required to continue to go to the same school and therefore regularly see their Ex. In contrast, an older person (though it may be inconvenient) has the option of taking a new job, or moving to a different city in order to give themselves literal space to heal and grow. This helplessness to protect themselves may intensify their trauma.

Trauma and control are correlated. For example, it was noticed as early as the First World War that the soldiers who appeared to be the most resilient to "shell shock," as PTSD was termed at the time, were those who had the most control and ability to protect themselves: pilots of aircraft. The ones who suffered the most intensely had the least amount of control or ability to protect themselves and had the most severe symptoms: soldiers floating above the battlefield in balloons. It's still true: the greater degree of control you have to protect yourself and get away from an emotionally dangerous situation, the better you will fare. Teens and young adults usually have the least.

Traumatic relationship losses during adolescence and young adulthood can have long-term emotional effects. Like newborn babies, adolescents have a burst of important brain development.

Their brains are overgrown by billions of new neurons, all ready to be pruned away by necessary new life experiences. In particular, their limbic brain—the part responsible for social awareness and feeling emotions—is developing rapidly. Because of this, adolescents experience emotions differently and more intensely than adults do. The things they experience about themselves and other people socially and romantically (particularly when colored by emotional traumas) can create blueprints for how they understand themselves and other people as they move forward into adulthood.

Messages about self-worth, value to other people, attractiveness, lovability, and inherent "goodness" are crystalized during adolescent social experiences. If social or romantic rejection teaches them that they are not valuable or worth loving, the damage to their self-esteem can be immense and difficult to repair. Furthermore, messages about the inherent trustworthiness of other people and potential for danger associated with romantic relationships can have reverberations for decades after. Many adults I've worked with in therapy who have deep insecurities about themselves or their relationships were not mistreated by their parents in early childhood, but rather bullied or rejected by their peers or love interests as adolescents.

The negative effects of relationship loss are often compounded by a young person's general inability to cope with such intensity and devastation. Whereas an older person may have learned how to soothe themselves, practice good self-care, and stay balanced emotionally, a young person has not yet had the opportunity to acquire those life skills. They literally do not know how to regulate their emotions. Older people also often have a life they can return to: hobbies, friendships, the satisfactions (or at least distractions) of a career. Young people may not have established these. Older people may also have a defined sense of themselves, an inner confidence and self-assurance that young people have not yet developed. For all of these reasons, when young people are dropped from a relationship they are much likely to go splat, rather than bounce back.

At it's worst, the devastation that adolescents face when they lose their primary attachment can quickly snowball into decimation of their entire social network. To many adolescents, their social lives are their world. The sun rises and sets on the good opinion of others, their inclusion in a group, and the messages of value and worth that accepting peers reflect back to them. The cascade of rejection, isolation, and abandonment can overwhelm an adolescent's ability to cope, entirely. Adolescents and young adults may cease to function, even dropping out of school. Inability to function during a critical time in their lives where they are laying the foundation for later growth and success can also have long-term consequences for their future.

In the midst of these catastrophic losses, adolescents are made even more vulnerable by the heightened emotionality and impulsivity of their still-developing brains. It is, tragically, not uncommon for fragile adolescents to be driven to the brink of suicide by the collapse of their entire social world and the messages of rejection and unworthiness that they internalize. Other adolescents may cope with the raging despair of these rejections through self-destructive behaviors or substance use. Establishing unhealthy coping skills during formative years may set them up for later (and potentially severe) addictive disorders.

For these reasons, it is essential that we stop dismissing young love as inconsequential. It is very easy for friends and family to roll their eyes at the "drama" of a wrecked teen and fail to see that they are experiencing a major life event that is not just putting them in immediate danger but that may have lasting impact on how they view themselves and other people. Instead, young people need support, guidance, and meaningful help to put the pieces of their lives—and themselves—back together again.

ADVANTAGES

Losing a cherished relationship traumatically during adolescence or young adulthood is undeniably difficult. However, there are some unique advantages to relationship loss in this phase of life. Even though you may not have as much control over your life, or as many inner resources as an older person does, you do have lots of distractions and opportunities. At no other time in your life will it be easier to make new friends, take up new interests, or go on new adventures. You may also have the support of many adults in your life. If you are in

Exaholics Breaking Your Addiction to an Ex Love

high school or college, you very likely have access to free counseling. You may be able to lean on the support of your parents, and if you do go through a period where you feel like you are falling apart, you may have the support and guidance to put your life back together and get a second chance.

The growth opportunities are enormous—going through this and successfully healing from it will teach you important life skills that will serve you well for the rest of your life. Everyone, sooner or later, goes through this experience. If you get it out of the way early, with a minimum of long-term consequences, you will be stronger and better able to negotiate emotionally intense situations in the future.

LONG-TERM RELATIONSHIPS: TWENTIES AND EARLY THIRTIES

Like the relationship losses of adolescence, love lost in the "prime years" of relationship building can have powerful and long-term consequences. In our modern culture, people pair up during their late twenties and early thirties. People are often actively seeking out mates: the person who they will marry, have children with, and with whom they will build a life.

During this period, many friends may marry. Couples, rather than individuals, become the social unit. New relationships are formed in the context of being in a partnership. People live together, sharing every aspect of daily life and forming deep attachments. They build lives around each other. In this stage of life, people may often move or travel together. They may accept or pass on jobs in service of their relationship, sacrifice in support of their partner's graduate education, and go into debt to buy furniture together. They nest, and may prepare for the next phase of life: children.

When relationships end during this pair-bonding era, it is often especially traumatic and devastating because it feels like the breakup is not just a loss in the present day, but also the destruction of a future. Marriage-minded individuals in particular may feel like the hopes and dreams they had for their lives are shattered. As they grieve the relationship itself, they often need to grieve the lost future they would have had with their partner.

This can be particularly true and especially agonizing for heterosexual women who have been in long-term partnerships extending into their thirties. A woman who dreams of a family but instead experiences a breakup at the age of thirty-two or thirty-three now has to deal with panic and anxiety about her hopes for her eventual family, as well as the despair, obsession, grief, and withdrawal that a relationship loss usually incites.

In the midst of their pain and grief, heterosexual women have enormous pressure to get back out there and find someone suitable to build a life with, becoming increasingly frantic as "all the good ones are taken." They may feel incredibly angry with their Exes for stealing their future and wasting their time. Regret, rage, and anxiety complicates their recovery process. I have worked with many women who, as they pine for their Exes, push themselves to date. Unfortunately, as they are not in a good space emotionally, it can be more difficult for them to find and attract a healthy partner. They may inadvertently infuse their first dates with awkward evaluations of net worth, marriageability, and family mindedness, leaving a prospective suitor feeling that he's just been on a job interview rather than a date. If they make it past the first few dates, a woman feeling vulnerable about her future may "rush the close," bringing up questions of commitment and intention too soon. Many men will pull away under these circumstances, and leave women feeling even more anxious, despairing, and vigilant about their future prospects.

Men who are interested in marriage and family may also take these losses hard, blaming their Exes for robbing them of their best years. I have sat with many men who have wept bitterly for the dreams that their Exes stole from them: little blond children with her big brown eyes, the comfortable home, and his connection to her extended family all must be mourned.

Feelings of anxiety and despair are often compounded as their peers are jumping the broom in droves. One of my twenty-nine-year-old clients was in (not just invited to but in—as in standing up there in an unflattering dress holding a bouquet) sixteen different weddings in one year. Her singleness at the time made her feel like the modern equivalent of a leper. She was the broken girl that nobody wanted.

Other clients are similarly triggered by pregnancy announcements, baby showers, and sweet baby pictures. They feel like the entire world is rolling on toward happy-family futures, leaving them behind. As they struggle through the normal Exaholic experience, an icicle of fear pokes at their heart, whispering, "You're going to be alone forever."

People ending same-sex relationships in this phase of life also often have the sense that everyone else in the world is in a long-term partnership except for them. The trauma, obsession, craving, and grief of a lost love are compounded by the shame of rejection and failure. Many people feel like the fish that got thrown back and must work to rebuild their self-esteem before they are able to open their hearts back up again.

The primary wound of relationships that end during this phase of life is often, "I wasn't good enough to marry."

This wound is often then scoured with salt as an Exaholic watches his or her future husband, wife, or life partner quickly pair up and often marry the next person they date. In no other group is obsessive gathering of information more intense (with the possible exception of people whose relationships end in infidelity). The need for data to compare themselves against is overwhelming, even if that information is painful. The torture that comes from comparing themselves with their lover's new partner inflames rage and hurt that can take years to recover from—years that a thirty-something Exaholic woman may not have.

For these reasons it is essential that people in the pair-bonding phase of life are assisted in moving through their healing process as quickly as possible. The sooner they can recover from their attachment to their Ex, the sooner they can begin to build the relationship that will carry them through the next chapter of their lives.

Advantages

The good news is that you are facing this issue at a point in your life when you have many options, and you may be at the peak of personal power and general attractiveness. More than any other group of Exaholics, you have independence and choices. You can move away, change jobs, go to grad school, lean on old friends, make new ones, immerse yourself in a satisfying career, and focus on yourself for as long as it takes to heal. You're still young enough to not get weird looks if you decide to hostel your way through Europe for six months. You can buy a motorcycle, get a dog, take a pottery class, and make it a point to talk to at least three new people every week. You can design your reality to be whatever you want it to be. You are in charge. And there are still some good ones left—I promise.

DIVORCE

Divorce is tragic. In addition to the pain and loss of losing their lover, life partner, and best friend, divorcing couples often struggle with enormous feelings of shame, anger, regret, and failure. On top of that, they have to make major and long-term legal, financial, and material decisions quickly—often at a time when they are not functioning very well cognitively and emotionally.

Ending a long-term, established, and formal partnership is a different experience than the searing loss of young love—though it can be just as emotionally and socially catastrophic. Generally speaking, if a couple has been together long enough to get married, the intensity of romantic infatuation has settled into a deep attachment. Your partnership is the fabric of your life: your social life, friendships, hobbies, shared interests, home, and family all center on your marriage. It is your home, both literally and emotionally.

Even though both people in every divorcing couple has reasons why the relationship was challenging, it is frequently the case that when divorce happens it is initiated by one person—and usually over the objections of another. One person is no longer willing to accept the disappointments and challenges of marriage and has pulled away emotionally. The one left behind in the ruins of a life often suffers terribly. They have been rejected and abandoned by the one person who promised to love them forever, through thick and thin. The sense of helplessness and powerlessness is overwhelming, as they watch their spouse go about taking apart their shared life.

Divorce may also have a dramatic impact on financial and material security. Two people working together are generally much better able to manage the responsibilities of life and get ahead. Two incomes going into supporting a household create more wealth and stability than one. Oftentimes, especially with kids in the picture, a natural division of labor is created where one person is in charge of earning money and the other person is in charge of running the show.

Tearing a family into two independent households, often with unequal childcare responsibilities and earning potential, can create a mess. This is particularly true for divorced women with children who chose to be stay-at-home moms or who deliberately chose under-employment in order to keep their schedules flexible for childcare. Divorcing women who had trusted the strength of their marriages to support them materially are often—even in our modern era—shoved under the poverty line by divorce. Subsequently, they can flounder for many years after the divorce, trying to build a career, raise children, and regain some financial security, as well as rebuilding their lives.

As a result, people who are divorcing are often very, very angry. "How could you do this to me?!?" is the refrain to the divorce song. It's understandable. A person whose partner has initiated a divorce feels helpless and victimized. They have made promises, bought real estate, pledged their lives, and made sacrifices that are now being ripped apart. They staked their claim: making a homestead for their entire lives and futures with this one person. A person who ultimately failed them.

"I feel like the rug was pulled out from under me."

"He is completely immature and self-centered and incapable of loving."

"I have been thrown out of my home."

"I've failed."

"This is humiliating."

Divorce feels like an injustice. Divorcing people are often kept awake at night not by longing for their idealized partner, but by resentment. Their Ex has stolen their secure future. They often feel like the person they once loved has died, replaced by a cold, vicious stranger who is out to get them. Under the surface they may have a craving for their lover, but not this one—they want the person who they married. Their longing is for the person they knew in the past, who may no longer exist.

Divorcing people are not just losing their primary attachment, the person to whom they've addictively bonded. They are losing their life partner, their family, and their homes. They are often losing financial security, social standing, and their future hopes and dreams. For many, it's an embarrassing failure. And they are pissed off.

To be rejected by your life partner, your husband, or your wife is the ultimate abandonment. To be unwanted by the person who knows and loves you the best is to say that you are not worth loving. That you are irredeemable. That you were simply not good enough. The hurt that comes from this rejection is abandonment rage at its most primal and ferocious.

The rage is also fueled by embarrassment. To stand up in front of God and everyone you know and pledge your love and devotion to each other, only to have the marriage collapse feels like a major, shameful failure to many divorcing couples. They fear judgment from friends, family, and society at large. To have to identify themselves as divorced feels like a lifelong stigma. Many people also often feel that they have let down their families, particularly if their families have been materially or financially supportive.

Furthermore, in their rage, despair, and trauma they must make major decisions: "Do we sell the house or do I buy her out?" "Should I ask for maintenance?" "Who gets the living room set?" I have worked with many people who were forced to make decisions—the best they could with the information they had at the time—and regretted some of those decisions deeply later on. The outcome of those decisions often led them to feeling that they'd been taken to the cleaners in their divorce and in doing so added a new layer of anger and resentment to their pain.

Ending a marriage is ending a major life segment that is defined by a home, a family, a social network, and once-pleasurable activities. Even if the relationship itself was seriously flawed, the loss of the life that was built on the foundation of the relationship is still incredibly traumatizing.

One difficulty that many divorcing people are surprised to encounter is the impact that a divorce has on their social network.

Once the dust of the divorce itself has settled—agreements have been signed, real estate sold, and new routines established—people can look around to see that their social landscape has changed considerably. After a certain age, our social units are couples rather than individuals. The comfortable friendships you have during your marriage may feel awkward to maintain as a single person. For that reason, being divorced can be very isolating.

Divorce is a major life trauma that impacts nearly every aspect of life.

ADVANTAGES

As difficult as getting divorced is, it does have advantages. First of all, by the time your relationship has deteriorated to the point where a divorce is in order, you no longer idealize your lover the way you once did. You've been burned, hurt, and disappointed so many times that frustration has probably replaced the tender feelings you once had for the person you married. Even though you have lots of losses to mourn, there were likely many aspects of this partnership that were not working for you either. Divorce may liberate you from an unsatisfying situation.

The primary work of getting divorced is grieving your old identity as a married person and then building a new one. It requires finding yourself again, amongst the rubble of the life you have been living. Divorce gives you the opportunity to discover the brightest and best pieces of yourself and reassemble them into a new (potentially better and more authentic) incarnation of you.

Furthermore, lots of other people are going through the same thing as you. Divorce is common. Between your parents, friends, extended family members, and co-workers you likely have lots of people in your life who can commiserate. There are meet-up groups, retreats, podcasts, and self-help books galore, all dedicated to the life and times of divorced people. You are in good company, and hearing the phoenix-rising-from-the-ashes stories of others may inspire you to create a new life that is much more fulfilling than the one you experienced while you were struggling in an unhappy marriage.

Couples With Children

Whether or not a divorce is involved, any time children are involved in a breakup it adds a new layer of pain and tragedy as well as complication.

No matter how badly you feel, no matter how enraged, obsessed, or broken you are after the relationship ends, you must continue to meet the emotional, material, and educational needs of your children—children who may be suffering enormously themselves. Despite how common it is, and how resilient children can be, having their parents split up is often extremely difficult for kids.

No matter how objectively questionable your Ex's parenting may have been, children are attached to their parents. Your kids' life may also have been just as disrupted as yours—maybe more so. Unless you and your Ex have chosen a child-centered nesting arrangement (where the two of you take turns living in the family home so that your children have consistency in their environment) your kids may now be living out of suitcases. This is difficult for anyone, let alone a young child with limited resources to cope.

Your children are likely confused, angry, and hurt about the split. They may blame themselves. They may blame you. They may feel ashamed of the situation. I work with many adults whose parents divorced when they were children. They often describe having a deep grief for their "normal life" that was lost when their parents split up.

Children are also finely attuned to the emotional state of their parents. Most kids become upset when their parents are upset. To see you suffering is worrisome to kids. They need to know that you are there to take care of them and protect them. Children who doubt your ability to keep them safe will quickly step into the role of caring for you—at great detriment to their emotional and psychological well-being.

In short: your children need you. They need you to be an adult who can comfort them, protect them, provide a stable environment, and help them put their little lives back together, at a time when you are least likely to have the emotional resources to do anything other than lay in your bed and cry.

If you are a parent, you do not have the luxury of falling apart entirely. You need to do whatever it takes to keep yourself in a place where you are able to be there emotionally for your children—not put your kids in the position of needing to take care of you or hide their own feelings of pain and anger so as not to upset you. So get into therapy, join a support group, practice good self-care, and lean on your friends.

The hardest parts for most Exaholics with children from the failed relationship is that you must continue to support their kids' relationship with your Ex. Above all else, as tempting as it may be, do not bad-mouth your Ex to your children. Even though they broke your heart, they are still your kids' mother or father. Your kids might wind up being just as disappointed and hurt by your Ex as you have been, but maybe they won't. Either way, your job is to help your kids develop the inner resources they need to be strong, healthy adults, with two human and imperfect parents.

An extremely difficult aspect of having children with an Ex is that as soon as your relationship is over you may have very little control over what happens with your kids while they are in your Ex's care. They might take your two-year-old bowling until ten pm, let them drink Diet Coke®, or introduce them to a variety of new girlfriends or boyfriends. Your kids might come home to you exhausted, confused, or hopped-up on sugar and caffeine. It might feel like you have to start over again in your efforts to establish good sleeping routines, discipline, or potty training every time your kid goes to your Ex's house. This is made all the more frustrating by the fact that you can't do anything about it. Learning to tolerate your frustration and anxiety while maintaining an emotionally safe and respectful environment for your children is the work of successful co-parenting with someone you may loathe.

While acceptance is a big piece of successful co-parenting, if you genuinely fear for your children's safety when they are with your Ex, you must protect them. If your Ex has a substance abuse problem that impairs their ability to safely care for your children, is verbally, emotionally, physically, or sexually abusive toward them, puts them in patently dangerous situations, or neglects their basic needs, you need to take legal action to protect your children. I have included resources for you to get help with this in Resources.

One of the biggest challenges for Exaholics who share children with their Exes is the need for ongoing communication with their Ex in order to co-parent and coordinate visitation. Under these circumstances you cannot make the clean break of no contact. Every time you speak with your Ex you will likely experience anxiety, pain, or anger, as well as an uptick in your obsessions and cravings. It may also be tempting to contact your Ex to "talk about the kids" as an excuse to simply connect with them when you are feeling especially low.

In these cases, choosing to not initiate unnecessary contact can be very helpful to you. While you will still have contact with your Ex, you can decide to be in control of yourself. What is necessary contact? Any communication required to make plans for visitation, coordinate the care of your children, or report important information. It's best if you communicate by email, if possible. This way you are buffered from the immediate interactions of phone and text and less likely to have your communication careen into the realm of the personal or painful. (We will talk more about not initiating contact when we discuss the Twelve Steps of Healing on page 209.)

ADVANTAGES

Having to co-parent children with an Ex is very challenging. Unlike Exaholics who do not share children with their partners, you do not get a clean slate. You can't start over in the same way that people without kids can and you don't have the freedom to make sweeping changes to your life. Nor do you have the luxury of collapsing into protracted, self-focused desolation. However, these circumstances are also the advantages of this situation: you have something to live for. You have a reason to be healthy and strong. Your path to recovery may be harder than that of other Exaholics, but your motivation to be healthy and well will be watching you eat your breakfast, holding your hand anxiously, and singing songs to you in the car. Being needed so desperately can give you the strength to carry both yourself and your children to a better place.

Furthermore, there is often a strong bond that occurs between single parents. Particularly if you have children of the same age, other single parents can come to feel like a chosen family of mutual support.

And there are lots of single parents in the same boat as you, many of whom are also eager to connect. Having a village of people around you who can commiserate, hang out on evenings and weekends, and offer practical support in terms of childcare and household tasks can reduce some of the enormous pressure that single parents feel to do it all.

INFIDELITY

Having a relationship end because your partner became involved with someone else unleashes a special kind of destruction. You may realize that you have been living a lie. The foundation of your life was built upon a false belief: that you were safe and loved. To find out that was not true can shake you to the core. You question your judgment, your ability to discern reality from fiction, and generally feel like an enraged, humiliated fool. If it stopped there, it would be bad enough. But for most people that is just the beginning.

Losing a relationship that you wanted to keep always triggers an avalanche of self-doubt. But when your Ex has rejected you through their actions, it's like they are saying, "Yeah I actually did like this person better," and the hurt and rejection you feel as a result are magnified a thousand fold. It is beyond devastating. It does more than leave a life in shambles. Infidelity slices into vulnerable, deep places, like your basic sense of value, self-respect, and ability to trust other people. These wounds can take a long time to repair, even after the relationship itself has ended.

Infidelity is incredibly damaging for a number of reasons.

First of all, it absolutely mangles your self-esteem. If your Ex willfully chose someone else over you, it seems like the only rational conclusion you can possibly come to is that the person they prefer is somehow better than you. That compared to them, you were not good enough to be worth loving and respecting. While any unwanted breakup leaves you sobbing, "Why?!?" a relationship lost to infidelity seems to coldly slide the answers across the table: the other person was sexier, younger, more attractive, more fun, more spiritual, more emotionally mature, smarter, or more successful than you. In the midst of the ordinary trauma of loss, you pick yourself apart until it feels like there is nothing left but ugly holes where you used to be.

But it gets worse. As we discussed in the last chapter, the sick reality of attachment loss is that when you are losing someone—even if that someone is a deeply flawed person of questionable character—you will go crazy with panic and ferocious desire to get them back. As angry as you are, as hurt as you are, as disgusted as you are, when you are losing your partner to someone else, you may have never wanted them more. The anxiety and uncertainty of this situation wrings out all the dopamine it seems like you have in your brain. You anxiously obsess and crave, idealizing your lost lover, and experiencing both enormous agitation and, frequently, lust. This reaction sends you into the most vividly juicy state of love—even if your relationship had previously been encased in the emotional cement of a desiccated long-term partnership. People in this position often see their partner through new eyes: desirable to someone else and infused once again in the glow of romantic attraction.

For this reason, obsession, craving, and addiction can be the fiercest in people who are losing their cherished person to another. They stalk information both online and in person. They drive past houses, restaurants, and offices, checking. They crack into bank accounts and email accounts, ferreting out information. Night and day, the whereabouts and emotional state of their straying partner is on their mind. And their need for information about their rival is just as intense as that for their partner. They want to know exactly what they look like, the clothes they wear, their mannerisms, and their personal habits. All the information is regurgitated and anxiously ruminated, endlessly, like a cow chewing its cud. Sleepless nights and foggy days, interspersed with searing lightning bolts of painful new information is the norm. People hate themselves for what they are doing, but cannot stop. Their mangled self-esteem is then topped with the cherry of shame.

Everyone says they would never do this. "If he cheated on me, I'd never take him back. We'd be done." Those self-righteous words are easy to say when you're not actually going through the experience. But the truth is, like most things, the actual experience is different than we think it will be. Your rational neocortex cannot factor in advance how it will feel to have the limbic storm of desire, obsession, and longing that will rage inside you when infidelity occurs. It sincerely believes that such a transgression would immediately cut you free from a relationship. This does happen, sometimes. But the majority of people whose partners cheat on them actually have a great deal of difficulty letting go. (Even in cases where the offending partner displays a lack of empathy and capacity for deceit that is downright sociopathic.) This bulldog nature of your limbic brain is the reason why such a significant percentage of relationships can recover from infidelity and even use it as a launching pad for enormous and necessary growth. However, in other cases, infidelity simply signifies that the person you are with is not able or willing to have a high-quality relationship with you. It can take a long time to figure that out. But eventually, if that is true, you will.

In cases where repair is not possible, after the limbic storm subsides and people are healed of their temporary insanity, they are often left feeling that the ultimate betrayal of infidelity was that they betrayed themselves. They didn't reject the offending partner immediately. They didn't act to save themselves from a crappy situation. They accepted the most profoundly humiliating mistreatment and then begged for more. They are left feeling that they've gone against their basic moral principles and were willing to accept anything if only their lying, cheating lover would take them back. It makes them feel pathetic, embarrassed, and ashamed.

Most major traumas that people experience, like a terrible car accident, a rape, or a life-threatening disease split your life into two: there is the time before and the time after. Finding out that your partner has been cheating on you (and then experiencing the shock of what happens to you in the aftermath) is an emotional trauma that takes an ax to your sense of personal safety. If you believed that you were loved, that there was commitment, and that you could depend on your beloved, only to find out that was not the reality of your life at all, your basic trust in other people is hacked apart. Because having a secure connection with an irreplaceable other is such a basic human need, to be rejected and abandoned for another person is a primary trauma. Worse, experiencing the madness that descends upon you in the aftermath can shake your trust in yourself, your ability to make good decisions, and to keep yourself safe.

Like other trauma survivors who have a grim wisdom about them that comes from having firsthand knowledge of the horror that is possible in the world ("You don't know what I've seen"), people who have been blindsided by an affair often struggle to trust again. They know what people are capable of.

In these cases, healing often requires a significant amount of work around forgiveness. Forgiveness for their Ex but, primarily, forgiveness for themselves. They may also have difficulty trusting people again in the future. Recovering from the emotional trauma of infidelity is one circumstance where it may be important to enlist the support of a competent therapist.

ADVANTAGES

It is difficult to consider, let alone appreciate the positive aspects of infidelity. However, individuals who go through the very hard work of recovering from a relationship that ended with infidelity often have enormous opportunities for personal growth. As they unpack their experiences, they often uncover truths about themselves that may have otherwise remained buried. Old self-limiting patterns, beliefs, or traumas may be identified. As difficult as the work is, it does provide you with an opportunity to learn about yourself, heal, and grow—an opportunity you may not have had otherwise. As you recover, you may repair wounds that you did not even know you carried until you were cut open by the trauma of infidelity. When you heal, you may be stronger and healthier than you were before.

BEING "THE OTHER"

Some of the most wrecked Exaholics I have ever met are the ones who have gone through the emotional meat-grinder of an affair with someone who is not available. They get spit out the other side, in pieces. Pieces that are often very difficult to stitch back together.

Affairs are the most addictive and emotionally destructive of all relationships. The highs are so much higher and the lows are so much lower that the biochemical storms unleashed by an affair will hook you through the gills.

Very few people set out to have an affair. (Though that does happen.) A recent poll of Americans conducted in 2013 found that all but 8 percent of the population believes that it is always wrong to cheat on a spouse. If you ask almost anyone if they would ever consider having a relationship with a person who is married, they would immediately say "No. I could never do that." Another self-righteous, definitive, and reasonable statement of truth that their neocortex wholeheartedly believes: having relationships with married people is illogical and immoral.

But the data tells us otherwise. While 92 percent of people believe that affairs are wrong, the research shows that around 20 percent of people—at some point in their lives—will in fact cheat on their partners.

What's happening, as usual, is that the limbic brain didn't get the memo. The limbic brain functions outside of morality and good intentions of the neocortex. The limbic brain notices sexy people and becomes romantically infatuated with them, whether or not the neocortex has decided to be married. This is a process that can happen without our intention or our consent. Being in close contact with a person (for example, someone you work with) who sends sizzles through your limbic system is bad news. Nearly all affairs begin with co-workers or friends that set off fun sparkles of dopamine in your reward center. Affairs often start gradually, before people realize what is happening to them. As infatuation begins to glow, the neocortex trots along behind, sputtering in denial. (*We're just friends. I'm not doing anything wrong. It's not like I'm cheating.*) Until the pleasure and excitement of being in this potentially unattainable person's presence grows too strong to fight. Then you're hooked.

As you know, people who are hooked can do bad things.

Most people in affairs understand that they are living in a way that goes against their core values, but they are under the influence of love. Just like any addiction that starts out slowly, a person in an affair starts crossing formerly unthinkable lines over a period of weeks and months. Their boundaries and rules are eventually all broken over time. Like an addict who progresses from trying it at a party to chasing it off the foil in their car on their lunch hour to nodding off on a dirty mattress in a house full of strangers with a needle in their arm—every step of the way they know, rationally, that what they are doing is a really bad idea for many reasons. But at some point they just don't care anymore. Something much bigger than their rational mind has possessed them.

So it is with people addicted to unhealthy relationships. The unquenchable craving for connection, the thrill of anticipation, and the pleasure of union overwhelms the best of intentions. As they descend into their addiction they find themselves doing shocking and once-unimaginable things. This is true for single people who fully understand that their fascination with a married person is not going to end well and married people who are profoundly attached to their spouses yet get swept away by the flash flood of romantic love for someone else.

While everyone in (and often in the proximity of) an illicit affair is damaged by it, this is especially true for the person who is actually available—The Other. The laws of love are simple and as constant as those governing physical reality. A dropped egg falls to the floor. The person who cares more about a romantic relationship always has less power. By definition, if a single person who is genuinely interested in and available for a real relationship falls in love with a married person, they are going to be at their mercy. They are the ones who go splat in the end.

To the person, everyone I've worked with who has been The Other in an illicit affair has spent the majority of the relationship in a state of fear, anxiety, resentment, and pain, punctuated by brief hours or days of relief in the moments when they have their occupied lover's attention. Most of the time, their lover isn't available when they want or need them. They don't get enough time with them. Their lover has to hide them. The Other is second. The simple knowledge that their cherished, beloved person is living with another, sleeping in the same bed (and possibly having sex with someone else), choosing to spend holidays with their real family, is absolutely devastating. The only times that The Other feels good are when they are with their beloved (but even then they are likely to feel resentment and an overwhelming need for reassurance).

Because The Other in an affair lives in such a state of churning anxiety, uncertainty, and pain, they are exposed to floods of restless, emotional dopamine and entirely cut off from serotonin. The result is that they are obsessive, agitated, hypervigilant, and often extremely emotional. The intense pleasure and reward they feel when with their lover are the only things that stop the pain. This neurological reality makes illicit affairs the most addictive kind of relationship, particularly for The Other.

The Other will often begin organizing their lives around their lover's availability. They accept that fact that The Occupied determines when they will talk, by what means they will connect, and when, if, and for how long they will be together. The unavailable lover dictates all the terms, and The Other feels that they have no choice but to go along. Many, if not most, Others in an affair feel that they debase themselves in order to maintain the relationship. They break their own boundaries. They tolerate behavior and mistreatment that they would never put up with before. They accept scraps and crumbs.

When you are with someone who has to hide and lie about your existence, it does something to you. We all want—need—to love and be loved. When you are with someone who can only love you sometimes, and on their terms only, you are not in an emotionally safe place. You are not getting your needs met. To be powerless in a relationship—entirely at the mercy of someone else—is a patently harrowing and destructive experience. Another person decides how much you are worth, how important you are, and whether or not you should be rewarded by their presence.

When these relationships ultimately end, as the vast majority do, The Other must deal with both a raging addiction to an unhealthy relationship plus an enormous amount of shame and self-loathing for allowing themselves to have been so profoundly mistreated. Because their biochemical experience of love has been so much more intense, due to the intense highs and lows they've been experiencing for months or years even prior to the breakup, they will have a much more intense pain response when the relationship is over.

Furthermore because of the guilt and shame they may feel about the affair, they tend to feel even more isolated than other people after a loss. Many people who are devastated after an affair ends feel entirely alone. Sometimes even their best friends don't know about what they've done. They hide their stories and suffer alone because they feel ashamed and think that they will be judged. Worse yet, someone might say, "Serves you right." Sadly, the ones who do confess their transgressions are often judged or rejected by their friends and family.

The Other in a failed affair will often feel that they have lost themselves entirely over the course of the relationship. "At the end, I didn't even know who I was anymore," is a common sentiment. Their actions, feelings, and experiences were so different from the person they thought they were that they feel dissociated from their core self. Others in affairs that have dragged on for a year or more may have been so focused on pleasing their unavailable lover, they may have lost the things they once loved and defined them. Friendships, hobbies, and their sense of satisfaction and contentment with life may have been obliterated in the inferno of the affair.

One of the most insidious aspects of an affair, in my opinion, is because the simple experience of being alive is so heightened in the context of an affair, some people feel that their everyday life—or safe and emotionally healthy relationships—are boring in comparison. After living on the edge, and feeling the exciting highs and lows of an affair, many people feel that life without that intensity is "meh." They therefore associate meaning and specialness with the time they spent with their lover and this only makes their recovery process harder. They are so dissatisfied with regular life that they grieve their lover even more deeply, not realizing that the context of the affair shook their neurotransmitters to a froth, like an energetic bartender shaking a margarita. They were under the influence of love and in the midst of a context that led them to have such intense feelings—not necessarily the person themselves.

In the aftermath of an affair the person who was partnered—The Occupied—is often left with a profound sense of shame and guilt. Even if they ultimately chose to go back to their primary partnership, they may struggle with feelings of obsession and craving for the person they had the affair with. They often wonder why the passion and the love was so intense with their lover and why the feelings they have with their spouse are so humdrum in comparison. They think that, because they felt such intense feelings for their lover, that love must have been more "real." It is difficult to understand the progression through lust, love, and attachment until you have lived it.

For example, I have worked with many people whose relationships began as affairs. The ones who made the choice to leave their spouses and families and formalize the relationship with their new lover inevitably experience the cooling of passion. This is simply what happens as relationships evolve. Sometimes they find that, once the party of romance is over—the fizzy champagne has been drunk, the decadent cake has been eaten, and the house is a wreck in the cold light of day—they have still made the right choice. They are now with someone who is a better match for them in terms of values, personality, and long-term compatibility.

Other times people realize, belatedly, that the lover they have chosen in the searing heat of passion is profoundly disappointing in the context of normal life. I can't tell you how many people I've talked to who grieve and mourn the safety, simplicity, and security of family that they lost, and bitterly regret destroying it for an affair that was ultimately hollow and hedonistic. Being in an affair is like living in an artificially constructed reality, like a luxurious nightclub in Vegas. It's only after you eventually walk out at dawn with your ears ringing and your wallet empty that you're finally able to see that the formerly effervescent temptress was just a morally questionable loudmouth, and the once irresistible bad boy was actually just selfish, immature, and irresponsible. The person carried away by their passions often comes to their senses in a deeply unsatisfying relationship with a person they don't like and don't trust. They realize too late that they traded a boring relationship for a bad one. And they can't go back home.

No matter what the circumstances, when relationships tainted by affairs end—whether you are The Other or The Occupied, the normal Exaholic experience is compounded by guilt, shame, regret, and very often self-hatred. If this is true for you, in addition to working through the steps of liberating yourself from your addiction you may also consider high-quality professional help if you find yourself struggling to forgive yourself and put the pieces of your life back together.

ADVANTAGES

Because these relationships are usually so terrible and toxic on every level, you have a major growth opportunity when they are over to do major work. Once the worst of the grief has passed you can do some serious exploration, and begin to ask yourself hard questions, like "How did that happen?" "Why was I so vulnerable to that kind of relationship?" And, "What do I do to keep myself from ever getting into that kind of situation again in the future?" The fact that you were in this situation is evidence that you have work to do, and I'd like to suggest that some good therapy is probably in order. Find someone qualified and get the support and guidance you need to do the work of healing.

LATER LIFE

A surprising number of couples successfully weather decades together, only to finally come apart later in life. Sometimes referred to as Gray Divorce, such losses can be profoundly hurtful and traumatic.

The breakup of very long-term relationships can be fueled by recognition in one partner that the time they have left to enjoy life is shorter than it was. Sometimes after children leave the partnership, couples realize their once-solid attachment has been neglected to the point of atrophy, and one person becomes unwilling to continue to live in the emotional or sexual desert the marriage has become.

Furthermore, as people age, their hormones change. On the other side of menopause, women often get less willing to put up with emotional neglect and refuse to continue to coddle and nurture selfish partners for the rest of their lives. As testosterone declines, men often soften and become more aware of their longing for meaning and emotional connection. After decades of knowing each other, partners often make assumptions about what is possible for the relationship and what is not—and sometimes, they are right.

The problem is that, generally speaking, later-life breakups occur unilaterally. One person decides to end the relationship over the objections of the other. Although the relationship may have been less than ideal for both, the other person has felt comfortable with it. The one-sided breaking of a "good enough" relationship often sends the person being left into despair.

The sadness, grief, craving, and loss of the one left are often magnified because of the longevity, importance, and deep attachment of the relationship. To have been with someone for twenty, thirty, forty, or even fifty years, only to be cast out by that person truly feels like being thrown out of the only home you've ever known.

People in this situation often feel like they are losing their whole lives. They may have to sell their longtime home, they might move out of a long-term community, and the routines and rituals that held their life together for decades are abruptly ended. They also have to cope with the anger and pain that comes from abandonment. They may have bitter regrets about choices or sacrifices they made for the marriage, only to be left alone in later life. Sometimes older people regret the choices they made while in the relationship, wishing they had listened to the complaints of their partner while they still had the chance to fix it.

Older people can feel very angry that after all this time, their spouse ended the relationship without giving them the opportunity to work on the problems together. Sadly, many of the spouses that do finally leave feel that they are only doing so after many, many years of frustrated efforts to change the relationship. At the end, they stop believing that change is possible. It is hard to convince them that their partner is capable of changing when they have years of evidence to prove otherwise. Then they give up. They often sail, relieved, into a satisfying new chapter of their lives, leaving their jilted partner behind to simmer in a bitter, bitter stew.

ADVANTAGES

Although losing a relationship later in life is often highly traumatic, there are a surprising number of advantages to it. Age often brings wisdom, perspective, and emotional resilience that younger people have not yet earned. Older people also frequently have long-established, supportive relationships. Additionally, they often have more single and possibly retired friends who are available to spend time with them. Certainly more so than a newly divorced middle-aged person whose contemporaries are in the thick of work and family life, and unavailable for a simple wine night unless it's scheduled three months in advance.

Older people often have a solid sense of themselves: they know what they like and what they don't. They know who they are. For many, being released from a long-term relationship gives them the opportunity to follow dreams that they never would have otherwise. Ending a relationship later in life, though painful, is often the catalyst for a vibrant new chapter.

Furthermore, couples that have been together for decades have often transcended romantic love and entered the soft strength of attachment a long time ago. They have been friends and companions for much longer than they were lovers. For this reason, in my experience, older people are much more likely to develop genuine friendships with their Exes after the shock and pain of the split itself has faded.

Many times, even though their couple-status has ended, older adults maintain their attachment to each other. They may share adult children and grandkids in common and still come together as a family for important events and holidays. They are more likely to accept and even embrace their Ex's new partner. They may have unconditional love for each other and genuinely want the best for each other—even if that means not being together anymore, which takes a great deal of maturity to do. In this way, older people can do a beautiful job of holding on to the good parts of their relationship, while also releasing each other into the freedom of independent being.

Many Loves, Many Losses

There are many more flavors of relationships that deserve a whole book's worth of discussion, much less a few pages of exploration about their endings. Same-sex relationships, second marriages with blended long-distance relationships, situations where one partner comes out, and never-married people in later life all have unique experiences when their relationships end.

It's also true that many relationships have factors common to several situations and developmental stages. Being a twenty-two-year-old woman with two young children left by her cheating, alcoholic husband is complex. The greater the complexity, the greater your need for support and guidance in healing.

Because there are many different kinds of relationships, and infinite variations in how they end, all relationship losses have unique challenges and opportunities. People have different personalities, hopes, dreams, life experiences, and core beliefs—all of which make a difference in the way individuals "do" relationships. But because we are all humans, with the same set of needs and standard-issue bonding equipment in our brains and bodies, we all go through a similar process as we recover.

PART 4
THE PATH TO RECOVERY

9

THE STAGES OF HEALING

"Denial helps us to pace our feelings of grief."

—Elisabeth Kübler-Ross

"IS THIS *EVER* GOING TO GET BETTER?"

"How long am I going to feel this way?"

"How do I get over this and move on?"

These are questions I hear from heartbroken clients all the time. They are suffering from the inside out, and can't escape the pain. It is especially hard for people who have been hurting for months or years to feel hopeful that their sadness, anxiety, and longing will ever come to an end.

I'm guessing you have probably asked yourself these questions too. As you survey the carnage of your smashed-up life from the depths of your despair, it can seem like recovery is impossible. In every direction is loss and pain. You can't go to the places you once enjoyed without being flooded by sadness, anxiety, and anger. Your relationships have changed—it can be hard to feel comfortable even with old friends. Your head is full of memories, replaying past and future conversations with the only person you can think about.

One of the hardest aspects of this is that it feels like you have lost yourself. Somewhere along this journey you went from being a confident, competent, and generally happy person to an anxious, consumed wreck who is addicted to a ghost, a person who no longer exists, at least not in the way you knew them before. The experience is so traumatizing and damaging on so many levels that it can feel like there is nothing left inside of you to help you find your way back.

This is a terrible place to be in. But I want you to know that this can and will get better and that there are specific things you can do to help yourself move through the healing process. Because relationships are by nature addictive processes, a twelve-step model of recovery can be very useful. However, for most Exaholics (like for most other addicts) the hardest part of the healing process is just getting to the first step: admitting that your attachment to your Ex is unhealthy and needs to end.

In order to get to the first step of true recovery you must slog your way through protest and despair, as well as the stages of change that all addicts move through before they are finally able to overcome denial and accept the fact that their relationship to their substance of choice must end.

Here's the trajectory in front of you:

- Precontemplation (not thinking about changing)
- Contemplation (thinking about changing)
- Determination (wanting to change)
- Action (changing)
- Maintenance (maintaining the change)

Like all addicts, an Exaholic goes through these stages of change before they are finally ready to admit that their continued attachment to their Ex is a problem and needs to end. Only then can they begin working the steps of recovery. Until then, many Exaholics are caught in a purgatory of longing as they suffer in the no-man's land between connection and emotional liberation: protest and despair.

As you probably know too well, it can take a very long time to come to grips with the reality that a relationship is over. Remember, because of the way your brain works, and how you were built to bond, even if you *know* it's over, you still don't *feel* like it's over. Your limbic brain is a wild creature and not subordinate to the will of your neocortex. It maintains your attachment to your Ex even when you don't want it to. But even worse, because it's hunger for reunion is so strong, it can trick your neocortex into believing that you should get back together with your Ex. The obsessive craving of protest throbs inside you, whether you want it to or not. The dark longing of despair consumes you, as you wait in hopeless hell for your lover to return.

Here's the problem: All addictions are sneaky, and relationship addiction is no different. Having a limbic need that is hungry for gratification can trick us into believing all kinds of things. For all their primitive mammalian brawn, our limbic brains are really quite savvy at getting our neocortexes to do whatever they want them to. When your limbic brain has an urge—an itch that wants to be scratched—primal feelings bubble up though the moist layers of your brain and finally emerge in your neocortex as delusional thinking. Your neocortex will obligingly twist itself into a pretzel to find evidence for whatever your limbic brain wants it to believe. Then your neocortex directs your behavior accordingly, self-righteously certain in it's justification.

In the terminology of the twelve-step movement, this phenomenon is referred to as denial.

- For example, the neocortex of an alcoholic can come up with eighty-five reasons why it is really in control of their drinking.
- "I only had three beers yesterday, and besides, it's Thursday night! Everybody drinks on Thursday night!"
- The neocortex of a smoker assures them that this time they really can just have one cigarette, and then stop again tomorrow.
- "I'll just buy the pack, smoke one, and throw the rest away. It's fine. It's totally normal to have an occasional cigarette."
- The neocortex of a panicky gambler helpfully calculates possible winnings and comes to the conclusion this is really an investment.

- "I'll pay off all the debt and have money left over to buy some real estate! Just like Dave Ramsey!"
- And, of course, your neocortex will always find lots of evidence to support the big lie of Exaholism: "We can get back together."

An Exaholic in the throes of their addiction is certain that reunion is possible. What happened was a terrible misunderstanding—just a nasty fight. They will come around and realize how deep their love is. They will be sorry and they will change this time. You will go on to have a better relationship than ever before and create an amazing love story of triumph over adversity. And in the meantime, you will be friends. Very, very close friends. That should tell each other everything and have sex together.

Until the reunion you hope for happens, your protest response will be making you think about your Ex constantly: on pins and needles, scanning and seeking them everywhere, eager for them to throw you a sign that they still care. If that doesn't happen, you'll descend into despair, miserably beating yourself up for all the mistakes you made over the course of the relationship, and for being so generally unlovable as to be rejected by the only person in the world who matters.

Precontemplation

Being at the mercy of protest and despair is the stage of change that is called "Precontemplation." In other words, you are not yet aware that you have a problem. You have bought into whatever your limbic brain wants you to believe, which is usually some variant of "we should be together."

The Precontemplation stage of change is ruled by King Denial. The Exaholic has not come to terms with the relationship being over and is emotionally flopping around like a fish out of water, desperate to return to their cool, green, watery home, where they were loved and all was well. Like a heroin addict who is single-minded on their mission for another fix, an Exaholic's heart and mind is completely focused on maintaining the attachment to their lover. If they can't literally reconnect with them, they will stay connected to them in their thoughts, fantasizing and rehashing, following their every move on Facebook and Twitter, and by attempting to gather information about them any way they can. In this way, they maintain their addiction.

Here's the really important thing to know about this stage: Even if you are not technically "with" your Ex, *you are still using*.

Just like romantic obsession and fantasy fuse you emotionally to your lover in the early days of enchantment, obsession and fantasy sustain your relationship even if it's technically ended. You are still having a relationship with your internalized lover in your head. This is because your limbic brain is not able to differentiate between things that are actually happening and things that you are thinking about. (When you think about something angering, you feel angry. When you think about something exciting, you feel excited. Et cetera.)

When you are thinking about or fantasizing about your Ex lover, you are still feeling all the same feelings: love, excitement, despair, longing, hurt, anger, and rejection. The thoughts themselves do nearly as good a job of wringing the dopamine out of your limbic brain as actual, in-person interactions with your Ex. And staying in contact with them through social media throughout the day is basically keeping an IV drip of dopamine in your arm. Obsessions and information feed the monkey just enough to keep it hooked but not enough to satisfy it, as you know oh-so-well.

Most Exaholics need to flounder around, chasing will-o'-the-wisps in the bog of hope for a long time before they are ready to let go and admit that their continued attachment to their Ex is problematic. They can't let go at first, because their attachment to their Ex is too strong (because it is working exactly the way nature intended, as we discussed in previous chapters). They are stuck in protest and are simply not ready to let go of their hope for reunion. They have a lot of emotional work to do before they can accept the fact that their continued attachment to their Ex is unhealthy for them.

This is purgatory—a mid-range ring of hell where you are not together, but not apart emotionally. You are still emotionally connected to your Ex, whether or not you are actually speaking. Perhaps you are still talking, or at least trying to. You might even hang out once in a while or even sleep together but then don't talk for days or weeks. You still have some of their personal items, which feels like an insurance policy guaranteeing future contact. You are in limbo, craving their presence and hoping for reunion. You can't bear to delete their number or block them. Even though you are not together, it still feels like they are yours.

Being in this space is very, very painful. You are deeply attached to someone that you are not able to connect with. Or, if you connect with them, you get hurt.

This is made worse by the fact that many relationships don't go out with a firm bang, but rather with a vague shrug. An, "I'm just not in a great place right now, but I really care about you," that leaves everyone confused about what is actually happening or not happening. (Note from a therapist who hears both sides: That isn't true. One person is usually actually pretty damn sure it's over, but the other remains bound by the hope of gentle let-downs that sound like future possibilities.)

So you twist in the wind, dangling on the end of a string that is still attached to your idealized Ex—high, high above you on the power differential. If they throw you a crumb of acknowledgment or affection you could cry with relief. If they ignore your pain, you burn in shame, self-loathing, and impotent anger. You pounce on any opportunity to win their affection, eager as an enthusiastic cocker spaniel hoping to win a cheese cube (oftentimes at great cost to your already destroyed self-esteem). It feels like the whims of your Ex have total control over your emotions, self-control, and future.

At some point (hopefully), after weeks or months of this torture, a small remnant of your healthy core self pipes up to say, "What the hell are you doing?"

At that point you move into Contemplation.

CONTEMPLATION

The Contemplation stage, or "thinking about changing" stage is defined by ambivalence. An alcoholic may understand (and hate) the fact that booze is destroying their family, but they are not ready to let go of the slurry abandon it brings. You are aware that you are not being treated well and that your life is suffering as a result of your attachment to your Ex, but you still feel an enormously strong connection to them. You might be very angry and hurt, but you still love them. It's a confusing, "I love you but I hate you" dance that pushes and pulls you one way and the other. You hate the way you feel, you hate what this is doing to you, you hate how much power your Ex continues to have over your life, and you might even hate them, *but* you still care about them. More important, you want them to love you, to like you, and to affirm you. You want them to want you. Your self-worth is still caught up in their opinion of you. It feels like the only way to get your self-esteem back is for them to desire you again.

In this phase, many Exaholics need to test the relationship before they can finally come to terms with the finality of the situation. They need to prove to themselves that it is really over before they can think about saying goodbye. So they try to contact their Ex and talk, "One last time." They go to therapy to show their Ex how much they've changed. They attempt to seduce or re-engage their Ex. They poke around to see if their Ex has changed and can finally be the person they need them to be. They may suggest dating again, "Just to see how it goes." It can take weeks to months of continued rejection, disappointments, and bad experiences for the scale of ambivalence to finally, definitively tip in the direction of letting go.

Every addict in recovery has a bottoming-out story to share: A Burroughs-esque *Naked Lunch* moment where they finally saw in stark clarity exactly what was impaled on the end of the fork they were about to put in their mouth. They were finally too impaired to do their job. They watched their spouse drive away with the kids. They woke up on a stranger's lawn. Or came-to in the midst of something much worse. Whatever the circumstances, they had an undeniable experience that shook them to the core and opened up their eyes to the fact that, "This has got to stop."

For Exaholics, the story of the bottom can sometimes be just as dramatic as those of ravaged addicts. When an Ex gets remarried, gets arrested, or does something so egregiously evil that your continued attachment to them is blatantly toxic, you are bounced off the cold stone of the bottom, whether you want to be or not.

Other times, the bottom for Exaholics can be more subtle and ambiguous, and builds over time. Loving someone is not objectively destructive the way that doing cocaine is. It is much easier to linger in denial, hope, and ambivalence when the problem is loving someone too much. The problem of a continued attachment to a person can be framed as wholesome, positive, and societally sanctioned by your ever-rationalizing neocortex. As a result, even when they experience immense pain, an Exaholic can remain trapped in ambivalence for a long time. However, there still comes a time when an Exaholic feels so low about themselves, or has been mistreated so badly, that they do hit their bottom and can no longer pretend that their attachment to their Ex is anything but hurtful and unhealthy for them.

At this point, your neocortex begins to gain a toehold. Your rational self starts actively wrestling with your limbic brain for control of your mind and soul. Your thinking mind becomes increasingly clear about the fact that this relationship should be over and that the person you are stuck on is simply not able or willing to love you in return. You begin to understand that your emotional dependence on this person is ruining you. That maybe, just maybe, you really want the relationship to be over too.

In other words, your neocortex finally begins to view the Ex cravings of your bulldog limbic brain as being a major problem. And that, believe it or not, is a good thing. Because once you begin to feel tired of your continued attachment you start to develop the motivation to change it. The more intense this frustration is the better. When you start to feel trapped by your unreturned love and sick of your slavish devotion to an unworthy person, you cultivate a genuine desire to break free of your unhealthy attachment and are ready to enter the Determination phase of change.

DETERMINATION
In the Determination phase of change, Exaholics are feeling motivated to change, and begin to plan how they will finally break free. Often, in this stage of change, people will begin looking for help, tools, or new ideas that will support their freedom. For an Exaholic, Determination comes from an awareness that they really need to let

Exaholics Breaking Your Addiction to an Ex Love

go of their attachment to their Ex, even if they don't feel like they can do it yet. They begin looking for resources, reading books (hi), and soliciting advice.

They can't let go emotionally yet, but they want to. The deck of evidence is stacked against the Ex, and their idealization of the relationship is being replaced by the reality of their disappointment. They are thinking about jumping into the twelve-step process, where they admit that they are an Exaholic and that their continued attachment to their Ex is unhealthy and problematic. But they're not completely, 100 percent sold. But they want to be. So they look for things that can help them firm up their resolve.

One of the most important and helpful things that an Exaholic can do at this point is connect with other people who are going through the same experience. People grappling with the confusing, consuming experience of protest and despair often feel like they are the only ones who are having the experience. As we've discussed, the true nature of love and the aftermath of love lost is simply not talked about or understood in our culture.

So when an Exaholic comes into contact with other people who feel the same things that they do, or even better—have begun to work the steps and heal—a major shift can happen: they can start to feel hope that they can change too. When they hear the stories of others, and how they finally hit their bottom and realized it was time to let go, they think about their own change process and whether they are ready too. When one Exaholic is able to bear witness to another about how their own healing process unfolded, it creates a lighthouse of hope—a path in the darkness that shows the way out. If you're in the Contemplation or Determination phase of change, I'd recommend looking around for stories of people who have been through what you're going through. Snoop around some online forums, or solicit authentic tales of heartbreak from trusted family and friends.

Your stages of change have already led you to this moment. The fact that you are reading this book is evidence that you are in either the contemplation or determination phase of recovery. To continue moving forward in your change process—meaning emotionally accepting that the relationship is over and beginning to heal—you need support.

Finding people who can validate your pain and offer both comfort and hope is a foundational part of the healing process. When I was going through my own small hell of rejection and despair, I was largely surrounded by teenagers so new to the world that most of them had yet to have the experience of being torn apart by rejection. They were confident in their judgment of me as being uniquely pathetic. The few adults I reached out to were so far beyond their own heartbreak they could only share with me what they knew to be true, which was, "It will pass." But I remember the comfort I experienced when I confided in one teacher, Mrs. Gray. She looked at me and really saw my pain. She shared with me that she was more traumatized by her high school breakup than she had been by her divorce. In that moment, my pain felt legitimized. It didn't make the pain go away, but it did make me feel less ashamed and broken. Knowing that someone else had also suffered horribly made me feel less alone. Knowing that someone had genuine compassion for me gave me the tiniest crumb of self-worth back.

You need people. Humans are not meant to go it alone. This is as true in your recovery as it's been since the moment you took your first breath on this earth. You need your tribe right now. Find someone: a buddy, a friend, or a therapist who can validate and support you. When you have supportive people throwing their weight behind you, you can lean harder against your limbic impulses and continue to stockpile reassuring information about what is happening and what the change process looks like. With support, you may even experiment with getting more physical distance from your Ex. Once your support system is firmly in place, then you can feel safe enough to take the leap of letting go. Then you can move into the Action phase, and your true healing can begin.

10

HOW TO COPE
WHILE YOU'RE RECOVERING

In case of emergency, break glass.

MY MOTHER'S FAMILY IS FROM A WORKING-CLASS TOWN
ON THE JERSEY SHORE. EVERY SUMMER, WE WOULD CRUISE
UP THE JERSEY TURNPIKE FROM VIRGINIA IN OUR THIRTY-
FOOT POWDER BLUE CHEVY IMPALA STATION WAGON. MY
SISTER AND I RODE OUT THE FOREVER-LONG DRIVE IN THE
FAR BACK ON PINK SATIN SLEEPING BAGS WITH HER MY
LITTLE PONIES, MY SWEET VALLEY HIGH NOVELS, AND
ALL THE SLIM JIMS WE COULD EAT. (IF SUCH OUTRAGEOUS
ACTS OF PHYSICAL AND NUTRITIONAL CHILD ENDANGERMENT
WERE TO OCCUR IN THIS DAY AND AGE—PARTICULARLY IN
MY NEW HOMETOWN OF DENVER, COLORADO—I AM SURE WE
WOULD BE IMMEDIATELY TAKEN INTO PROTECTIVE CUSTODY.)

After spending the first several hours of our visit being made fun of by our cousins for our Southern accents ("Say 'firefly' again!" "Oh my gawd they sound just like Scarlett O'Hara! Har har!"), eventually they'd get bored of us and we'd all go down to the board-walk. My mom, aunties, and Nanny would quickly succumb to their Irish magical thinking and stand riveted for hours, gambling quarters on the ticking Wheel of Fortune®. My sister and I were left to wander the gift shops, fascinated by the little shell-encrusted boxes, floating shark fetuses, and random, wacky, and entirely useless souvenirs.

One of those always stuck with me. It was a little wood and glass box with a single cigarette and match inside. Printed on the front in red letters it said, "In case of emergency, break glass." I had fun imagining what kind of emergency might cause a frantic adult to go scrabbling for the box and inhale its carcinogenic contents with shaking hands. Burnt dinner? Team lost? Heard a bad joke? There's nothing on TV?

As silly as my imagined catastrophes were, I liked the idea of having an emergency action plan. Something about knowing what to do when the shit actually does hit the fan is still reassuring to me.

Why am I bringing this up? Because you, my friend, need a plan.

You don't need me to tell you this, but I'm going to say it anyway: What you are going through right now is very difficult, emotionally, socially, and even physically. And, unfortunately, moving through the stages of change as you emotionally prepare to let go can take a long time. Before you arrive at the cusp of acceptance and can really begin your healing process, you may need to endure weeks or even months of painful and disappointing experiences. Even worse than the terrible things your Ex may or may not be doing to you during this time are often the inescapable experience of your own mind: the obsession, craving, seeking, and decimation of your self-esteem.

The time is nigh, y'all. This is it. It's time to break the glass and do something to help yourself cope.

While I would never suggest smoking cigarettes as a particularly helpful or productive strategy for dealing with a crisis, the truth is, you do need to do something to help yourself get through this. The bad thing just happened, and it's time to smash the glass and enact your emergency action plan. The time between when your relationship officially ends and you come to acceptance and start healing can be enormously confusing. This chapter is intended to be a crisis manual—a guidebook for how to handle yourself in the first days, weeks, and months after a breakup, before you're ready to cut the cord for good.

General Advice on How to Handle Yourself

Unless you are under the influence of positive feelings, it is always better to act based on your values rather than your emotions. Emotions come and go. Your values are different. They are the lighthouse of your authentic truth. Your values come from the highest and best part of yourself and are at the core of your personality. They don't change. Values may become obscured by emotions, or be forgotten, but they are the unseen architecture of your personality, your choices, and your life.

Right now, and for probably at least the next several weeks or months, you are going to be feeling really bad. Your emotions will rage and make you feel like doing all kinds of things. Some of those things could support good outcomes, but, generally speaking, when any of us act on feelings of fear, hurt, anger, and panic, it generally doesn't go well. The truth is that for the time being, listening to your feelings will likely run you off the road. You might feel like throwing a chair out the window, sideswiping a certain someone's car in a parking lot, quitting your job, or even killing yourself. But acting on any of these things will only unleash more pain and destruction. Following your values will keep you safe.

Acting from your values instead of your feelings will help you create good outcomes even when you are feeling terrible. For this reason it is very important for you to get clear about who you are underneath the pain you are feeling right now and use your commitment to your core values to guide your actions.

Before we go any further, let's check in with those values. What are they? Make a list of the qualities, circumstances, and characteristics that are most important to you. Unconditional love, security, health, compassion, adventure, fun, passion, success, meaningful work, order, reliability, service to others, respect, enthusiasm, friendship, authenticity, family, growth, creativity, peace, emotional safety . . . this is just a short list to get you started thinking about what kinds of things are really and truly important to you. Write down what your most important values are. When you get clear about your values, you can draw upon them to guide your behaviors in the weeks and months to come.

Make the choice right now: accept your feelings. Honor them, process them, soothe them. But only *act* from your values. Besides, it is always your job to make these values manifest in your life anyway— not expect and wish that they be given to you. If you value security, reliability, health, and order, it's on you to demonstrate that through your decisions and behaviors. The way you operate in reality is how you cultivate a values-based life.

In addition to whatever other values you identified as being important to you, I would like to strongly suggest that you choose to incorporate physical health, mental and emotional wellness, and respect for yourself and others as foundational values to focus on in the coming months. You're going to need them to get through this.

Mental and Emotional Self-Care

Now let's talk about how to handle yourself in specific situations. How to take care of yourself, how to manage your thoughts and feelings, how to stay in control of your behaviors, how to stay safe, and how to deal with hard moments, like seeing your Ex.

Processing

If you are like most people, you are feeling absolutely flooded with out-of-control thoughts, feelings, and obsessions in the first days, weeks, and months after a breakup. You are probably feeling some combination of hurt, angry, scared, sad, rejected, abandoned, guilty, lonely, resentful, victimized, relieved, and tormented by longing all at the same time. This is a lot to process and it's important that you have some kind of outlet to work through these feelings.

Consider keeping a journal in which you can give voice to your feelings, joining an in-person or online support group for people dealing with breakups, or enlisting the support of a competent therapist. All of these options give you the opportunity to begin engaging in a psychological process that is akin to dumping out a messy snarl of yarn with clumps of gum and broken bits stuck in the strands. Every time you talk or write through your thoughts and feelings, it's like combing through one small section. Putting nebulous, confusing feelings into language creates order and understanding. Over time, you straighten everything out in your head and heart. As you make sense of what happened, you write a new narrative of yourself and your life. Ultimately, this is the core of how people reclaim themselves and move on. Find a safe environment in which you can do this important work, and use it.

Spirituality

There are several important things to consider about spirituality when you are going through a major crisis.

1. Spirituality can be a source of incredible comfort and guidance for you right now. A meaningful spiritual practice can provide a touchstone of support and reassurance that feels like it comes from the inside out. This is particularly true if you have already established a relationship with a spiritual practice, a church, or a higher power. Spirituality can be one path toward making sense of your experience and finding hope for the future. Spending time in meaningful spiritual activities may be more important for you than ever. Consider making it a priority.

2. You may also feel angry with God, the Universe, or whatever deity you usually pray to. Your faith may have been shaken. Being angry and feeling abandoned is a completely normal and expected part of the healing process. Also consider that you may be more needy and impressionable than usual and seeking answers to unanswerable questions. Beware of getting involved with any group, investing in any product, or embracing any practice that promises an effortless cure or quick transformation. And whatever you do, don't join a cult.

3. If you're an atheist, you can find cold comfort in having one more piece of evidence for why there is no God.

Mourning

Back in the old days, when people experienced a death, they went into a period of mourning. They dressed in black or wore black armbands to both convey respect for the deceased but also to signal to other people that they were not well emotionally. This lost custom served an important psychosocial purpose for grieving people, helping to rally the support and empathy of their communities. Emotionally fragile people were given a pass on social activities, responsibilities, and big decisions. They didn't get invited to parties, expectations of them were lowered for a while, and people were extra-gentle with them. It was just generally understood that they were not going to be okay for a while. Like, a year.

Unfortunately in our modern culture, such grace is not generally extended to us. The people around you may have limited capacity for your emotional devastation. We're expected to get ourselves together again, and quick. No excuses: it's the American way. Your circumstances may require you to hold up the "I'm fine" façade, even if you are not.

Because the world at large is probably not going to respect or support the fact that you are going through an incredibly fragile time, you must respect and set boundaries around the legitimacy of your grief. No one else is going to do this for you. But you can decide to go into mourning and take extra-special emotional care of yourself for as long as you need.

Mourning has two parts: internal and external.

Internal mourning involves simply giving yourself permission to not be okay for a while. I hope that reading this book (particularly the chapters that explain why this is such an enormous, real, and agonizing loss for you) helps you to develop some compassion for yourself. No matter what kind of messages you get from the world that wants you to hurry up and get over it, you must not allow yourself to get tricked into believing that they are right. You are experiencing a major loss on a primal level. There is absolutely no reason why you *should* be okay right now. Do not feel ashamed of the way that you feel. Do not put yourself in situations where you are going to be judged for feeling the way you do. Instead, find safe environments that honor, respect, and allow your authentic feelings, and that allow you to mourn and heal.

On that note, it might also be a good time, if possible, to avoid making any major life decisions. The immediate aftermath of a breakup is not the time to quit your job, move away, buy real estate, or get a tattoo. Give yourself some time to heal and start feeling like you again. When the dust settles, then you can make new plans. For now, just accept the fact that you're not going to be okay for a while as you go about the important work of grieving and healing. If you must make major decisions (especially in a divorce situation), surround yourself with trusted advisors who can help you think through things clearly and rationally, rather than emotionally.

External mourning is creating a healing environment for yourself. Decide that you deserve the time to be quiet and do some reflecting. Understand that now is a uniquely fragile and vulnerable time of grieving, processing, and healing. You don't have to force yourself to go to parties, make new friends, or expend a lot of unnecessary energy unless you authentically want to. Think about what activities feel genuinely soothing and nurturing to you and give yourself permission to make them a priority. Say no to everything else. Avoid judgmental friends, high-impact social situations, and taking on stressful new projects. If your circumstances allow, find a good yoga class, spend time in nature, and do a meditation retreat. Now is the time to focus on you.

COPING WITH OBSESSION

One of the most difficult things for Exaholics in the weeks and months after a breakup are the nonstop, obsessive thoughts. It's because they feel so out of control. You can throw all your stuff in the back of your car and drive away. You can curl your texting fingers into fists that you jam in your pockets. You can pack your calendar with yoga, coffee dates, and cooking classes. You can buy a dog. But you can't stop thinking about your Ex.

Waking up from another nightmare in which you are victimized, abandoned, or ignored by your Ex, you lay in the darkness. Memories of conversations you had, or wanted to have, play in your head like movies until it's time to get up in the gray light of morning. Coffee. Shower. Driving. Working. No matter what you're doing, throughout your day the bulk of your mind is focused on your Ex. What they are doing, or not doing, or who they're doing it with. The other 10 percent of your attention steers you, on autopilot, through the rest of your life.

Your brain has been bound up in a tight, elaborate knot by an unsolvable riddle: "What the hell happened?" It works to free itself by wrestling with old memories or speculations, one by one. If it could only understand—emerge the victor from one of these skirmishes—you might be released from the cage of obsession. But there is no final victory. The memories are indestructible and crowd together in a mob that has no end. Your mind is stuck, hemmed in on every side by ghosts of your former life.

You've moved on physically. But I don't have to tell you that moving on mentally and emotionally is very, very difficult. It feels impossible to get away from your Ex when they, and their army of ghosts, have taken up residence in your own head.

The path to reducing obsessions and starting to get control of your mind lies in mindfulness and learning how to be here now.

Here's a quick primer:

1. **Stay in the present.**

   If you pay attention, you'll notice that there is a distinct difference between what is actually happening, literally, right now, and the things that you are thinking about. Thoughts about your Ex are time travelers. They are memories of things that happened in the past or worries about things that could happen in the future. In the actual, literal, present moment, very little is usually happening. You're sitting in a chair reading a book. Your feet are on the floor. You're probably wearing clothes. You're breathing. That's it.

   When an intrusive or triggering thought pops into your mind, simply being able to notice, "I am having a thought about something that is not happening right now," and coming back into physical reality will help you be able to step back and develop your meta-cognition. (Metacognition is your ability to think about what you're thinking about.) This strengthens your neocortex and helps build the ability to intentionally shift away from obsessive thoughts. Use the present moment as an anchor to reality and steer yourself back into the present over and over and over again. Over time, as your mind is freed from obsessive rumination that reinforces your addiction (by releasing surges of dopamine), your obsessions themselves will lessen.

2. Stop and replace.

Another way of helping yourself with rumination is to use the stop and replace technique. This involves planning in advance what you'd like your replacement thought to be. This might need to be a new thought, unique to each day. But it needs to be something that is pleasant and enjoyable: an upcoming vacation, getting a new fish for your fish tank, lunch—whatever. When you notice you're self-obsessing about your Ex, just say to yourself, "Stop." And then intentionally shift to thinking about your ski trip this weekend. I'll also add that if you don't currently have many things that are pleasant in your life to think about, you need to get some.

Another fantastic replacement strategy is to use mantras to break your obsessions. A mantra is a word or sound that is traditionally repeated to help you concentrate while meditating, but you can use one to bring yourself back to safety when you find yourself thinking about your Ex. A simple "We are no longer together and I release you to the universe," can release you from these intrusive thoughts.

3. Be tolerant of yourself.

Cognitive techniques require practice, and you will have to do them over and over again throughout the day. They are not going to "heal" your obsession—only meaningful growth work will do that, and that is going to take time. Just like if you break your arm, it's going to hurt. The pain that your obsessive thoughts generate is your brain's way of saying, "I'm hurt! Take care of me!" We have to respect pain and allow it to guide us to the work we need to do. You have been injured, and it is okay for you to not be okay for a while. Accept the fact that right now your mind is an obsessive pain factory, that this is normal, and that it's going to get better.

Mindfulness, shifting, and acceptance, when applied consistently, will give you some respite, allowing you little moments of sanctuary from the torment of your thoughts. And feeling even a little bit more in control of your mind is worth a lot.

Maintaining Contact Through Social Media

At no other point in history has it been easier to torture yourself by spying on your Ex. In the past you would only have had access to the same level of information about them if you were actually hiding in the bushes outside their house, cupped ear to the wall. Now you have it all, and more, available to you twenty-four hours a day. You can know what your Ex had for lunch, what they think about the *Game of Thrones*® season finale, and read a real-time, blow-by-blow description of the amazing party they are at without you right now, photos and all. Lucky you.

Of course, you are craving this knowledge. Your social media relationship probably feels to you like a lifeline of connection. If you're like most Exaholics, the idea of losing that contact fills you with fear. We will be discussing the process of achieving acceptance and abstinence in the next chapter, but for now, please consider what having this information about your Ex actually does to you.

Each "contact" with your Ex reinforces the connection, biologically. Every new morsel of information zings you with dopamine, creating an explosion of anxiety, torment, and longing inside of you. It is also helping keep you on the hook. Having new information to obsess about is simply prolonging your madness.

I cannot tell you what to do, but I would like to suggest that you may feel much, much better on a daily basis if you are not continually assaulted by new, hurtful, angering, or confusing information about your Ex. The less you think about them, the better. I know that you may not feel able to cut yourself off from this electronic conveyor belt of painful information right now, but I sincerely hope that when the time is right, you will.

When Your Ex Is Sleeping with Someone New

This is a toughie. Even if you've been doing okay in the first weeks and months after your relationship ends, there is still something about knowing that your Ex is with someone new that will send you into a frenzy of emotional pain, obsession, craving, and desire.

It may be related to the primal response that evolution has designed in us: mate guarding. The same way that bull walruses wrestle each other to bloody blubber, and female magpies angrily flap away seductively sidling rivals, humans freak out when former—even unwanted—mates pair up with a new person. It's an automatic, immediate reaction to fight for our mate and protect our primary attachment from external threats. A hundred thousand years ago, the angst, anger, lust, and fear that floods you when you think about your Ex having sex with someone else would have provoked you into running off your rival with screams, sticks, and stones. But now you just spy on them both through the window of your iPhone, in impotent rage.

And It. Is. All. You. Can. Think. About.

Are they on the motorcycle right now? He's probably taking her to that restaurant I always wanted to go to that he said was too expensive. Are they holding hands right now? I bet they're kissing. Maybe they are having sex right this very second. They probably skipped the motorcycle ride and decided to spend the day in bed. We used to do that . . .

In your mind's eye you play out scenes from your life together. Except your role is being played by someone who might be sexier, more fun, or more interesting. You see your Ex—the happy, sweet, fun one you first fell in love with—sharing the best parts of themselves (and hiding the rest). It feels incredibly unfair.

It's worst at night, when there are no distractions. The joy and passion you envision for them is made all the more cruel by the stark contrast to your own silent bed. You lay sleepless, writhing in agony at the injustice. You want to stop thinking about it but you can't. You feel trapped in your own head.

As with any obsession, remember that part of your brain that feels things cannot differentiate between something that you're thinking about and something that is actually happening. So when you're imagining your Ex and their new sex partner making out on the couch, you react to it emotionally (and physically), as if you were seeing it happen right in front of you: Your heart starts racing, you feel nauseated, and you are filled with pain and rage.

Being victimized by these intrusive images is incredibly traumatizing. Ruminating does not bring any value to your healing process. Instead, it keeps you from moving forward. In order to rescue yourself from the impotent madness of this obsession, you must double down on your cognitive skills of mindfulness and shifting.

Differentiate between what you're thinking about and what is actually happening. Notice that you are having an internal experience—not an actual experience. It sounds simple, but it's very easy to get swept away in our thoughts without even noticing what's happening, particularly when they are as emotionally charged as imagining your Ex having sex with a new person.

Recognize that your vivid thoughts are activating all these scary, painful feelings, but in reality nothing bad is actually happening to you right now. You are sitting at a table, eating a bowl of cereal. You are breathing. Anchoring yourself to the reality of the present moment by using your senses creates a protective barrier between you and intrusive thoughts.

Once you've broken the obsession and are in the safe space of reality, you can shift your thoughts elsewhere. Use a mantra, or make plans. Shifting is important because the thoughts we habitually think about get stronger. When you practice shifting, the intrusive thoughts about your Ex will get weaker.

Shifting your awareness or distracting yourself does not mean that you are avoiding or stuffing your feelings. Obsessing is not the same thing as processing. It's mentally picking at a scab that you are not allowing to heal. You have to get unstuck from the obsession phase in order for healthy new growth to occur.

The Stranger

"I don't even know who this person is anymore," is a common sentiment of people ending their relationships. It seems like the person you love has been transformed into some twisted, callous version of the person who once loved you. When love is blown out like a candle it can seem like there is nothing in the eyes of your former lover but hardness or contempt. No empathy. No softness. No desire. Whatever loving being had previously inhabited them is simply gone—leaving a shell that looks, walks, and talks like your beloved. It's like the moment when life leaves the body of a being, immediately transforming it into nothing but dead meat. Your partner is still there in body, but the person you knew is gone.

Much of the protest phase is attempting to illicit some kind of response or acknowledgment from this sudden stranger inhabiting your Ex's body. Exaholics will work very hard to prod and rouse an Ex into showing that they still care.

If this is true for you, I suggest that it can be very helpful for you to consider that the person you knew has ceased to be. They no longer exist in the world. The mystifying stranger that has replaced your lover must be treated differently than the person you loved. This new person has a proven record of hurting you or not caring about you as much as you cared about them.

The truth is, it takes a long, long time to get to know people. We need to observe people over time, and in many different situations, to truly get to know their personality, their values, and how they cope with stress or other dark feelings. In the meantime, before we have all the information, we fill in the blanks with whatever we prefer to believe, constructing dopamine-fueled fantasies about our lover that may or may not be true. It can be very traumatizing when, as we get to know people better, they are not actually who we thought— or hoped—they were. Many relationship conflicts come from people being upset about who the other person actually is. When relationships end, reality breaks through the fantasy once and for all. For many Exaholics, losing the dream of who they believed their partner was is as painful as losing the relationship itself.

Think about what reality has taught you about who your Ex is (or is not) and what you should expect from them. When you have more information about a person, you get to make new decisions. In this case, you have new information that your Ex is not the person you thought they were. They are an unknown quantity. Therefore, new boundaries are called for.

What kind of boundaries do you have with strangers or people that you don't know very well? What about strangers or acquaintances who are known to have done hurtful things to people? Do you call them up and try to talk to them? Do you expect to be cared for? Is it appropriate to tell them personal things about yourself? What would you expect to gain by demanding attention or affection from them? Not so much, is the correct answer to all of the above.

Your Ex is no more. They are now a stranger to you. Conceptualizing the shift in their entire way of being can help you get the psychological distance you need to start setting new boundaries, adjusting your expectations, and restructuring your attachment to them. It will also help you understand that your continued attachment to them is only harmful to you.

The person you thought you were having a relationship doesn't actually exist. Treating it like a death, with the ceremony and mourning you would allow yourself if you literally lost a person, will help you cope.

WHEN YOU SEE YOUR EX OUT AND ABOUT

Exaholics I work with are often worried about what they'll do if/when they run into their Ex. They should be. Every interaction with your Ex will buy you another one to three weeks of rumination and suffering, particularly if it doesn't go well.

Here are some general tips:

1. It will be better for you, you will heal faster, and you will have less angst if you do not see your Ex—particularly when you are in a vulnerable state. Any encounter or sighting will set you back significantly in your healing process. Truthfully, any contact with your Ex at all will prolong your suffering by a week or two. (We'll be talking more about not initiating contact in the next chapter.) But for now, think about where you are most likely to see them and attempt to avoid those areas for awhile.

2. If you can't avoid seeing your Ex, or you are likely to run into each other even if you try not to, it is vital that you plan in advance how you want to handle it. Having a plan will make it much more likely that you will handle the encounter in a way that feels healthy and positive to you.

Your plan should be based on your core values: Who do you want to be when you encounter your Ex? A disheveled shrieking banshee? A sobbing wreck with mucus bubbling out of your nose? A pathetic, drunk, slurring fool begging for another chance? Or a cool, collected, confident, and attractive person?

Hint: Experiencing you as any of the first three will only reinforce your Ex's desire to be out of the relationship, as in, "Thank God I don't have to deal with that anymore." Seeing you glide on by with your act together has a much greater likelihood of eliciting a twinge of regret and longing in your Ex. So get clear about your values and think about who you are when you are at your best. Are you intelligent? Well dressed? Fit? Composed? Friendly? Figure out the image you want to project.

Also, get clear about when an encounter is most likely to happen. Where will you be? In a certain neighborhood? At the farmers' market? At a certain time of day? I'd prefer (for your sake) that you use this information to avoid these situations, but if you can't, then at least prepare: take a shower, put on mascara, and rehearse your actions or responses.

Remember: You are fragile, vulnerable, and in the midst of a healing/grieving process. You need to have boundaries with the person who hurt you. They have shown you that they are not an emotionally safe or available person for you. If you attempt to reconnect with them—particularly at a time and place when they are not emotionally prepared to go there—you are going to get rejected again. Any free-range interaction with your Ex is just going to briskly rub salt into your already bloody wounds. Remember that the person you see tomorrow at the farmers' market is not the person you were in a relationship with. That person is gone, having been replaced by your Ex. Let go of any reunion fantasies and act accordingly.

BOUNDARIES

The most powerful and healthy thing that you can do when you see your Ex is to protect yourself. You do this by communicating your boundaries. Ideally, you do this without actually interacting with your Ex and thereby opening yourself up to painful or embarrassing moments. For example, if you look straight at your Ex, make eye contact, and then look away and keep walking it communicates very clearly, "I see you. We have nothing to discuss. Don't talk to me."

Ignoring them can make them think that you don't see them, and increase the likelihood that you get a tap on the shoulder.

COMMUNICATION

If you must talk to them (as in, if they speak to you first), be cheerful, be light—and be extremely brief. Do not ask for or offer any personal information. Remember, they lost their privileges to access your inner self when they showed you that they were not an emotionally safe person for you. When they rejected you, or behaved so badly that they forced you to reject them, they taught you that you need to have very strong boundaries with them. If you don't, you will get hurt. Therefore, they don't get to know how badly you are hurting.

What Not to Do, Example A: Freak-Out

Setting: Farmers' market, Saturday morning
Ex: Hey. How've you been?
Exaholic [snarling]: How do you think I've been?
Ex: Yeah, well. I know. Okay, well . . .
Exaholic [tearing up]: You don't care at all about how I'm feeling! You never have!
Ex: I have to go.
Exaholic [screaming]: Yes, go! Go, you uncaring asshole!!
[Strangers fifteen feet away stop fondling tomatoes and look up to take in the unfolding drama.]
[Ex walks away shaking their head.]
[Exaholic leaves to go home and ruminate and cry for two weeks.]

What Not to Do, Example B: Oversharing

Setting: Farmers' market, Saturday morning
Ex: Hey. How've you been?
Exaholic: Oh I'm okay. How are you?
Ex: I have good days and bad days. Sometimes I miss you.
Exaholic: Me too. I feel so sad all the time, you're all I can think about.
Ex: Yeah. Well. We can never work. You know that, right?
Exaholic: [starts to cry]

Ex: I have to go.
[Strangers' eyes fixate on your tear-streaked face as they walk by.]
[Ex walks away shaking their head.]
[Exaholic leaves to go home and ruminate and cry for two weeks.]

What to Strive for, Example C: Good Boundaries

Setting: Farmers' market, Saturday morning
Ex: Hey. How've you been?
Exaholic: Oh I'm okay. [sips coffee and pointedly offers no other personal details or chitchat]
Ex: Yeah, me too.
Exaholic: Okay, see you around.
[Exaholic feels mildly victorious, but still goes home and stews over the encounter for a week.]

WHAT TO DO IF YOU SEE YOUR EX OUT WITH SOMEONE NEW

Keep walking. Don't stop. Pay the tab, call a cab, and get the hell out of there. You are likely to become so flooded that you will lose control of yourself. Any interaction is going to end badly (and when I say badly, I mean embarrassingly). You will regret it. Just go home. If you know you are going to be in a situation where this type of encounter is a possibility, try to go with a friend who can take charge and muscle you out the door if necessary.

COPING WITH DIFFICULT DAYS

In addition to difficult moments, there are certain days—or even seasons—that may be harder than others. Days when families come together to celebrate holidays, situations that have memories with your partner attached to them, or times when it seems like every one else but you is with their partner are going to be difficult at first. As the wheel of life twirls around the first year of Thanksgiving, Christmas/ Hanukkah, New Year's, Valentine's Day, St. Paddy's Day, Easter/ Passover, Memorial Day, Fourth of July, Labor Day, and Halloween (with a few more solstices, fasts, or feasting days depending on your persuasion), you will be confronted by the absence of your partner and harassed by old memories.

During your relationship, you spread layers of memories over every shared event—possibly for many years. Now special days seem encased in those memories. You can't even get close to them without getting triggered into a flood of sadness, anger, regret, or longing for what was. For many people, birthdays and anniversaries are the hardest: the days that were just yours may have especially tender memories attached to them, particularly if in the past you or your partner worked hard to make them meaningful and special.

Holidays also shine a bright and unforgiving spotlight on your current social landscape. The drumbeat of rituals that hold social systems together through time can seem to mock you at first. When everyone else in the world seems to be having a fabulous time with the people they love the most, you are acutely aware of your losses. The absence of your partner, their family, your shared friends, and your old rituals can be enormously painful. If you have children who now need to split newly awkward holidays, it can feel like you are losing them on special days too, as well as having to help them cope with the pain of their own lost family memories and traditions.

Holidays and special events also push you into contact with people you don't see all the time, and who want to know what's happening in your life. Thanksgiving is often especially hard because of having to acknowledge the new absence of a partner to your extended family, having to answer questions about your relationship, and having to hear unsolicited advice. Christmas or other religious holidays can be painful for the same reasons, but also because of the loss of the rituals and the specialness that you may have created together in years past. Not having a most important person to love and be loved by on these important days can send you into a tailspin of grief.

However, the worst of all is often Valentine's Day: the day that everyone in the world must go on a date and do something fabulous to celebrate their romance. Not only are you awash in memories of Valentines' past, in terrible grief and longing for your love, and acutely aware of your singleness, but everyone from your hairdresser to the cashier at Target® feels entitled to ask you what you are doing to celebrate. Many people I've worked with feel like hiding, from the days just past New Year's when the red hearts start appearing everywhere like mushrooms after a rain, until they are finally replaced by the non-threatening green shamrocks of early spring. After months of glittery, lonely, and needling holidays, you may be very much looking forward to putting on a stupid green hat and losing yourself in the anonymity of a sweaty, beer-drinking mob on St. Paddy's Day. (Unless of course old memories follow you there, too.)

So how to deal?

You may not like this very much, but here is the unvarnished truth: You're going to feel bad on holidays and anniversaries at first. However, the good news is, holidays help move you forward in your healing process because they give you a natural opportunity to grieve. The work of grieving is sitting with pain and allowing yourself to fully feel and make sense of your experiences. You need to do this sooner or later. So, especially in the beginning, you might consider using holidays as a special "time out" for you to be alone, do some journaling, go to a retreat, or book an extra-long therapy session. Trying to be happy on days when you're not will likely backfire anyway: Forcing yourself to be with people when you don't feel like it, putting yourself in awkward social situations, and imitating cheer is only going to make you feel worse. Obey your sad feelings and give yourself the time and space you need to heal. Remember, this is a special time—you're in mourning. Give yourself a pass. Honor and respect your feelings instead of trying to make them change. The only way out of this is through it.

Once you've had time to do some honest grieving, you need to lay down some new memories. The keyword here is new. You can do new and different things in your old environment, thereby shellacking it with a few new layers of fresh experiences that will give you distance and protection from the ghosts of the past. You can also follow the example of Willy Wonka and push the "Up and Out" button in your life—going through the roof into something entirely novel and different. Do not attempt to replicate the past but rather put effort into creating completely fresh experiences and rituals. If you usually spend Christmas with your family, maybe this year you should treat yourself to a ski vacation or trip to Mexico instead. Go out for a fancy Vietnamese dinner on Thanksgiving. Host a dance party for single friends on Valentine's Day. Be bold—the more energy you put into creating amazing new memories, the sooner your past with your Ex will feel like it happened to a different person.

How to Handle Intrusive Questions or Invalidating Comments

When you're going through a bad breakup, you need to have a plan in place for how to handle people. This is often especially true around the holidays, but even in random moments when you're not expecting it, friends and acquaintances might ask about your Ex. This can be hard, because it pushes you into the truth of your feelings at times when you might not be emotionally prepared to feel it, much less talk about it. And the last thing you need to do is spill your guts to your wide-eyed dog walker or kid's preschool teacher.

You need boundaries. Plan in advance what those boundaries are, and rehearse your lines. What do you want strangers or distant acquaintances to know about your relationship? A simple, "We're not together anymore," is just fine. Closer friends or family members may ask intrusive questions seeking details about why and how. If you don't feel like talking about it, you don't have to. A simple, "It's a long story, and I don't really feel like getting into it right now, Grandma," or "I'll tell you more when I'm feeling up to it," is appropriate. If you're worried about hurting someone's feelings by withholding information, consider that they are the ones asking insensitive questions and putting you in an awkward position in the first place. You don't have to discuss anything you don't want to.

The hardest part can be the responses you might get back when you do open up to people you trust about how you're really feeling. When you share with one of your closest friends that you're devastated, that your Ex is all you can think about, and that you miss them terribly, and get a, "At least you're still young! How about Match.com?" it can feel incredibly isolating and invalidating. It's like brightly telling a woman who just had a miscarriage, "Well, you can always adopt!" How do you handle people who can't respond to you with empathy and sensitivity?

You have two choices. You can let them know how to help you by telling them. Saying, "I know you just want me to feel better, but the truth is that I'm probably going to be really sad about this for awhile. You don't need to do anything to fix me or help me—actually just letting me talk about how I feel without judgment or advice is really helpful." This kind of direct strategy can help your friends and family learn how to help you through their empathetic presence.

However, if the people in your life cannot be coached into responding more helpfully (or if they express irritation or impatience with you for your feelings), you will need to move to plan B and set boundaries with them too. If they aren't able to respond to your truth with sensitivity, they lose the right to hear about it. You cannot get blood from a stone, and you can't get emotional responsiveness from some people—and it will only hurt and frustrate you if you keep trying. You need to find other people who are able to meet you where you are. This may involve actively finding a person or people who are in the same boat, or a compassionate therapist or coach who can non-judgmentally hold a space for you to work through your feelings and make sense of your story.

PHYSICAL SELF-CARE

I hated the therapist I saw in high school for suggesting that I would feel better if I got more exercise. It felt incredibly invalidating to me and made me feel like she didn't understand the depth of my pain at all. It felt like she was suggesting I should use some Neosporin and a bandage on the bloody guts that had just fallen out of me and onto the beige carpet of her office.

Here's what I wish the too-cheerful, inexperienced shrink with the puffy hair had been able to tell me when I was in high school: Self-care is not going to change anything about your circumstances, and it is not going to solve your problems. But it will give you more strength, energy, and resilience to cope with what is happening. It's also a way of showing yourself that you are still valuable and worth taking care of.

The fact is, when you are going through a terribly painful, stressful, and traumatic experience, you need to get really serious about taking care of yourself because no one else is going to. Nourishing yourself in some basic ways—eating, sleeping, exercising—is the fastest, cheapest, and easiest thing that you can do to help yourself right now. You can't control anyone else, you can't control this situation, and you might not be able to control yourself very well in the days and weeks immediately after an unwanted breakup. But you can, and really must, take care of yourself as you're going through it.

I know that doing basic things like eating, sleeping, and exercising can be surprisingly hard when you feel shattered and mad with obsessive grief. But it is these exact moments when you are in most dire need of physical grounding and nourishing.

Let me put it this way: You are going to feel bad anyway, but you will feel worse if you don't follow through with these basic self-care strategies.

1. **Eat something.** We are all familiar with the clichés of binging on ice cream and powdered donuts in the aftermath of a breakup. If that is all you have to help yourself feel better, by all means, do it (though I hope your repertoire of coping skills expands as you go through your healing process). But here's the deal—chaotic spikes and dips in your blood sugar will swing your mood around with it, making you feel crazier and more emotional than you already are. So do yourself a favor and be sure to eat some protein with every meal.

    If you find that you cannot eat . . . well, that can be a common side-effect of heartbreak too. That was certainly my experience in the weeks and months following my own traumatic breakup. Talk to your doctor to see if there are nutritional supplements that you can use to increase your caloric intake in healthy ways. Personally, I lived on chocolate and strawberry meal replacement shakes and the occasional BLT sandwich for what felt like months. Clearly, not optimal—but it was better than my alternative of existing solely on Pepsi, cigarettes, and fingernails. Do whatever you have to do to nourish yourself.

2. **Supplements.** Unless there is a medical reason for you not to, consider taking a good multivitamin. Deficiencies in vitamins and minerals, including vitamins B6 and B12, vitamin D, Iron, Selenium, and Magnesium are frequently found in people who

struggle with depression and anxiety. Ensuring that you are not deficient in them is a simple investment in supporting yourself emotionally.

3. **Fish oil.** The compounds in fish oil help your body produce the calming neurotransmitter serotonin. Adding these to your daily routine may help you feel somewhat better emotionally and could potentially protect you from having your sadness and despair develop into full-blown depression.

4. **Probiotics.** The quality and quantity of gut bacteria supported by probiotic supplements has been found by research to impact mood. Believe it or not, your gut is rich with neurotransmitter-producing nerves. It produces serotonin and other neurotransmitters in quantities that rival that of your brain. Popping a daily probiotic is one of the easiest things you can do to smooth your mood.

5. **Water.** Research has also found that even mild dehydration is associated with higher anxiety, reduced ability to concentrate, and a lower tolerance for frustration and emotional distress. Drinking more water than you think you need will help you feel more competent and even-keeled.

6. **Caffeine.** Remember when we talked about the neurotransmitters in your brain and the different roles they played? Especially the part about how dopamine makes you feel agitated, anxious, restless, and obsessive? Caffeine amplifies that effect. If you are having anxiety, racing thoughts, and a hard time sleeping, consider reducing or eliminating caffeine. You are probably still going to feel all of these things, but you will feel them to a less extreme degree than you will if you're jacking yourself up with an unnecessary stimulant.

7. **Sleep.** It is very likely that in the first days, weeks, and even months after a breakup, your sleep will be disrupted. You may find yourself having a very hard time falling asleep or waking up

in the middle of the night and not being able to go back to sleep. If you tend toward depression naturally, you might feel like all you want to do is sleep.

Not getting enough sleep has been found to have a major impact on mood, cognitive functioning, and emotional resilience. You may consider doubling down on good sleep hygiene skills, including winding down at the end of the day, having a soothing evening routine, and going to bed and waking up at the same time every day. Sleep training or mindfulness programs may also be helpful.

If you are literally not able to sleep because of the intensity of your distress, do not be a white-knuckled hero. Get some help. Not sleeping is only going to make whatever else you are dealing with worse. Go to your doctor and find out if it might be appropriate to get some short-term medical support to help you sleep while you are coping with this crisis.

8. **Exercise.** I know that right now you feel like all the wind has been punched out of you and all you feel like doing is lying in the fetal position on your floor, staring at the crumbs and cat hairs imbedded in your carpet. Go ahead and do that. Be one with the cat hairs and crumbs. You have every right and reason in the world to feel devastated right now. The thought of even finding your shoes, let alone mustering up the energy to walk out your door probably makes you feel exhausted. I get that. And I can hear you shouting "Die, Shrink!" at me in your mind as I wind up to remind you about how helpful and important it is for you to get exercise right now. Trust me, I understand. I totally resented the horrible therapist who advised me to get more exercise too.

Before you throw this book across the room, hear me say that I'm only here to help you. I can't tell you what to do; I can only provide you with information. Here is the information:

Research has found that doing even thirty minutes of anything that raises your heart rate is about as effective in reducing symptoms of anxiety and depression as anti-depressant medication. Besides possibly feeling somewhat better emotionally if you exercise, you will have more energy, sleep better, be better able to regulate your emotions, and think more clearly. You do not have to kill yourself at the gym or do anything painful to achieve this effect. Briskly walking fifteen minutes away from your house, and then turning around and walking back again is just fine. You can cry while you're doing it if you want to—just wear sunglasses. It will take about two weeks to feel the benefits of regular exercise, so don't give up if it doesn't seem to help right away.

That is all I'm going to say about exercising. Just look at the crumbs some more and think about it.

9. **Drinking and drugs.** In the first days, weeks, and months after an agonizing breakup, you may feel like obliterating yourself in a bottle or sliding out of reality for a little while via the fuzzy buzz of pot. It's a common desire. Research shows that there is an uptick in drinking and drug use in individuals going through a major relationship loss. And yes, getting drunk or high is a reliable way of artificially stimulating the reward center that aches so intensely inside of you. If you get drunk, you very well may feel better . . . momentarily at least.

But we both know you can't stay drunk forever. Anesthetizing yourself doesn't make the pain go away, it only postpones it. Coping with this is hard enough. Deferring your pain until you are fat, haggard, ashamed of yourself, and chronically hungover is not helpful. Furthermore, you could have a much, much bigger problem on your hands if you go that route. Aside from feeling like crap about yourself, you risk the very real potential of ruining your life in much more spectacular, embarrassing, and difficult-to-repair ways than you would by just dealing with the pain of your loss. It is not worth it.

The pain you are in, as terrible and endless as it seems, is temporary. Embrace the fact that you're going to feel bad for a while and stop trying to run away from it. The pain itself is not going to hurt you. Having emotions does not damage you in any way. You are simply having an experience. It doesn't hurt you, it heals you. The work of grief is feeling and processing your emotions. In contrast, suppressing emotions or avoiding them through drugs and alcohol most certainly does cause harm. Right now, you are doing the work of grieving: allowing yourself to feel, and cope with, the legitimate pain of your loss. This emotional pain will only persist to the degree that you resist it. Put the bottle down and go stand in the shower and have a good cry instead.

In Summary

There are many things in your life that are extremely difficult to deal with right now. Drinking a couple extra glasses of water, swallowing some vitamins, and making sure you eat something is not that hard, comparatively. Taking supplements and eating protein is not going to change your life, but making sure that you're not deficient in anything important is one easy way to take care of yourself right now. There is so much happening in your life that you cannot control right now. At least with everything else going on in your life, you can make the choice that you're not going to get dragged down by physical circumstances that absolutely are in your control to improve.

Now that I've sufficiently annoyed you by telling you a bunch of stuff you probably already knew about what you should be doing to take care of yourself, I'm going to drive this golf cart into the darkness and bring you with me—we need to talk about some scary things.

How to Not Become a Stalker

Neither of us wants to have this conversation, but I'd be an irresponsible therapist and a bad friend to you if we didn't go here. We're going to talk about how to manage compulsions, the fine line between compulsions and stalking, and what to do if you feel genuinely out of control of yourself.

Managing Compulsions

The experience of losing a primary relationship is having nonstop obsessive thoughts about it. Expect to have intrusive, constant thoughts about your Ex, and plan accordingly. (Practice those mindfulness and shifting skills.)

Compulsions—feeling compelled to do something—are the behavioral manifestations of your thoughts. You may be wondering constantly what your Ex is doing, where they are, who they are with: those are thoughts. Thoughts only exist in your head. Thoughts don't bother anyone except you. Compulsions are when you act on your thoughts. Compulsions are behaviors you engage in, in attempts to pacify your compulsions . . . and behaviors can have consequences.

Most of the Exaholics I meet with in therapy engage in some form of compulsive behavior, particularly in the very first days and weeks following an unwanted split. Most of this is benign. Checking a Facebook page where someone is publicly posting information is not illegal or immoral. Texting or calling someone you've been emotionally connected to for years in efforts to patch things up is understandable. Writing a letter or leaving a meaningful gift can be an important part of the process of closure for both of you.

Unfortunately, it is also not unusual for Exaholics to engage in more intrusive information-seeking or more aggressive attempts to contact their Ex. This is understandable, when you consider it from a neurological level of protest. Remember, when you are in love, it floods you with dopamine and drops your serotonin. This neurotransmitter combo is then heightened when you are in scary, emotionally intense situations (like the loss of your primary relationship). Low serotonin makes you obsessive. Dopamine makes you impulsive, among other things. And above all else, love is addictive. When you are cut off from the source of your love, emotional security, and pleasure, you go into withdrawal and become intensely focused on reconnection above all else. These circumstances conspire to create a churning chemical froth inside your brain that makes you not just frantic and obsessive, but more likely to act on your negative feelings.

But here's the deal: Even though the urges to do so are common, acting on your obsessions is never a good idea. Behaviors that arise out of your fear and pain are rarely helpful or productive. Most of the time they only make things worse for you. I have never had an Exaholic (including myself) find out some new piece of information about their Ex and then think, "Ahhh. Knowing they spent the weekend in Cabo with their new boyfriend has made me feel *so* much better." The only thing that comes from ferreting and snooping is that you remain stuck in angst. I have also never had an Exaholic on my couch who benefitted from aggressively contacting their Ex against their wishes. No one has ever said to me, "You know, the fortieth phone call did the trick—I screamed at him so loud that time, he realized how much he loved me and then we got back together."

In addition to being emotionally destructive to you, indulging compulsions can make you do bad things. Even criminal things. For example, calling repeatedly after your Ex has communicated they do not want to talk to you, showing up at your Ex's home, work, or school to confront them, or accessing private email or bank accounts to monitor their activity is not okay. It is a violation of their boundaries, and it is illegal.

It is stalking.

While I have never seen frantic, obsessive, or intrusive behaviors lead to successful outcomes for an Exaholic, I have seen their negative impact on the Ex—and that's where it gets sad and scary. I have worked with many Exes who have ended relationships for legitimate reasons only to become victims of stalking and emotional coercion by out-of-control Exaholics. As in, having to take out restraining orders and pursuing legal action against their Exaholic.

There is a fine line between being heartsick and mad with obsessive grief, and then acting on those thoughts in pathological and illegal ways. The latter is stalking. Stalking is defined as unwanted pursuit or obsessive following of someone who does not want you to do so. It can be a slippery slope between garden-variety Exaholic compulsions and criminal stalking. Therefore, you need to have a strategy in place for managing compulsions so that they don't escalate and get you in trouble.

You have to, because allowing yourself to get out of control can put you into the position of being an abuser and a perpetrator of domestic violence. Scary to think about, but true. I can't tell you how many people I've worked with who feel trapped in unhealthy relationships and afraid to leave for fear their partners would rage at them, berate them, harass them with dozens of calls and texts, kill themselves, take the kids away forever, install themselves in front of their home or work, litigate them into poverty, call their employer with false stories, or enter their homes (via a key or garage door opener they couldn't get back) to confront or intimidate them, or threaten them. So they stay, against their will. This is not love. Coercion, harassment, and intimidation are all aspects of domestic violence.

Your perceptions of what is happening in these moments may be very different from those of your Ex. Seriously. Even if it feels to you like, "We just need to see each other. We just need to talk," your Ex may experience your attempts to reconnect as dogged pursuit and feel badgered and harassed. They may experience you as a perpetrator of emotional abuse who is trapping them in an unwanted relationship. They can't tell you this because of their fear of consequences from you. But they tell me—their therapist. And I'm telling you: You need to respect their boundaries. No means no. If someone tells you they don't want to be with you anymore, you don't get to override that because you don't want the relationship to end. You have to deal with it. Refusing to accept that, or acting out on your hurt and anger can put you in hard-core perpetrator or stalker territory.

There are two different kinds of stalking: one is essentially stranger stalking, in which people develop an intense, obsessional interest in strangers, or acquaintances who reject them. The second is stalking that happens in the aftermath of a relationship loss, when one partner continues to pursue, follow, and harass their Ex. About 50 percent of stalking cases develop when a romantic relationship ends. Over their lifetime, 15- to 20% percent of all women and 5 percent of men will experience some form of stalking. This difference in stalking reports between genders is likely because most stalkers (80 percent) are men.

There is an arc to the phenomena of stalking.

1. It starts with excessive preoccupation with an Ex, and obsessive thinking about them. Obsessive thinking is the most prevalent feature of a stalker (as well as anyone going through an unwanted breakup).

2. Obsessive thinking turns into compulsive watching and information gathering, in escalating violations of personal rights and privacy. The first stage of this is proximity and surveillance: being physically near the Ex and watching them—either literally or virtually. (Note: All people going through breakups are biologically pulled to maintain proximity with their Ex and soothe their obsessions through information gathering. While the desire to do so is normal the behavior itself must be controlled.)

3. The next tier of stalking is when watching turns into invasion. Invasion means that you are violating boundaries, privacy, and security. Examples of invasion are leaving unwanted gifts, showing up at an Ex's home, work, or school, attempting to recruit their friends or family members to "talk sense into them," and continuing to contact them after they have asked you not to. Invasion also includes accessing private information via bank accounts, phone records, and email accounts. Around this point, the intended target stops becoming an Ex. The correct term now is "victim." As in, "victim of criminal stalking." All of the above are legitimate legal reasons for them to be awarded a restraining order against you.

4. Stalking may also come to involve proxy surveillance of the victim. This means recruiting other people to help you watch the victim or gather information about them. This includes using private investigators, location identification apps, and installing spyware on their phone or computer, as well as attempting to involve their friends, family, and co-workers.

Exaholics Breaking Your Addiction to an Ex Love

5. As unchecked stalking intensifies, it may come to involve outright intimidation, including harassment such as continued unwanted calls, letters, or texts. The tone changes, disintegrating into threats or demands. The stalker may aggressively attempt to confront their Ex or threaten to harm them in some way. They may threaten to kill themselves or harm others. They may engage in shocking manipulation tactics in efforts to re-engage their Exes. Stalkers have been known to fabricate life-threatening illnesses and pregnancies in efforts to manipulate the affections of the victim. (For real: I once worked with a man trying to get away from a woman who insisted that she was both pregnant with their triplets and suffering from brain cancer, even to the point of fabricating fake doctors' letters.)

6. If these attempts to control the victim are unsuccessful, the stalker can escalate to increasingly serious forms of coercion such as blackmail or imposing financial, circumstantial, or legal consequences, or efforts to constrain the victim—up to and including kidnapping.

7. The apex of stalking is physical violence toward the victim, their property, other people, or suicide.

I know you think that you could never be violent, but if you are engaging in any behaviors from number three to seven, you are at risk of being violent. Here's why:

In all stalking cases combined (including the 50 percent of cases where people develop an obsessional fixation on a stranger or acquaintance) there is a 25 to 40 percent chance of having at least one violent episode, where the stalker physically assaults the victim. However, if stalking occurs in the context of a failed romantic relationship, the percentage of violence toward ex-lovers rises to 55 to 89 percent. The intensity of the attraction, attachment trauma, abandonment, rage, and overall emotional reactivity in these cases leads to a much greater risk of violence.

Generally speaking, violence is the norm among stalkers who have had a prior romantic relationship with their victim. In nearly all cases, the violence is unplanned and born of the heat of the moment. Imagine the scene of a confrontation: You're already in a heightened state from simply being near your Ex and in the throes of the anger, hurt, frustration, rejection, abandonment, and embarrassment that you want to communicate. Frustrated efforts to talk turn to yelling, and yelling turns to pushing or blocking exits. You become flooded with blind rage, and the next thing you know, you could physically hurt your Ex. It happens. It happens to people who don't think they are capable of violence. And they're not . . . until they are in that specific, intense state of anger and agitation.

Again, it makes sense when we consider the impact of romantic relationships on brain chemistry. Remember, high dopamine increases agitation, energy, and impulsivity. Love lowers fear, making it more likely that people will take potentially dangerous risks. Low serotonin increases obsessional thoughts and compulsions. Plus, if you're doing things that are already intrusive, you are demonstrating that you struggle with boundaries and accepting limits, or at the very least with impulsivity. This is a combination that makes you vulnerable to being swept away by your emotions and doing something bad in the heat of the moment.

What to Do If You're Afraid You're Stalking

It is common to feel very, very upset in the aftermath of a breakup. It is normal to feel angry, jealous, and terribly hurt. It is one thing to feel the desire to inflict pain on the one who has hurt you, or to destroy or damage something that you cannot have. These are just thoughts and feelings that need to be honored and processed. It is quite another to act on these feelings.

If you find yourself acting on these dark feelings, (or planning to act on them) you need to get help. Stalking behaviors are often a prelude to violence. If you can't control your compulsion to call your Ex repeatedly, show up at their work or home, write them letters, and attempt to connect with them after they have clearly told you that your efforts are unwanted, you are stalking. If you cannot control your efforts to contact them or violate their boundaries, you have no evidence that would support your being able to not behave violently if you felt provoked. You are already committing a criminal act and you must get help.

Am I scaring you? Okay, good—that is showing you that your core values are peace, restraint, safety, and lawfulness. Hold on to those values and let them carry you to a better place.

Here's what acting on those healthy values looks like:

1. Doubling down to manage those obsessive thoughts. All stalking is born from obsessions. Practice your mindfulness and shifting skills.

2. Feel as mad, sad, hurt, and terrible as you want to, but act from your values. Do some journaling about who your values are calling you to be, and behave accordingly.

3. Understand that your continued attachment to your Ex is bringing out the worst in you. Think of this as being your bottom. Allow this to motivate you to admit that you have a problem and move to Step 1 of healing: acceptance and abstinence.

4. If you find yourself having trouble not acting out on your compulsions, get into some good counseling with a therapist who has experience with domestic violence offenders. I know that is a scary term and may be difficult to take on, but therapists with this specialty are the people who will be able to help you the most. There are specific options for you in the Resources section at the back of the book.

5. Consider seeking medical support from a physician or psychiatrist. Getting on the right medication while you are in the process of healing can help reduce vulnerability to both obsessions and compulsions.

OTHER TIMES TO GET PROFESSIONAL HELP

I know that the trauma you are experiencing right now may be literally life shattering. It may feel like the most important things in the world to you have just been destroyed. Your primary relationship, your children, your friendships, your home, your financial security, the things you loved, and your ability to function may just have been ripped away from you. It can feel like a nuclear bomb just went off in the middle of your life. And in the midst of it, you are having to cope with very real and very serious psychiatric events: abandonment rage, protest panic, attachment withdrawal, and brain chemistry that makes you unspeakably anxious, depressed beyond words, plus obsessive and impulsive. You may very well feel trapped in the worst pain of your life, and that pain may overwhelm your ability to cope.

Here are times when you need to get professional support:

1. If your current circumstances are pushing you beyond your coping skills and you are unable to function in vital ways (like being able to meet the needs of your children or complete required tasks at work or school), you need to get professional help.

2. If the only ways that you know to help yourself feel better are self-destructive, such as cutting, burning, or hitting yourself, acting out sexually, or relying on drugs or alcohol to cope with your feelings, you need to get professional help.

3. If you are fantasizing about ending your own life, you need to get professional help.

Remember: As terrible as this current life-space is, it is transient. It may take a while, but it will pass. Emotionally damaging your children, dropping out of school, tanking your career, ruining your personal and professional reputation, carving scars into your arm, acquiring AIDS or an unwanted pregnancy, developing a major substance abuse problem, or ending your own life are not going to make your current situation any better. Doing self-destructive things will only create more pain and bigger messes to clean up. In the worst cases, you can create permanent destruction in efforts to solve a temporary problem.

If you're feeling exposed right now because you recognize these traits and behaviors in yourself, I am genuinely sorry for how difficult this has been for you. I understand that the loss you are going through now is probably one of many difficult experiences you've had to cope with in your life. I hope that you refer to Resources for emergency options, and use them.

11

HEALING THROUGH THE TWELVE STEPS OF EXAHOLICS

IF YOU ARE READY TO ADMIT THAT YOUR CONTINUED ATTACHMENT TO YOUR EX IS A PROBLEM, YOU HAVE ARRIVED AT THE DOORSTEP OF HEALING.

The work of step one is radical honesty. It's been said, "The truth will set you free." It can be incredibly empowering to accept the truth: The relationship is over, it needs to be over, and it's time to move on. When you understand that your craving for contact and obsession with your Ex is holding you back and creating pain for you, it helps you to see your thoughts and feelings about your relationship in a new light; you begin to see that it is toxic. The shift that occurs in an alcoholic who becomes aware that their raging craving for alcohol *is* the problem—not how much they were drinking, or when, or why—is liberating in itself. They have discovered the true face of the enemy. In this case, the enemy is your craving for contact, your continued obsessions, and the feelings your Ex can still trigger inside of you.

With any addiction, once you admit that the thing you're addicted to is a problem, you have to stop doing it. An alcoholic who is still drinking is not in recovery. An Exaholic who is still talking to their Ex, watching their every move on Twitter, and fantasizing about their reunion is not in recovery either. An Exaholic doesn't take the first action of healing until they are no longer initiating contact with their Ex. Not initiating contact is the abstinence of Exaholics.

The distinction between not initiating contact and no contact is important. Your addiction is to a person who, unlike a bottle of Chardonnay, can actually jump out at you and make you interact with them. You can't control whether your Ex texts you selfies of how happy they are, calls you demanding that their sinus irrigator be returned immediately, or happens to be browsing the lonely individually wrapped portions of chicken alfredo in the frozen foods aisle at the same time as you are. You cannot control contact.

You can, however, control whether you initiate that contact. For many Exaholics, committing that they will not text, dial, or instigate confrontations is hugely empowering. It means that they are now officially on the path of healing. The longer you go without contact, the weaker your attachment to your Ex will become. Not initiating contact puts you back into control.

Not initiating contact also means disengaging from your Ex online. (Sorry.) Social media is a communication tool. Even if it's one-sided, when you are following them and watching them online, you are initiating contact with them. It's time to block, unfriend, and unfollow. Delete your entire account if you need to remove your ability to "check." It's the Exaholic equivalent of dumping the booze down the sink. You can't have them "talking to you" right there on your phone at ten pm on a lonely night, reinforcing your attachment to them with every post. As long as you keep yourself open to their online presence, you are actively using. Please do not worry about "hurting their feelings" or "making them mad" or "seeming immature" by unfriending or unfollowing them. The damage to your relationship has already been done. Now it's time for new boundaries.

Are you having a hard time letting go of social media connections because you are secretly holding on to the idea that they may still see (and/or care about) your posts? That if you snip the digital cord, they may never see your future tanned abs, envious vacations, and eventual engagement announcement? (And then weep bitter tears of regret?) Let it go. Give it up. Your desire to create any emotional reaction in them—also known as communicating—is a trap that is only holding you in the past and keeping your addiction alive.

Of course, there must be a loophole for necessary contact. If you co-parent, run a business together, or are actively in the process of taking your shared life apart, you are going to have to communicate with your Ex. You can manage this and maintain your abstinence if you do not initiate contact with your Ex for emotional reasons (i.e., "I was thinking about how much I missed us today," or "How have you been?," or "I need to tell you how much I hate you," are all examples of you falling off the wagon). You can, however, convey necessary information.

I would highly recommend communicating necessary information by email. That way you can slow down, be clear about what you want to say, and censor out anything not necessary before sending. In comparison, talking to or texting your Ex in real-time is too dangerous. Speaking to or texting your Ex without extremely clear and firm boundaries is the Exaholic equivalent of an alcoholic walking into a bar, ordering a drink, and just . . . holding it. It's not going to end well.

Many Exaholics count their days of not initiating contact and consider them precious days of sobriety. Amassing days where they were in control, they felt empowered, and like they were breaking free of their relationship helps give them confidence as well as continued motivation to stay away. Focusing on the days you don't initiate contact also helps you stay away from global, scary thoughts like, "We're never going to see each other again," that throw your limbic brain into an anxious frenzy. Instead you can take it one day at a time, one hour at a time, or one minute at a time. "I am not initiating contact right now" feels like a righteous victory that also helps you stay in the present.

As good as it can feel to finally take your power back, the true work of step one lies not just in your abstinence, but also in your acceptance of the end. This is a loss. It is a death. As liberating as step one feels, it also brings feelings of grief and despair as you come to terms with the relationship really being over. Step two is ready and waiting to help you cope with this.

STEP TWO

> *We have come to believe that those in our support network, who share in our distress, are the ones to turn to for love and support.*
>
> *"People in grief need someone to walk with them without judging them."*
>
> —GAIL SHEEHY

THE WORK OF STEP TWO IS TWOFOLD: GRIEVING AND REACHING OUT FOR SUPPORT. GRIEF TRAILS BEHIND ANY ACCEPTANCE OF LOSS. WHEN YOU HAVE LOST A PRIMARY ATTACHMENT, YOU HAVE LOST ONE OF THE MOST IMPORTANT AND BASIC OF HUMAN NEEDS FOR CONNECTION. WHETHER YOUR PERSON HAS ABANDONED YOU, REJECTED YOU, ABUSED YOU INTO FLEEING, OR ACTUALLY DIED DOESN'T MATTER. YOU MISS THEM, AND YOUR EVOLUTIONARY, EMOTIONAL, AND EXISTENTIAL REASON FOR BEING HAS BEEN CRUSHED.

In some ways, a literal death can be easier to accept and deal with than the loss of a cherished primary relationship when your partner chooses to leave you. When someone dies of cancer, or in a tragic accident, it's not a direct rejection of you. In contrast, when you want desperately to be with someone who does not want to be with you (or who can't or won't be the person you need them to be), losing them feels like a statement of your worth. It's personal.

Once Exaholics have given up the fantasy of reunion and accepted the fact that their lover is not returning, does not love them back, or is simply not the person they hoped they were, grief, fear, and despair close in. These feelings were often held at bay by continued attachment and information gathering. When you stop "using," the pain rushes in. The work of grief is allowing yourself to feel the pain of the loss. This requires getting very serious about your physical, emotional, and cognitive self-care, and giving yourself permission to be sad for a while. If you have not done so already as you prepared to let go, it is now vitally important that you assemble a reliable support system for yourself.

During this time it can be tremendously comforting and healing to connect with other people who have genuine empathy and respect for your experience.

As simple as it seems, reaching out for support is a profoundly important step of healing because one of the primary experiences of being an Exaholic is isolation. Breakups strain relationships, making once easy friendships awkward. As discussed in previous chapters, people's tolerance for your pain only extends so far. And most of the well-meaning advice you get just feels like invalidating nudges to do something that you are incapable of. And you are not exactly in the place where you're able to make new friends. Like any addict who faces judgment or possibly pity from people who have never felt enslaved by a destructive force, Exaholics rarely have a safe harbor of non-judgmental understanding except with helping professionals, friends, or family who have recently gone through their own healing, or other (current or former) Exaholics.

The heart and soul of any twelve-step program lies not just in the steps themselves but in the community of survivors that is working through the steps together. To have a group of people who are in the same emotional space you are—and therefore understand exactly how you feel—is incredibly validating. People who are going through the same thing have empathy for your experience that is impossible to find elsewhere. There is patience, acceptance, and genuinely helpful guidance from people who are struggling to find their own way through the darkness of relationship loss.

For all these reasons, consider joining a support group for people going through breakups if there is one in your area. A simple Google

Search™ for "divorce support groups" or "breakup support groups" will turn up options in your area. There are also various online communities available to you, including the forums through www.exaholics.com.

You may also enlist the support of a good therapist and rally friends and family who have genuine empathy and understanding of your current experience—avoid well-meaning friends who inadvertently make you feel invalidated or judged. (You can still spend time with them, obviously, but only share your feelings with others who, in the beautiful words of Brené Brown, have "earned the right to hear your truth.")

When you've been through so much rejection, pain, and shame, simply sharing your feelings is an act of bravery. For some, just knowing that others are hurting as badly as they are can feel comforting. This isn't taking pleasure in the misfortune of others, but rather it is the incredibly validating experience of knowing that you are not alone in your heartache and that what you are experiencing is normal.

Human connection soothes pain. I know that the connection of a caring community is not the same as the comfort you'd find in the arms of your Ex, but allowing other people to be there for you and to support you during this time is a key step of healing.

Find your people, and let them be there for you now.

Step Three

> *We place our faith in this kindred network of unconditional support and trust that with their support we have the power to heal and grow.*
>
> *"We belong to each other."*
>
> —Mother Teresa

THE WORK OF STEP THREE IS RENEWING YOUR FAITH IN OTHER PEOPLE. YOU DO THIS BY ASKING FOR AND RECEIVING HELP. AGAIN, THIS SOUNDS LIKE A SMALL THING, BUT THE IMPLICATIONS ARE HUGE. ASKING FOR HELP CONTAINS THE

IMPLICATION THAT YOU ARE TRUSTING THAT OTHER PEOPLE
WILL HELP YOU. FOR SOMEONE WHO HAS BEEN MANGLED AND
ABUSED BY THE PERSON WHO WAS SUPPOSED TO LOVE THEM THE
MOST, TRUSTING THAT ANOTHER HUMAN BEING WOULD BE KIND
OR HELPFUL TO YOU CAN BE A BIG LEAP OF FAITH. IT ALSO STARTS
TO RESTORE HEALTHY BONDS TO OTHER PEOPLE.

Start small. Ask for the wisdom of other people who are going through the same thing that you are, or who are knowledgeable on the subject of healing. How are they coping? What strategies do they use to avoid initiating contact? How did they finally realize that their attachment was a problem? How do they deal with the obsessions?

You will get many, many answers. Some will work for you and some will not. However, they will all push you into deeper contact with what feels right or wrong for you. And through conversations, book recommendations, links to articles, podcasts, and TED Talks, your community can become your new best friend. As you learn from others, you'll get new ideas about how to handle yourself in the days, weeks, and months to come. Learning is evolving.

This third step feels good. It feels good to reconnect with people, and it feels good to be validated and understood. But on a deeper level there is something much more important happening that is neurologically based. At this stage you still have a throbbing attachment to your unresponsive and/or emotionally dangerous Ex. You know you can't connect with them, but you still need connection. Your need for secure attachment is basic and primary, and it doesn't go away just because you don't have anyone to attach to. When you connect with a community, you begin to attach to them. Your throbbing, attachment-craving reunion with your Ex is soothed, somewhat, by nurturing human contact with others. Your attachment is transferred from a dangerous place to a safe one.

Think back to the junkie rats we discussed in chapter 6. (For those of you who are just flipping through and have no idea what I'm talking about, please refer to page 96.) Rats, like humans, are often healed of their addiction when they are involved in a positive community that satisfies the need to bond and connect. Having a supportive person or community for you to temporarily transfer your attachment, and get your emotional needs met, is the vehicle through which healing happens. You were harmed in a relationship, and you will be healed through a relationship. If you are not able to connect with an Exaholics community, a good therapist can serve the same role in your life: a temporary safe person to attach to while you are healing. I know it sounds weird, but simply having a healthy, affirming relationship is about 75 percent of the healing power of therapy.

Having healthy, new relationships are a crucial part of your recovery process. At first, the safest relationships for you will be with other Exaholics or with supportive, non-judgmental, and compassionate people. As you become stronger, I'd like you to find and actively pursue other platonic relationships. This may include strengthening relationships with people already in your life such as family members or friends you've fallen out of touch with. Meet-up groups centered on a common interest, book clubs, or recreational sports teams are also fabulous ways to simply interact with other people in a low-stress way. You may also set a goal for yourself of simply being friendly to strangers—chatting up random people is how we develop acquaintances and then eventually make friends. These people do *not* need to know all about your breakup or your current emotional reality.

I also understand that feeling able and ready to go out in the world and have the energy, self-esteem, and interest in forming new relationships may feel out of reach emotionally right now. But when the time is right, challenge yourself to broaden your social circle. Doing so will help you heal.

But the first healing and stabilization will happen in the cocoon of your group of trusted people. Through their support and your practicing of the physical, mental, and emotional self-care strategies we discussed in the last chapter, you will begin to trust other people and yourself again. As you experience trust and emotional safety, you can start to learn about yourself and others on a deeper level that will catalyze your healing process.

STEP FOUR

We begin to accept our support network as an integral part of our lives, allowing the love and acceptance we find here to help us heal and rebuild our strength.

"You are worthy of love and belonging."

—BRENÉ BROWN

THE WORK OF STEP FOUR INVOLVES RECLAIMING YOURSELF AS BEING WORTHY AND VALUABLE. THIS IS CRUCIAL, BECAUSE BREAKUPS SHRED YOUR SELF-ESTEEM. WHEN THE PERSON YOU ARE MOST STRONGLY ATTACHED TO REJECTS YOU, IT CREATES A PRIMARY WOUND THAT OOZES HURT AND SHAME. IT'S HARD NOT TO FEEL LIKE THERE MUST BE SOMETHING WRONG OR BAD ABOUT YOU IF THE PERSON WHO KNEW YOU THE BEST DOESN'T WANT TO BE WITH YOU ANYMORE. THIS EXPERIENCE SIMPLY CRUSHES YOUR SELF-ESTEEM—THERE'S NO OTHER WAY AROUND IT. STEP FOUR IS ALL ABOUT HELPING YOU PUT IT BACK TOGETHER.

For most people, it is much easier for them to have empathy and compassion for other people than it is for them to be empathetic and compassionate with themselves. When you become involved with other people who are going though a traumatic breakup and hear their stories, you naturally feel for them. You see their side of things. You feel their pain. You understand what they cannot: that they weren't being treated very well and that it would be healthier for them to take control of the situation and decide to end it on their own terms.

But, when it comes to you, it's hard to believe that you weren't rejected by a really great person because you weren't good enough. Or that the love you had wasn't the most passionate and intense thing you'll ever know, and you're doomed to a life of isolation or settling. The seething limbic emotional storm boiling in your brain obscures your vision. It prevents you from looking at your own situation as clearly and rationally as you can see the circumstances of others.

When you become an active member of a support group, you develop psychological distance and perspective for your own situation through your interactions with others. You hear their stories and feel compassion, empathy, and hope for them. Over time, you can begin to realize that you are no exception: that you are worthy of support, compassion, and empathy too. That there is nothing wrong with you. That going through this is not a statement of your value as a person—it happens to all kinds of fantastic people. In fact, being rejected happens at least once to just about everyone. Not everybody is going to love you the way you want them to. Not all relationships are a good match in terms of values or temperament. Sometimes people get emotionally hooked on people who are not good long-term partners. You come to realize this through the stories of others. Eventually, you come to realize that this is true for you too.

Once that happens, you can begin to accept the support and encouragement of your community. In doing so, you revise your story about what just happened. You shift from being the victim, or the unlovable ogre, into just another person whose relationship didn't work out. As you develop a new story about what happened, you begin to experience an emotional shift. You begin to reclaim your self-esteem.

As you help other people develop compassion and empathy for themselves, you also develop compassion and empathy for yourself too. You realize that your story is not that special or unique. Pain is pain. Loss is loss. Rejection is rejection. Just because you're going through it doesn't mean that you are a bad person.

The Myth of Closure

In the process of patching your self-esteem back together, you will likely come across a gaping hole hungering for something that you may or may not have been consciously aware of before: closure.

Closure is a fantasy that many Exaholics hold on to long after they've crossed the line of letting go. The idea that there will eventually, someday, be a reckoning—a judgment day—for what's been done. That you will finally have the answers to the questions that have been painfully digging in your brain. (Answers that will provide you with evidence that will protect you from the sneering voice of shame, telling you that it was all your fault and that you were unworthy of love.) That your Ex will squirm in guilt and regret for the pain they caused you. That you will someday emerge from all this, triumphant—fit, tanned, confident, popular, and successful—and that your Ex will see your resplendence and realize how stupid they were. The myth of closure tricks you into believing that there will be a Hollywood moment, a final ending that wraps everything up in a neat bow of understanding,and will allow you to feel at peace with the past.

True peace comes from the acceptance of ambiguity. You will probably never have closure. You will probably never really understand what happened, or why. There will not likely be any meaningful justice for what's been done to you. You may never get to show your Ex what an amazing person you really are and what a huge mistake they made. Needing closure means that you still crave your Ex's approval of you and desire for you. It means that your self-worth is still tied to your Ex's opinion of you. When you let go of the myth of closure, you take back your power once and for all.

Here's your new mantra for step four:

"Nobody gets to decide what happened, or who I am, or what I'm worth . . . except me."

STEP FIVE

> *We resolve to become stronger, wiser, happier*
> *people as a result of what we learned from our*
> *past relationships, so that we might have stronger*
> *and more loving relationships in the future."*

> *There are no mistakes, no coincidences.*
> *All events are blessings given to us to learn from."*
>
> —ELISABETH KÜBLER-ROSS

THE WORK OF STEP FIVE IS GROWTH. ONCE YOU HAVE WORKED THROUGH YOUR GRIEF AND USED HEALTHY RELATIONSHIPS TO REBUILD YOUR SELF-ESTEEM, YOU CAN BEGIN DOING THE REAL WORK OF RECOVERY, WHICH IS FIGURING OUT WHAT THE HECK

HAPPENED AND USING THAT INFORMATION TO GROW.
HOW DID YOU GET SO DEEPLY ADDICTED TO A PERSON WHO
WOUND UP DISAPPOINTING YOU SO TERRIBLY? THE PURPOSE OF
THIS EXPLORATION IS NOT TO CHASTISE OR BEAT YOURSELF UP,
BUT RATHER TO GAIN INSIGHT THAT WILL HELP YOU HAVE MORE
SUCCESSFUL AND FULFILLING RELATIONSHIPS IN THE FUTURE.
THIS HAS NOTHING TO DO WITH WHO YOUR EX WAS (OR WASN'T,
AS THE CASE MAY BE). IT HAS TO DO WITH YOU.

Most Exaholics, around this stage, notice a marked shift in the way they feel. Some call it the "pivot point." They begin thinking less about their Ex and more about themselves. The first four steps are really about working through the pain of the loss, figuring out how to cope with the absence of your cherished person, learning to trust people again, and reclaiming your self-esteem. During that phase of healing, people tend to talk about their Exes a lot. And that is okay. But around the time of step five, particularly once people have wrestled the myth of closure into submission, there is a shift. People become less interested in their Exes than they are in themselves. They are detaching emotionally from the relationship. Once they have the headspace to think about something besides their Ex, they often turn their attention back to their own process.

This is a fragile and challenging time where you may be confronted by your own vulnerabilities, mistakes, and opportunities for growth. I think a great way to crack into this work (if you don't have access to a good therapist) is to either engage with a group who is willing to ask you hard questions, or to do some journaling and reflecting.

Questions to consider asking yourself include:

What were my circumstances before I got involved in this relationship?

What attracted me to this person?

Were there early red flags that I chose to overlook?

Did I confuse passion for a healthy, secure attachment?

How did I handle my anxiety in this relationship?

Am I dependent on the good opinions of others for my own self-worth?

Were there mistakes I made that impacted the quality of this relationship?

The true opportunity of loss and pain is growth. The goal of step five is to begin to understand the vulnerabilities that allowed you to become so deeply addicted to an unhealthy relationship and learn from that experience.

Step Six

> *We use the feedback of our support network to help us develop a more complete understanding of who we are, and where we need to grow.*
>
> *"We all need people who will give us feedback. That's how we improve."*
>
> —Bill Gates

THE WORK OF STEP SIX IS DEVELOPING THE COURAGE TO LOOK AT YOURSELF HONESTLY. IN STEP FIVE YOU BEGAN TO CONFRONT YOURSELF AND UNDERSTAND WHERE YOU HAVE OPPORTUNITIES TO GROW. AND YET WE ALL HAVE BLIND SPOTS. WHEN IT COMES TO OURSELVES, WE OFTEN DON'T KNOW WHAT WE DON'T KNOW. OUR INSIGHT IS BOUND BY THE LIMITATIONS OF OUR PERSPECTIVE. FOR THAT REASON HAVING THE FEEDBACK OF A COMMUNITY IS ESSENTIAL TO YOUR CONTINUED GROWTH. BECAUSE YOU CANNOT CHANGE WHAT YOU ARE NOT AWARE OF.

Step six therefore involves asking other trusted and emotionally safe people for feedback. Think about the people who are most familiar with both you and your Ex. Are there people in your life who were there for the entire relationship? More importantly, did they have the opportunity to observe you as you fell into love and then fell out the other side?

Consider asking them their opinions of what they witnessed as you went through the relationship, and be open to their answers.

Family members are often the best sources. The permanency of their relationship with you can give them the permission to be honest with you in ways that newer friends might not. Support groups who are very familiar with your story are often good too—those are the people who have your permission to be honest with you, as you've been honest with them. Just be sure to ask people that you trust. Mean-spirited criticism or judgment is never helpful, but authentic perspectives are.

You might hear people say that they felt worried about you when you entered into the relationship and that they saw early red flags that you missed or chose to overlook. You might hear them say they felt like you lost yourself in the relationship. You may learn how your Ex appears to others who are not wearing "love goggles." They may point out things that you did that they perceived as contributing to the failure of the relationship. The last kind of feedback is the hardest to hear, particularly if you have felt legitimately victimized by your Ex. You don't have to accept the opinions of others as gospel. Just put it in the hopper and think about it, and see if there is any value to you in considering the possibility that there is some truth to what they are saying.

Taking feedback non-defensively is difficult. Everyone is vulnerable to something called the fundamental attribution error, the psychological principle that underlies defensiveness. In short, it means that we all have a tendency to judge others and attribute their bad behavior to their character, while making excuses for ourselves and attributing our bad behavior to our circumstances. Understand that people will therefore make sense of things that happened in your life differently than you will, because you were living the experience, not observing it. Try to resist the impulse to meet their feedback with a "Yes, but." Rather, breathe and listen to what they are saying about how it looked from an outsider's perspective. Practice gratitude for the gift of insight you are receiving. Try to be glad that you have people in your life that care enough about you to be honest with you.

If your community is primarily your therapist, getting the feedback you need for growth can potentially be tricky. Direct feedback can be hard for some breeds of therapist, particularly those who have been schooled in non-directive, person-centered forms of therapy. If you ask your therapist for his or her opinion of how your behavior, choices, or underlying motivations may have impacted your experience and just keep hearing, "It's not important what I think—what do *you* think?" You may need to rephrase your question to get through the impasse. Starting the request with, "In your professional opinion," might help. Also, helping them understand that you are seeking feedback in order to improve your self-awareness and future outcomes may make them more comfortable with giving you their opinions. If you have a therapist who would rather discuss your need for information from them (implying that there is something pathological about the need itself) than answer your questions, you may consider asking them about why they are so uncomfortable with having authenticity in your therapeutic relationship. Or you might just move on to a professionally trained therapist who also has a background in coaching as opposed to just counseling, and who can better support your needs in this phase of your recovery work.

(Side note for those of you considering seeking professional help: Anyone—I mean anyone—can call themselves a "Life Coach" and hang a shingle. A "Life Coach" doesn't need any formal education or training at all, and in most states there is zero regulation of the profession. It is not even recognized as a profession by most state regulatory agencies. Your windbag real estate agent can get inspired by a Tony Robbins book this afternoon, build a website this evening, and start taking clients tomorrow. Buyer beware.)

STEP SEVEN

> *We made the decision that we were ready to improve ourselves with the help of our support network, our higher power, and/or inner wisdom.*

> *"Make the most of yourself, for that is all there is of you."*

> —RALPH WALDO EMERSON

STEP SEVEN PREPARES YOU TO START BUILDING A DIFFERENT FUTURE. IN STEPS FIVE AND SIX, YOU CHALLENGED YOURSELF. YOU CHALLENGED YOURSELF BY ASKING HARD QUESTIONS, AND YOU CHALLENGED YOURSELF BY ASKING OTHERS FOR THEIR FEEDBACK. NOW IT'S TIME FOR YOU TO TAKE ALL THAT NEW INFORMATION AND THINK ABOUT HOW TO MAKE IT WORK IN YOUR LIFE.

The sweetest revenge there is for you is to genuinely be happy and well, and to love your life. In step seven, you figure out what makes you happy and how to get better results in your life.

Throughout steps five and six, you gained insight and self-awareness. These insights can take many forms. Maybe you became aware that you have a tendency to put the needs of others before your own. Perhaps you realized that your anxiety made you controlling. Maybe you discovered that you shut down and avoided conflict, or avoided having difficult conversations that may have lead to greater intimacy. You might have learned that you were overly reliant on your partner for social and emotional fulfillment. Sometimes the big takeaway is that you moved too fast, allowing yourself to get emotionally invested in a person before you knew the truth of their character.

Once you have the information, you can begin planning what you want to change for the better. During this phase, Exaholics can make contact with their hopes for themselves.

It's time to start asking yourself some exciting new questions:

- What would have been different for you now if you'd done things differently in the past?
- Knowing what you know now, what kind of person would you like to be with in the future?
- Who do *you* want to be in your next relationship?
- How will you know if your next relationship is working? How will you know if it isn't?

As you work through these questions, you begin to have clarity about your core self, your values, and what you need to do next time in order to have a truly happy and satisfying relationship. You begin to envision your new future and develop a plan that you can then implement in step eight.

STEP EIGHT

> *We ask our support network to help us identify*
> *and remove all of our unhealthy relationship*
> *patterns, and we commit to practicing healthy*
> *new relationship skills with our network.*
>
> *"Wax on. Wax off."*
>
> —MR. MIYAGI, *The Karate Kid*

THE KEYWORD OF STEP EIGHT IS ACTION. STEPS FIVE THROUGH SEVEN HAVE GIVEN YOU INSIGHT INTO YOUR CHALLENGES AND OPPORTUNITIES FOR GROWTH, AND DIRECTION ON WHAT TO DO IN ORDER TO CHANGE. IN STEP EIGHT, YOU BEGIN PRACTICING THE SKILLS THAT WILL HELP YOU DEVELOP BETTER RELATIONSHIPS IN THE FUTURE.

Through your exploration, did you realize that you tend to hide, minimize, or suppress your feelings and attend to the feelings of other people instead? In step eight, your job is to figure out what you feel and what you need, and practice communicating more openly and assertively. Practice with your community or with friends and family with whom you have emotionally safe relationships.

Did you uncover the fact that you get controlling and demanding when you are anxious? In step eight, you have the opportunity to practice managing your anxiety directly instead of attempting to change other people in order to help you feel better.

Did your explorations in the previous steps teach you that you are overly eager to jump into relationships with people who ultimately hurt you? In step eight, you can practice meeting new people and not oversharing, overcommitting, or over-relying on them until they have earned your trust.

Did your life feel like an empty desert until your Ex swept in, making everything seem okay? All right then, your step eight will involve taking steps to build a satisfying, independent life. Take some classes, make some new friends, and get a hobby or three.

Insight is not enough. Just knowing that you are a certain way, or why you are the way you are, doesn't change anything. You have to actively change it through your behaviors. In step eight, your job is to practice the new ways of being that you've identified as being important.

Practice your new skills on your friends, your family, and with your community of support. Expect new ways of being to feel weird and unnatural at first. Remember—act from your values, not your feelings.

Wax on. Wax off.

Step Nine

Make a list of all the persons who our unhealthy relationship patterns have injured in the past, and who we must make amends to.

"I did then what I knew how to do. Now that I know better, I do better."

—Maya Angelou

A SURPRISINGLY DIFFICULT BYPRODUCT OF PERSONAL GROWTH CAN BE FEELINGS OF GUILT AND REGRET FOR THE THINGS YOU DID BEFORE YOU KNEW BETTER. I'VE HAD MANY PEOPLE WEEP BITTERLY ON MY THERAPY COUCH FOR THE MISTAKES THEY MADE WHILE IN THE GRIPS OF A RELATIONSHIP ADDICTION, BEFORE THEY HEALED AND GREW.

There are a few important things to remember as you work through this step and come to terms with the fact that, before you got to the place you are now, you may have done things you feel badly about.

For example, once you've gained sobriety and are no longer under the influence of love, you may be disappointed, or even embarrassed, by the things you did in efforts to maintain connection with your Ex. You may have accepted mistreatment from them, or given up things that were formerly very important to you. You may feel like you lost yourself in your efforts to be accommodating and pleasing to your unworthy Ex. You might feel that the ultimate betrayal you experienced over the course of your relationship was your betrayal of yourself.

You might also feel really bad about things that you did to other people while you were out of your mind with toxic love. Remember that pain makes everyone self-focused. For example, if you just broke your arm, you wouldn't be able to be really interested and excited about your friend's new promotion—you'd want to tell them about how much your arm hurt and ask them to please drive you to the hospital. Whatever they have going on would just not feel that important to you in the moment because what was happening to you was so major and immediate. The problem with Exaholism is that the emotional pain is as fierce as that of a broken bone, but it can persist for many months.

When you were in the depths of your Exaholism, you might not have been at your best as a friend, mom, dad, daughter, son, sister, brother, or co-worker. Even before your breakup, you may have been so obsessed with the person who is now your Ex that maybe you neglected your other relationships. After your relationship ended, you may have been so wracked by hurt, anxiety, rage, and rejection that you probably needed to unload a lot of heavy stuff on your friends, bail on plans, and forgot to ask how they were doing (or be present enough to hear the answer).

If you have kids, you may not have been the parent that you would like to be while you were consumed by your feelings about your Ex. They may have seen you hurt, angry, or preoccupied—perhaps at a time that they really needed more emotional support from you. Your family and closest friends may have ridden out this hurricane with you, encouraging you, talking to you for hours as you obsessed about your Ex, keeping you company, and perhaps even supporting you materially or financially. In other words, you may have made many "withdrawals" from various relationship accounts without putting much back in.

As crappy as this is to think about, it's also normal. This has been a hard time.

This has also been a period of immense growth as you have worked through your recovery. As you have been working your steps, you learned, you opened up, and you changed. As you did, in a very literal way, you have grown into a different person.

In changing, you may have become more aware of how your old patterns impacted other people. You may be aware that your negative old patterns were harmful to your children, your Ex, your family, your friends, and even yourself. As you make a list of the people who were hurt or damaged when you were in the grips of your addiction, you may begin to feel very sad or guilty.

Guilt, unlike shame, can actually be a very healthy emotion. Where shame tells you, "You are bad," guilt tells you, "You hurt someone." Feeling bad about doing harm gives you the motivation to learn from your mistakes, right wrongs, and be a better person going forward.

Make a list of the people who have been harmed by your addiction. When you are done, go back and write your own name at the top.

Step Ten

Directly apologize and make amends to these persons except in cases where it might injure them or others.

"Compassion is the basis of morality."

—Arthur Schopenhauer, *On the Basis of Morality*

CAN YOU FORGIVE? CAN YOU FORGIVE YOUR EX? CAN YOU FORGIVE YOURSELF?

At the core of forgiveness is compassion. Can you, compassionately, revisit your story and understand why you did the things you did, through the truth of the person you were? Can you forgive yourself for being that person?

One way that I have found to be helpful to my clients who have difficulty forgiving themselves is to remind them that the fact that they feel badly about the past mistake is evidence that they care and that they have grown sufficiently to realize what they've done. In growing, they are a different person than they used to be. The mistakes they made, as terrible as they feel now, were an important experience—maybe even a vital one—without which they would not have had the same opportunity to heal, grow, and become stronger, wiser people.

To achieve gratitude for the hard times that catalyzed your growth is the epitome of healing.

With clients for whom gratitude for their misfortunes feel like too big a leap (or simply too soon) I often ask, "Would the person you are today do the things that you did in the past?" Is your answer no? Then that means that you are now a different person than the one who did those things. And those shameful or regrettable acts were part of the path to becoming the person you are today, for better or for worse.

There are many paths to forgiveness. For some people, forgiveness is spiritual. They feel that only God has the power and depth of love to forgive anything. If your belief system involves asking for forgiveness from a higher power, then by all means do so. If your flavor of religion has specific rituals around forgiveness and redemption, then use them. (Say whatever you want about Catholics, but the act of confession and absolution is a psychologically powerful healing tool.) For others, psychological and secular forgiveness is the path to peace. That involves understanding, with compassion, the person you were versus the person you have become. The psychological equivalent to spiritual forgiveness is appreciating your own growth.

When you feel at peace, feel forgiven, and have made amends to yourself, then you can ask for the forgiveness of others, too. Forgiving yourself first will put you in a sturdy enough place psychologically that you will be okay if they can't or won't forgive you. Remember, asking for forgiveness, expressing remorse, and making amends isn't about you—it's about them. If you *need* someone to forgive you before you can feel better, you are displacing responsibility and making it about you again. Your job now is to be unconditionally loving and supportive to people you may have hurt in the past, not dependent on them to forgive you so that you can feel better.

Making amends also allows you to rebuild healthy relationships with people who want to give you a second chance. Doing this work and repairing or deepening your relationships can help you have a more stable and fulfilling life. It is also an important part of your continuing to recover your self-esteem and self-confidence.

Let's discuss the process of forgiveness and of rebuilding trust in damaged or strained relationships. There are several steps to this process:

1. Acknowledge harm done. Letting the person who was hurt during your Exaholism know that you understand the harm that was done to them. That you neglected your relationship with them, undervalued their advice, or took more than you gave for a while.

2. Allow the person you hurt to tell you about what the experience was like for them, if they want to. When people experience you as being open and willing to hear them, they will feel safe enough to open up to you. You may hear things that make you feel badly. Your job is to breathe, stay grounded in love and generosity, and non-defensively accept the truth of their experience.

3. Again, let them know that you understand their feelings and that their feelings are important to you. Sharing your feelings of regret or guilt about the events goes a long way in repairing trust. "Sorry" isn't good enough—you need to be able to communicate that you understand why what happened hurt them.

4. Talk about how you would handle the situation if it happened again in the future. What would you do

differently, if you could get a do-over? Be explicit.

Expect that some people may not be interested in forgiving you or in repairing their relationship with you. They don't need to forgive you or take you back in order for you to be okay. Your job is to acknowledge the hurt, make sincere attempts at amends, and then practice honoring the feelings of others—whatever they may be.

5. Words are only a start. To repair trust and good-will you must show people that you are sincere through your actions. If you've neglected a relation-ship or been self-focused, you must show up: call, text, check in, invite people places—show them you mean what you say and that they can trust you again.

6. All of the above needs to apply to you too. I have never worked with an Exaholic in the latter stages of healing who hasn't expressed remorse and regret for the toll their addic-tion has taken on them, personally. Oftentimes, a recovering Exaholic squirms in shame or embarrassment for the extent to which they lost control of themselves, or how far their behavior was from their values. (I know this was certainly true for me, too.)

You may consider writing yourself a letter, acknowl-edging what you did that was hurtful to you. Did you fail to protect yourself from abuse or mistreatment? Did you allow your addiction to make you behave in a way that was incongruent with your core values? Did you lose yourself in this relationship? It's okay—that's what it means to be an Exaholic. However, by acknowl-edging the ways that you failed yourself, you can restore trust with yourself. It sounds odd, but addictions often damage an individual's confidence in themselves to make good choices and protect themselves from harm. In your letter to yourself, write about what you've learned and how you will handle yourself in the future.

7. Deep breath here: I want you to consider writing a letter of forgiveness, and perhaps even apology, to your Ex. It may not be a good idea to actually send this letter (I trust your judgment one way or the other), but the act of simply writing it can be profoundly emotionally healing for you. Did you behave really well all the time over the course of your relationship? Were there mistakes you made that negatively impacted your Ex? Write about them, and acknowledge how your behavior may have affected your Ex. Also, be sure to write about how their behavior and choices impacted you. If you can forgive them for their transgressions (not approve of or condone, but forgive), it will be enormously healing for you. You can stop being hurt and angry and simply acknowledge that things happened. You are then released from the negativity that might be trapping you in the past.

STEP ELEVEN

We continue our efforts to understand ourselves and admit our character flaws without delay. We continue to strengthen our relationships within our network.

"It's in your moments of decision that your destiny is shaped."

—TONY ROBBINS

I KNOW IT PROBABLY SOUNDS UNBELIEVABLE, BUT MANY TIMES WHEN EXAHOLICS ARE IN THE LATER STAGES OF HEALING THEY WILL SAY THINGS LIKE, "YOU KNOW, THAT WAS A HORRIBLE EXPERIENCE. BUT IT TAUGHT ME SO MANY IMPORTANT THINGS ABOUT MYSELF THAT I AM GLAD NOW THAT IT HAPPENED. WITHOUT GOING THROUGH THAT, I WOULDN'T BE THE PERSON THAT I AM TODAY."

When you are in step eleven, all of the things that you've learned come together. You are actively out in the world, being a new you. You are maintaining the positive changes you've worked so hard to develop. These might include:

- Practicing good self-care
- Managing your emotions in healthy ways
- Handling obsessive or negative thoughts through mindfulness and shifting
- Having clarity around who you are and what you need to be happy and well
- Building positive things into your life, based on your values
- Being your best self in healthy, non-romantic relationships
- Maintaining good boundaries and having realistic expectations of others
- Practicing healthy, open, and appropriately assertive communication
- Creating emotional safety for yourself and others
- Opening yourself up to the possibility of a healthy, new relationship
- Feeling wiser and more mature as a result of your growth

You have been planting important seeds over the course of your recovery. In the early stages of healing it feels like your emotional landscape is a desert of destruction and desolation. When flowers start to bloom, and your core self starts to feel like a lush garden of joy and possibility, you realize that all the crap that you had to go through to get here was the fertilizer.

Step Twelve

Having had a spiritual rebirth through the practice of these steps, we now carry this message to other Exaholics who are suffering today.

"When you get, give. When you learn, teach."

—Maya Angelou

ONE OF THE MOST MEANINGFUL THINGS THAT YOU CAN DO TO SUPPORT YOUR OWN WELLNESS AND RECOVERY IS TO BE OF SERVICE TO OTHERS WHO ARE STRUGGLING. WHEN YOU CAN BE GENUINELY EMPATHETIC, A TEACHER OF SKILLS, AND AN ENCOURAGER OF FORWARD MOVEMENT, IT ONLY REINFORCES YOUR GROWTH. FOR MANY PEOPLE, THE MOST MEANINGFUL ACTIVITIES THAT BRING THEM THE MOST AUTHENTIC JOY LIE IN HELPING OTHER PEOPLE.

When you have "arrived" and feel free from your addiction, you have the opportunity to help other people heal and grow too. Your ability to have empathy for the reality of the pain and trauma that others are currently enduring means more than you know. Your presence in the life of someone else can represent hope that they too may someday overcome their own pain.

Furthermore, being in the role of a teacher, mentor, and guide will help you continue to learn and grow and give you continued motivation to maintain your own recovery.

So seek out opportunities to connect with people who are hurting. Lurk on message boards. Take an obviously suffering co-worker out to lunch. And above all else, resist the temptation to tell people, "You have to let go and move on." Even though that is true, remember how invalidating that was for you to hear when you were in the depths of your own despair.

Try this instead: "You are normal and you're not alone."

"When you find yourself in the position to help someone,
be happy and feel blessed because God is answering that person's
prayer through you. Remember: our purpose on earth is not
to get lost in the dark but to be a light to others,
so that they may find a way through us."
—Alberto Casing

Acknowledgments

This book is about you and for you, because you and I are sharing the human experience. Being humans, we are on the same journey of love together: longing for it, attempting to understand it, seeking it out, keeping it close, wrestling with it when necessary, and finding the courage to allow it to grow and expand our souls. When the highest and noblest form of love is present in our lives we experience grace that transcends everything . . . and lifts us up.

I am profoundly grateful for the true love and grace that has been at work in my life, lifting me up, and allowing me to create this book for you. It's been present in the form of my endlessly supportive husband, the patience of our son, the selflessness of my mother, the encouragement and support of my sister, father, and friends, and the trust of the clients who have shared their secrets and stories with me. This book is their gift to you.

And, of course, without the vision of Bobby the Mastermind, and without the intellectual generosity of the generations of researchers whose shoulders I am currently standing upon, including Helen Fisher, John Bowlby, Mary Ainsworth, Lucy Brown, and Susan Johnson—this book would not have been possible at all.

Resources

EMERGENCY RESOURCES

National Suicide Prevention Lifeline: 1-800-273-8255, (24/7/365), English & Spanish, **www.suicidepreventionlifeline.org.**

The National Domestic Violence Hotline: 1-800-799-SAFE (7233), (24/7/365), English & Spanish, **www.thehotline.org** **

*** (Note: This hotline is available for both victims/survivors of abuse as well as perpetrators. If you are struggling with compulsions to stalk your Ex, or are engaging in abusive/harassing behaviors and need emergency help in redirecting yourself, please call this hotline for support.)*

United Way: Call 2-1-1 from any phone and you will be connected to a person in your community who can help you access resources ranging from emergency shelter, to crisis lines, low-income housing, emergency childcare, support groups, and mental health treatment (in all states besides Illinois and Arkansas: in those states please do a general Internet search for "emergency resources for _____").

United Way resources are accessible nationwide at **www.211us.org**.

PARENTING SUPPORT

If you struggle with parenting and feel helpless, or at risk of becoming out of control with your children: 1-855- 4A PARENT (1-855-427-2736) or go to **www.nationalparenthelpline.org** to speak immediately with a trained advocate who can help you.

CHILD ABUSE OR NEGLECT

If you know or suspect that a child is being neglected or physically or sexually abused:

Call 800-4-A-CHILD (422.4453) or 800.2.A.CHILD (222.4453, TDD for hearing impaired) **www.childhelp.org**. This organization provides multilingual crisis intervention and professional counseling on child abuse. Gives referrals to local social service groups offering counseling on child abuse. Operates 24 hours, seven days a week.

If you are a minor and need help, call: National Youth Crisis Hotline: 800-442-HOPE (4673). This organization provides counseling and referrals to local drug treatment centers, shelters, and counseling services. Responds to youth dealing with pregnancy, molestation, suicide, and child abuse. Operates 24 hours, seven days a week.

If you are caring for a child who is struggling with the effects of past trauma, you can find support here: National Child Traumatic Stress Network: **www.nctsn.org**

THERAPY RESOURCES

If you determine that it would be helpful to get connected with a therapist or coach, the first step is to familiarize yourself with the different kinds of licensures and professions.

Online Guide to Finding the Right Therapist:
http://bit.ly/1f7Zqvu.

Once armed with knowledge, then you can do an online search for practitioners in your area or call your health insurance provider for a list of practitioners who are in-network with your plan.

NOTES

CHAPTER 4: BUILT TO LOVE

44   **evolutionary biologist Dr. Helen Fisher identified** . . . Helen Fisher, Arthur Aron, and Lucy Brown, "Romantic love: An fMRI study of a neural mechanism for mate choice," *Journal of Comparative Neurology*, December 2005, 493(1), 58–62.

54   **a psychiatrist named John Bowlby** . . . John Bowlby, *Attachment: Attachment and Loss, Vol 1* (New York: Basic Books. Penguin Books, 1971; 2nd edn, 1982).

55   **young children become extremely distressed** . . . John Bowlby, *Attachment and Loss, Vol 2, Separation: Anxiety and Anger* (New York: Basic Books. Penguin Books, 1975).

55   . . . **stopped growing and wasted away** . . . John Bowlby, *Attachment and Loss, Vol 3, Loss: Sadness and Depression* (New York: Basic Books. Penguin Books, 1981).

55   . . . **the account of Frederick the Second** . . . Thomas Lewis, Fari Amini, and Richard Lannon, *A General Theory of Love* (New York: Random House, 2001).

57   . . . **of behaviorists with baby monkeys** . . . Harry F. Harlow, "The nature of love," *American Psychologist*, 13 (1958), 673–685.

57   . . . **monkeys totally deprived of maternal** . . . Harry F. Harlow, Robert O. Dodsworth, and Margaret K. Harlow, "Total social isolation in monkeys," *Proceedings of the National Academy of Sciences*, 54 (1), July 1965.

57   **study beginning in 1969 Mary Ainsworth** . . . Mary D. Salter Ainsworth, Mary C. Blehar, Everett Waters, Sally Wall, *Patterns of attachment: a psychological study of the strange situation* (New York: Psychology Press, 1978, *2nd Ed. 2014*).

61   **adults physically coregulate** . . . Darby Saxbe and Rena L. Repetti, "For better or worse? Coregulation of couples' cortisol levels and mood states," *Journal of Personality and Social Psychology*, 98 (2010), 92–103.

62   **just like tiny babies depend on** . . . David A. Sbarra and Cindy Hazan, "Coregulation, dysregulation, self-regulation: an integrative analysis and empirical agenda for understanding adult attachment, separation, loss and recovery," *Personality and Social Psychology Review*, 12 (2008), 141.

63   **called Emotionally Focused Couples Therapy** . . . Susan Johnson, *Hold Me Tight* (New York: Little, Brown and Company, 2008).

64   **in her article on happiness and perfection** . . . Brené Brown, "Want to be happy? Stop trying to be perfect." cnn.com, November 2, 2010, accessed June 1, 2015, http://www.cnn.com/2010/LIVING/11/01/give.up.perfection.

CHAPTER 5: THE NATURE OF LOVE

67　**In 1994, Dr. Fisher published** . . . Helen Fisher, "The nature of romantic love," *The Journal of NIH Research* 6(4) 1994: 59–64, Reprinted in *Annual Editions: Physical Anthropology*, Spring 1995.

76　**lust, romantic love, and attachment** . . . H. Fisher, A. Aron, D. Mashek, G. Strong, H. Li, and L. Brown, "Defining the brain systems of lust, romantic attraction and attachment," *Archives of Sexual Behavior*, 31:5 (2002), 413–419.

76　**feelings of lust reside in** . . . Helen Fisher, "Brains do it: lust, attraction and attachment," Dana.org, January, 2000, accessed June 1, 2015: http://www.dana.org/ Cerebrum/Default.aspx?id=39351.

78　**romantic attraction . . . in an emotionally turbulent** . . . Donald G. Dutton and Arthur P. Aron, "Some evidence for heightened sexual attraction under conditions of high anxiety," *Journal of Personality and Social Psychology*, 30(4), 1974, 510–17.

79　**marriage and divorce statistics reveal** . . . Helen Fisher, "The nature of romantic love," *The Journal of NIH Research*, 6(4) 1994: 59–64, reprinted in Annual Editions: *Physical Anthropology*, Spring 1995.

80　**lust, love, and attachment . . . related but separate** . . . Helen Fisher, Arthur Aron, Debra Mashek, Haifang Li, and Lucy Brown, "Defining the brain systems of lust, romantic attraction and attachment," *Archives of Sexual Behavior*, 31:5 (2002), 413–9.

CHAPTER 6: ADDICTED TO LOVE

83　**"Love includes obsessive behaviors and** . . . Joseph Frascella, Marc N. Potenza, Lucy L. Brown, and Anna Rose Childress, "Carving addiction at a new joint? Shared brain vulnerabilities open the way for non-substance addictions," *Annals of the New York Academy of Sciences*, 1187 (2010), 294–315. Retrieved on June 1, 2015 doi: 10.1111/j.1749–6632.2009.05420.x.

84　**compared the brain activity of participants** . . . Helen Fisher, Arthur Aron, Lucy Brown, "An fMRI study of a neural mechanism for mate choice," *Journal of Comparative Neurology*, 493:1 (2005), 58–62.

88　**brain activity in cocaine addicts . . . love** . . . Robert C. Risinger, Betty Jo Salmeron, Thomas J. Ross, Shelley L. Amen, Michael Sanfilipo, Raymond G. Hoffmann, Alan S. Bloom, Hugh Garavan, Elliot A. Stein, "Neural correlates of high and craving during cocaine self-adminstration using BOLD fMRI," *NeuroImage*, 26:4 (2005), 1097–1108.

88　**area is associated with cigarette craving** . . . Brody AL., Mandelkern M.A., Olmstead R.E., Jou J., Tiogson E., Allen V., Scheibal D., London E.D., Monterosso J.R., Tiffany S.T., Korb A., Gan J.J., Cohen M.S., "Neural substrates of resisting craving during cigarette cue exposure," *Biological Psychiatry*, 62:6 (2007).

89　**people with Obsessive Compulsive Disorder** . . . Donatella Marazziti, Hagop Akiskal, Alessandra Rossi, "Alteration of the platlet serotonin transporter in romantic love," *Psychological Medicine*, 29 (1999), 741–745.

90　**manufacturing opiate-like serotonin, vasopressin** . . . Bianca P. Acevedo, Arthur Aron, Helen E. Fisher, and Lucy L. Brown, "Neural correlates of long-term intense romantic love," *Social Cognitive and Affective Neuroscience* (2011), accessed June 1, 2015. doi:10.1093/scan/nsq092.

91　**as attachment deepens, serotonin levels rise** . . . Bianca P. Acevedo, Arthur Aron, Helen E. Fisher, and Lucy L. Brown, "Neural correlates of long-term intense romantic

love," *Social Cognitive and Affective Neuroscience* (2011), accessed June 1, 2015. doi:10.1093/scan/nsq092.

87   **a great book on the subject is** . . . Esther Perel, *Mating in Captivity: Unlocking Erotic Intelligence* (New York: Harper, 2007).

88   **thinking about their sweetheart more than** . . . Roy F. Baumeister, Sara R. Wotman, Arlene M. Stillwell, "Unrequited love: On heartbreak, anger, guilt, scriptlessness and humiliation," *Journal of Personality and Social Psychology*, 64:3 (1993), 377–94.

93   **you feel "Love" much more vividly** . . . Helen E. Fisher, "Lost love: The nature of romantic rejection," in *Cut Loose: (mainly) Midlife and Older Women on the End of (mostly) Long-Term Relationships,* Nan Baurer-Maglin, (Ed) (New Jersey: Rutgers University Press, 2006).

94   **substance abuse neurophysiology may be based on** . . . Joseph Frascella, Marc N. Potenza, Lucy L. Brown, and Anna Rose Childress, "Carving addiction at a new joint? Shared brain vulnerabilities open the way for non-substance addictions," *Annals of the New York Academy of Sciences,* 1187 (2010), 294–315. Retrieved on June 1, 2015 doi: 10.1111/j.1749–6632.2009.05420.x

95   **Substances that ease physical pain soothe** . . . C. Nathan DeWall, Geoff MacDonald, Gregory D. Webster, Carrie L. Masten, Roy F. Baumeister, Catilin Powell, David Combs, David R. Schurtz, Tyler F. Stillman, Dianne M. Tice and Naomi I. Eisenberger, "Acetaminophen reduces social pain: Behavioral and neural evidence," *Psychological Science,* 21:7 (2010), 931–37.

95   **function without the comfort of drugs**, Gabor Mate, *In The Realm Of Hungry Ghosts: Close Encounters With Addiction* (Berkeley, CA: North Atlantic Books, 2010).

96   **Without normal attachment, emotional regulation** . . . P.J. Flores, *Addiction as an Attachment Disorder* (New York: Jason Aronson, 2004).

96   **In his 2015 piece on "The Cause of Addiction** . . . " Johan Hari, "The likely cause of addiction has been discovered, and it is not what you think," Huffington Post, January 20, 2015, accessed June 1, 2015, http://www.huffingtonpost.com/johann-hari/the-real-cause-of-addicti_b_6506936.htm.

96   **conducted in the 1970s by Dr. Bruce Alexander** . . . B.K. Alexander, R.B. Coambs, and P.F. Hadaway, "The effect of housing and gender on morphine self-administration in rats," *Psychopharmacology*, 58 (1978), 175–9.

CHAPTER 7: WHEN LOVE IS LOST

113   **Sbarra and Hazan point out** . . . David A. Sbarra and Cindy Hazan, "Coregulation, dysregulation, self-regulation: An integrative analysis and empirical agenda for understanding adult attachment, separation, loss and recovery," *Personality and Social Psychology Review*, 12 (2008), 141.

110   **. . . rejected by someone they loved intensely**, Roy F. Baumeister, Sara R. Wotman, Arlene M. Stillwell, "Unrequited love: On heartbreak, anger, guilt, scriptlessness and humiliation," *Journal of Personality and Social Psychology*, 64:3 (1993), 377–94.

112   **we are galvanized by the protest response** . . . Thomas Lewis, Fari Amini, and Richard Lannon, *A General Theory of Love* (New York: Random House, 2001).

113   **fMRI scans of heartbroken people revealed** . . . Helen E. Fisher, Lucy L. Brown, Arthur Aron, Greg Strong, Debra Mashek, "Reward, addiction, and emotion regulation systems associated with rejection in love," *Journal of Neurophysiology*, 104:1 (2010), 51–60. DOI: 10.1152/jn.00784.2009.

116 **replaying memories reactivates the same** . . . Helen E. Fisher, Lucy
L. Brown, Arthur Aron, Greg Strong, Debra Mashek, "Reward, addiction, and emotion
regulation systems associated with rejection in love," *Journal of Neurophysiology*, 104:1
(2010), 51–60. DOI: 10.1152/jn.00784.2009.

116 **Having mental representation of attachment** . . . Naomi I. Eisenberger, Sarah L.
Master, Tristen K. Inagaki, Shelley E. Taylor, David Shirinyan, Matthew D. Liberman,
and Bruce D. Nailboff, "Attachment figures activate a safety signal-related neural region
and reduce pain experience," *Psychological and Cognitive Sciences*, 108:28 (2011),
11721–11726.

119 **rage towards your rejecting lover** . . . Ellis B.J., Malamuth N.M., "Love and anger in
romantic relationships: a discrete systems model," *Journal of Personality*, 68:3 (2000),
525–56.

120 **impact of rejection on physical pain** . . . Ethan Kross, Marc G. Berman, Walter
Mischel, Edward E. Smith, and Tor D. Wager, "Social rejection shares somatosensory
representations with physical pain," *Proceedings of the National Academy of Sciences*,
108:15 (2011), 6270–75.

121 **dying, particularly of heart attacks**, Elizabeth Mostofsky, Malcolm Maclure, Jane
B. Sherwood, Geoffrey H. Tofler, James E. Muller, and Murray A. Mittleman, "Risk
of acute myocardial infarction after the death of a significant person in one's life: the
determinants of myocardial infarction onset study," *Circulation*, 125 (2012), 491–6.

122 **Shame is believing that you** . . . " Brené Brown, "Listening to Shame," TED
Talk filmed March 2012, accessed June 1, 2015 at http://www.ted.com/talks/
brene_brown_listening_to_shame.

124 **animals experience depressive symptoms**. . . Thomas Lewis, Fari Amini, and Richard
Lannon, *A General Theory of Love* (New York: Random House, 2001).

125 **Men are also more likely to stalk** . . . J. Reid Meloy and Helen Fisher, "Some thoughts
on the neurobiology of stalking," *Journal of Forensic Sciences*, 50:6 (2005), 1472–80.

125 **Women who have been rejected** . . . Helen E. Fisher, "Lost love: The nature of romantic
rejection," in *Cut Loose: (mainly) Midlife and Older Women on the End of (mostly) Long-
Term Relationships*, Nan Baurer-Maglin, Ed. (New Jersey: Rutgers University Press,
2006).

125 **Grace Larsen, of Northwestern University** . . . Grace M. Larsen, David A. Sbarra,
"Participating in research on romantic breakups promotes emotional recovery via
changes in self-concept clarity," *Social Psychological and Personality Science*, 6:4
(2015), 399–406.

CHAPTER 8: TYPES OF LOSS

151 **poll of Americans conducted in 2013** . . . Gallup.com, "Once taboo, more behaviors
acceptable in the US," accessed June 1, 2015 http://www.gallup.com/poll/183455/once-
taboo-behaviors-acceptable.aspx.

151 **While 92 percent of people report believing** . . . Tom W. Smith, "American sexual
behavior: Trends, socio-demographic differences, and risk behavior," *National Opinion
Research Center, Topical Report No. 25*, updated April 2003, accessed June 1, 2015,
http://publicdata.norc.org:41000/gss/DOCUMENTS/REPORTS/Topical_Reports/
TR25.pdf.

CHAPTER 9: STAGES OF HEALING

182 **evolution has designed** ... "Mate Guarding," David M. Buss, "Human mate guarding," *Neuroendocrinology Letters Special Issue*, 23:4 (2002), 23–9.

195 **bacteria supported by probiotic supplements** ... Javier A. Bravo, Paul Forsythe, Marianne V. Chew, Emily Escaravage, Helene M. Savignac, Timothy G. Dinan, John Bienenstock, and John F. Cryan, "Ingestion of lactobacillus strain regulates emotional behavior and central GABA receptor expression in a mouse via the vagus nerve," *Proceedings of the National Academy of Sciences of the United States of America*, 108:38 (2011), 16050–55.

195 **mild dehydration is associated with** ... Lawrence E. Armstrong, Matthew S. Ganio, Douglas J. Casa, Elaine C. Lee, Brendon P. McDermott, Jennifer F. Klau, Liliana Jiminez, Laurent Le Bellego, Emmanuel Chevillotte, and Harris R. Liberman, "Mild dehydration affects mood in healthy young women," *The Journal of Nutrition*, 142:2 (2012), 382–88.

197 **reducing symptoms of anxiety and depression** ... Peter J. Carek, Sarah E. Laibstain, Stephen M. Carek, "Exercise for the treatment of depression and anxiety," *The International Journal of Psychiatry in Medicine*, 41:1 (2011), 15–28.

197 **uptick in drinking and drug use** ... Charles B. Fleming, Helene R. White, Sabrina Oesterle, Kevin P. Haggerty, and Richard F. Catalano, "Romantic relationship status changes and substance use among 18- to 20-year-olds," *Journal of Studies on Alcohol and Drugs*, 71 (2010), 847–56.

201 **There are two different kinds of stalking** ... J. Reid Meloy and Helen Fisher, "Some thoughts on the neurobiology of stalking," *Journal of Forensic Sciences*, 50:6 (2005), 1472–80.

203 **percentage of violence toward ex lovers** ... J. Reid Meloy and Helen Fisher, "Some thoughts on the neurobiology of stalking," *Journal of Forensic Sciences*, 50:6 (2005), 1472–80.